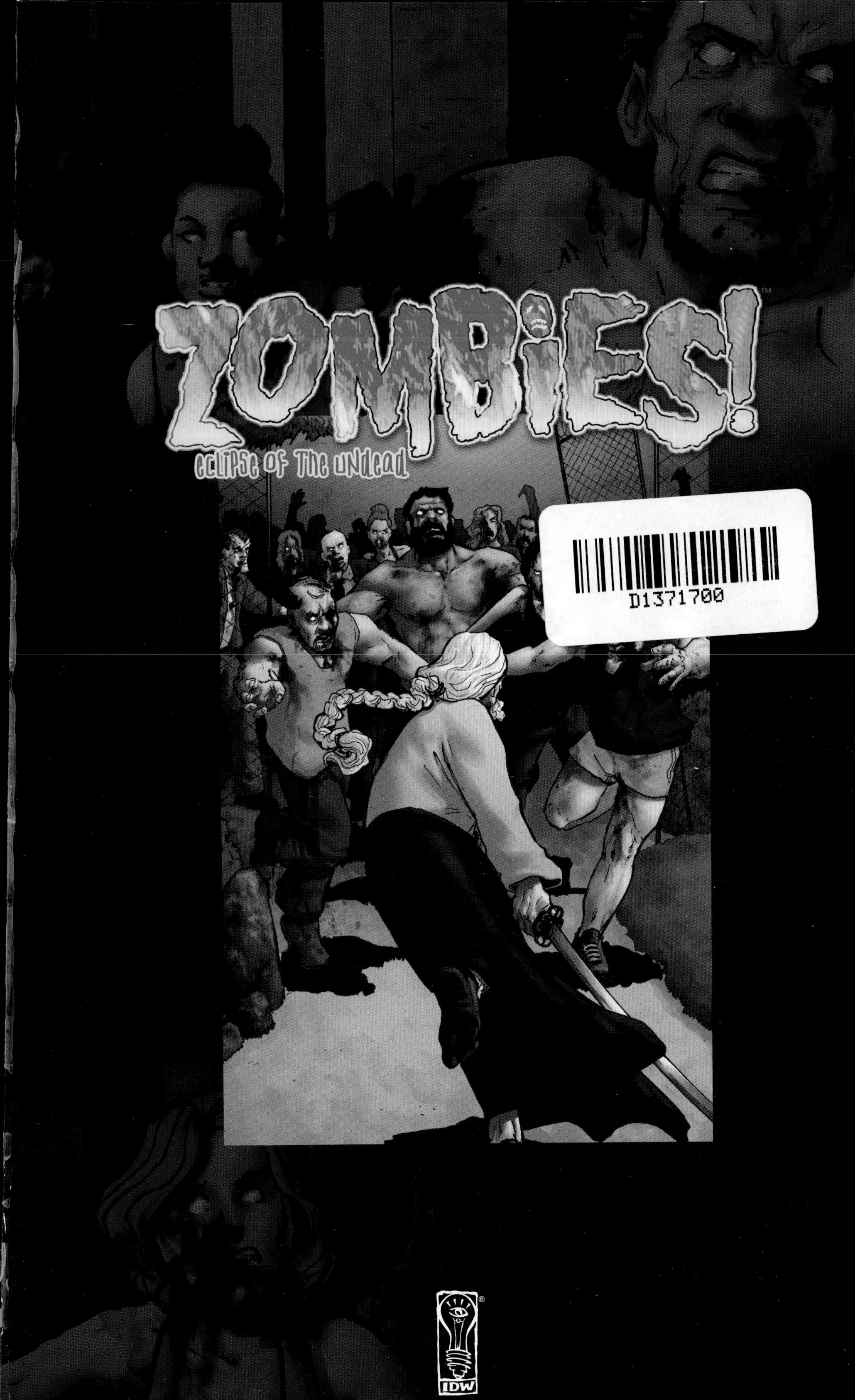
ZOMBIES!™
eclipse of the undead
IDW

IDW PUBLISHING • SAN DIEGO, CA

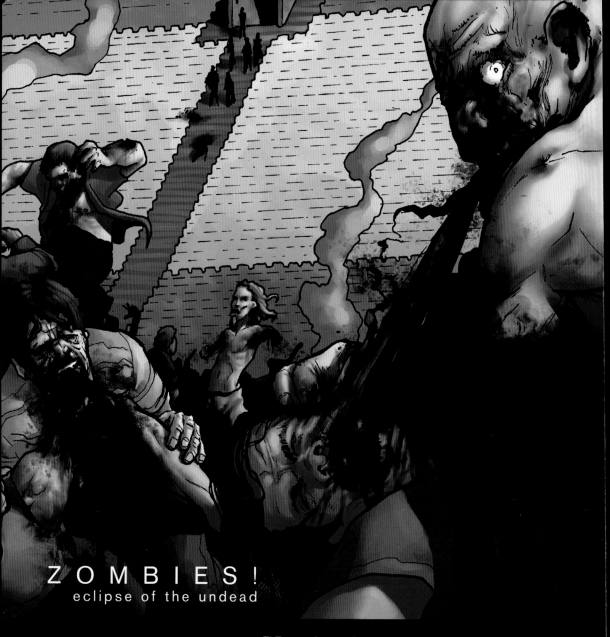

ZOMBIES!
eclipse of the undead

written by **El Torres**, Sulaco Studios

art by **Yair Herrera**, Sulaco Studios

letters by **Sulaco Studios**

cover by **Yair Herrera**, Sulaco Studios

book design by **Robbie Robbins** and **Neil Uyetake**

collection edits by **Justin Eisinger**

original series edits by **Chris Ryall**

DW Publishing is:
Ted Adams, Co-President
Robbie Robbins, Co-President
Chris Ryall, Publisher/Editor-in-Chief
Kris Oprisko, Vice President
Alan Payne, Vice President of Sales
Neil Uyetake, Art Director
Dan Taylor, Editor
Justin Eisinger, Editorial Assistant
Chris Mowry, Graphic Artist
Matthew Ruzicka, CPA, Controller
Alonzo Simon, Shipping Manager
Alex Garner, Creative Director
Yumiko Miyano, Business Development
Rick Privman, Business Development

ISBN: 978-1-60010-069-7

10 09 08 07   1 2 3 4 5

www.IDWPUBLISHING.com

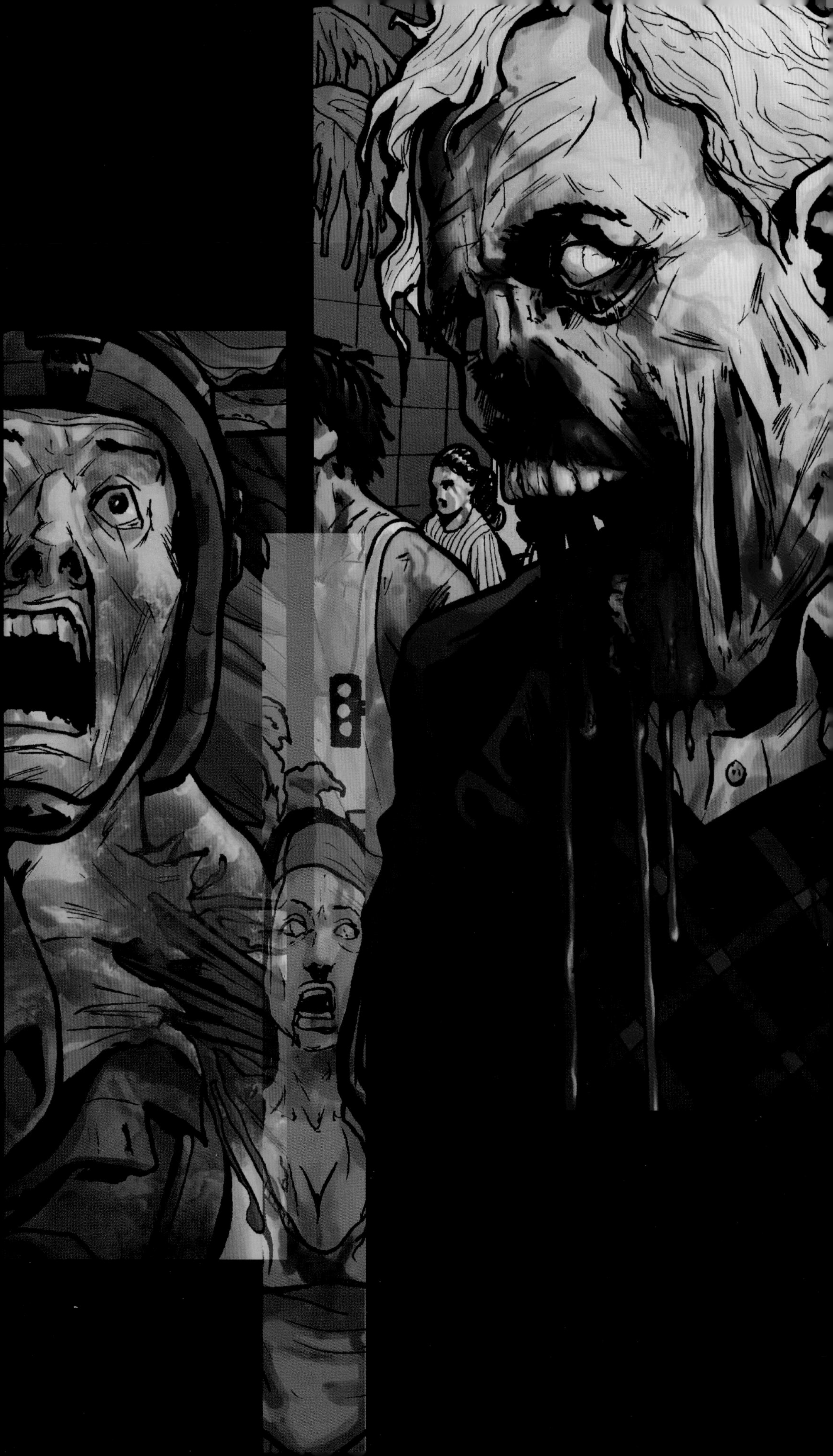

CHAPTER ONE

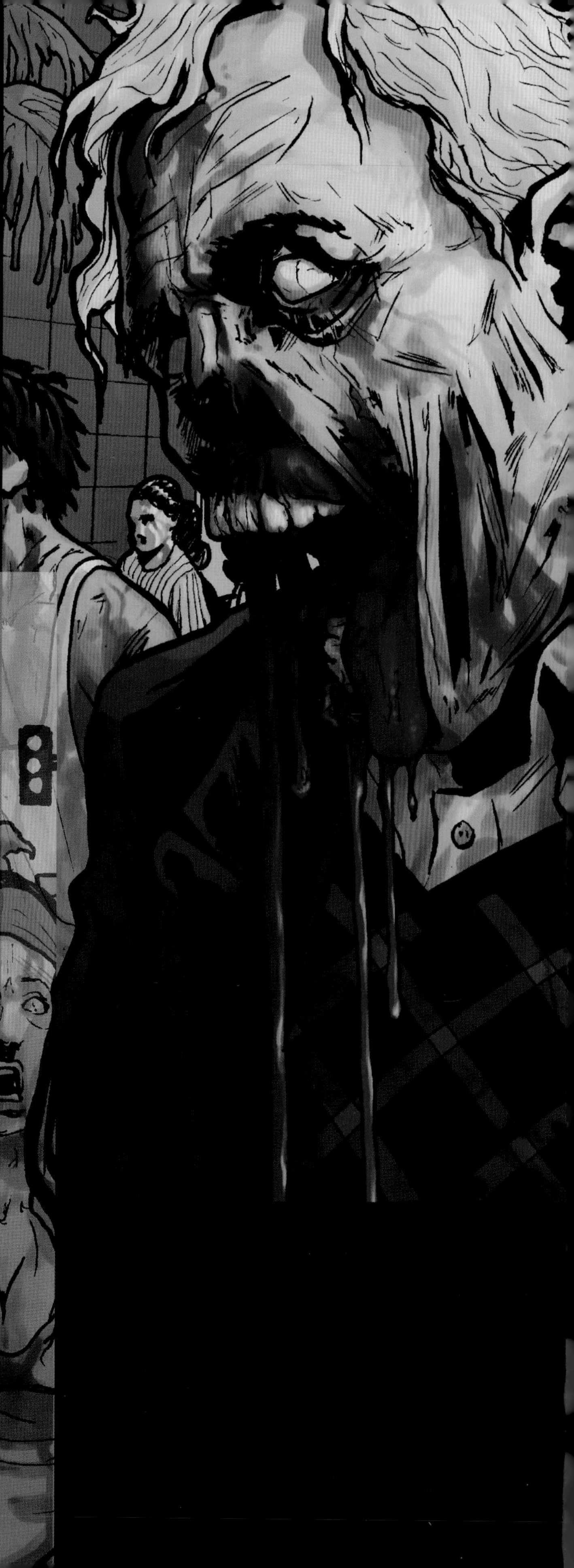

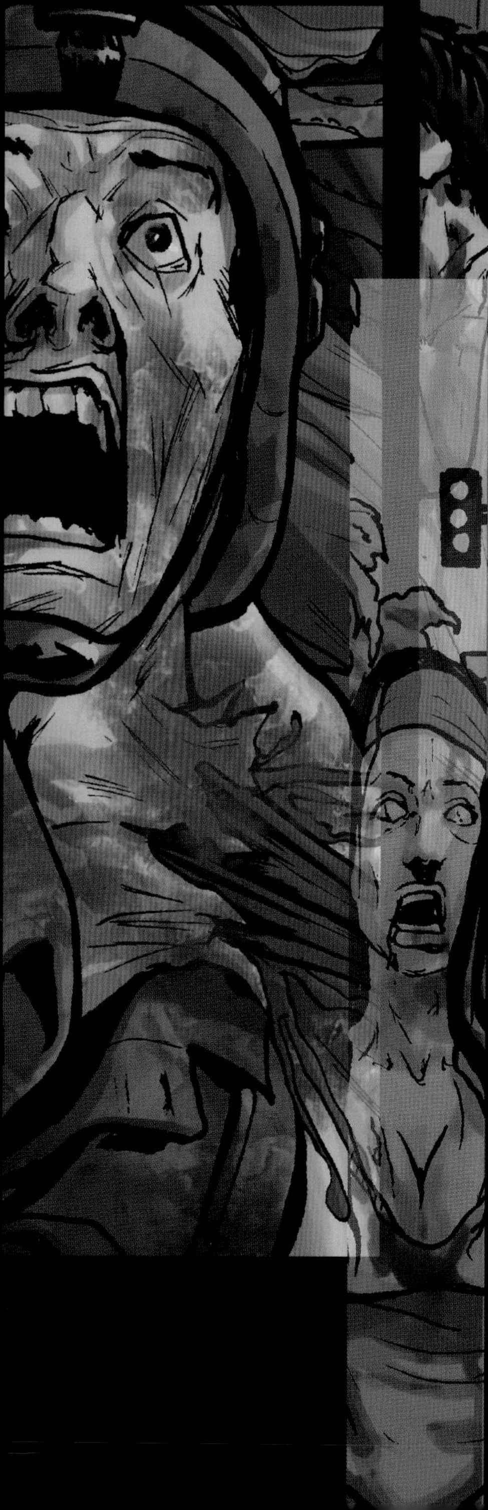

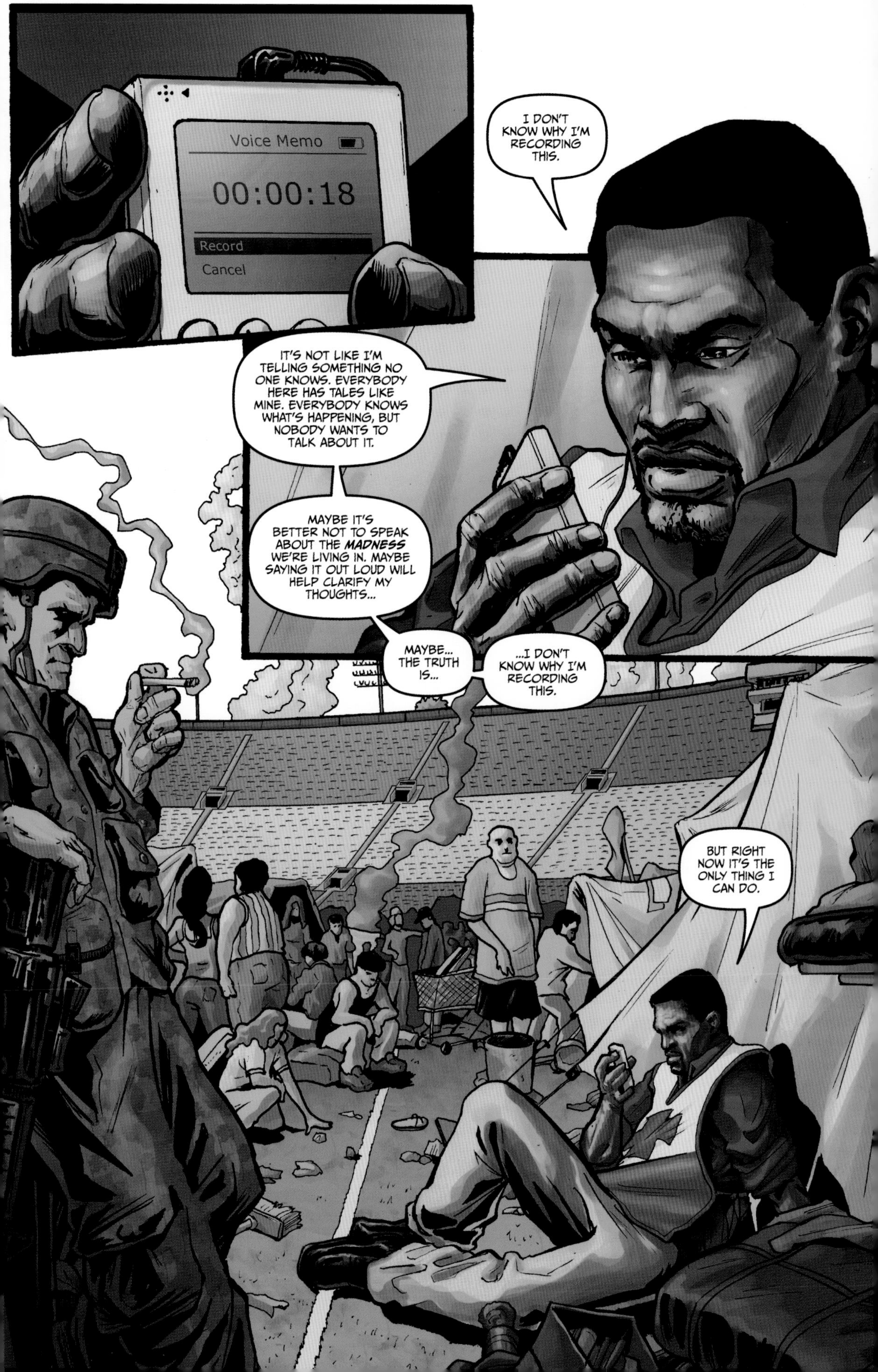
Voice Memo
00:00:18
Record
Cancel
I DON'T KNOW WHY I'M RECORDING THIS.
IT'S NOT LIKE I'M TELLING SOMETHING NO ONE KNOWS. EVERYBODY HERE HAS TALES LIKE MINE. EVERYBODY KNOWS WHAT'S HAPPENING, BUT NOBODY WANTS TO TALK ABOUT IT.
MAYBE IT'S BETTER NOT TO SPEAK ABOUT THE MADNESS WE'RE LIVING IN. MAYBE SAYING IT OUT LOUD WILL HELP CLARIFY MY THOUGHTS...
MAYBE... THE TRUTH IS...
...I DON'T KNOW WHY I'M RECORDING THIS.
BUT RIGHT NOW IT'S THE ONLY THING I CAN DO.

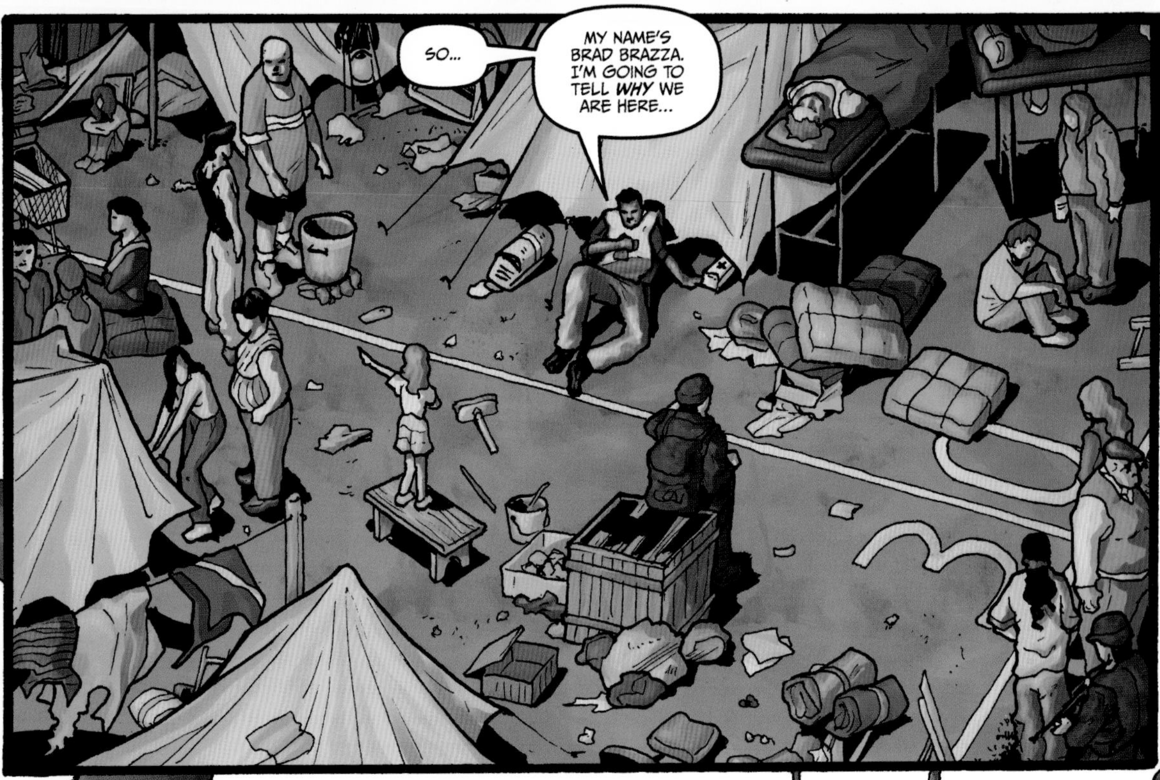
SO...
MY NAME'S BRAD BRAZZA. I'M GOING TO TELL *WHY* WE ARE HERE...

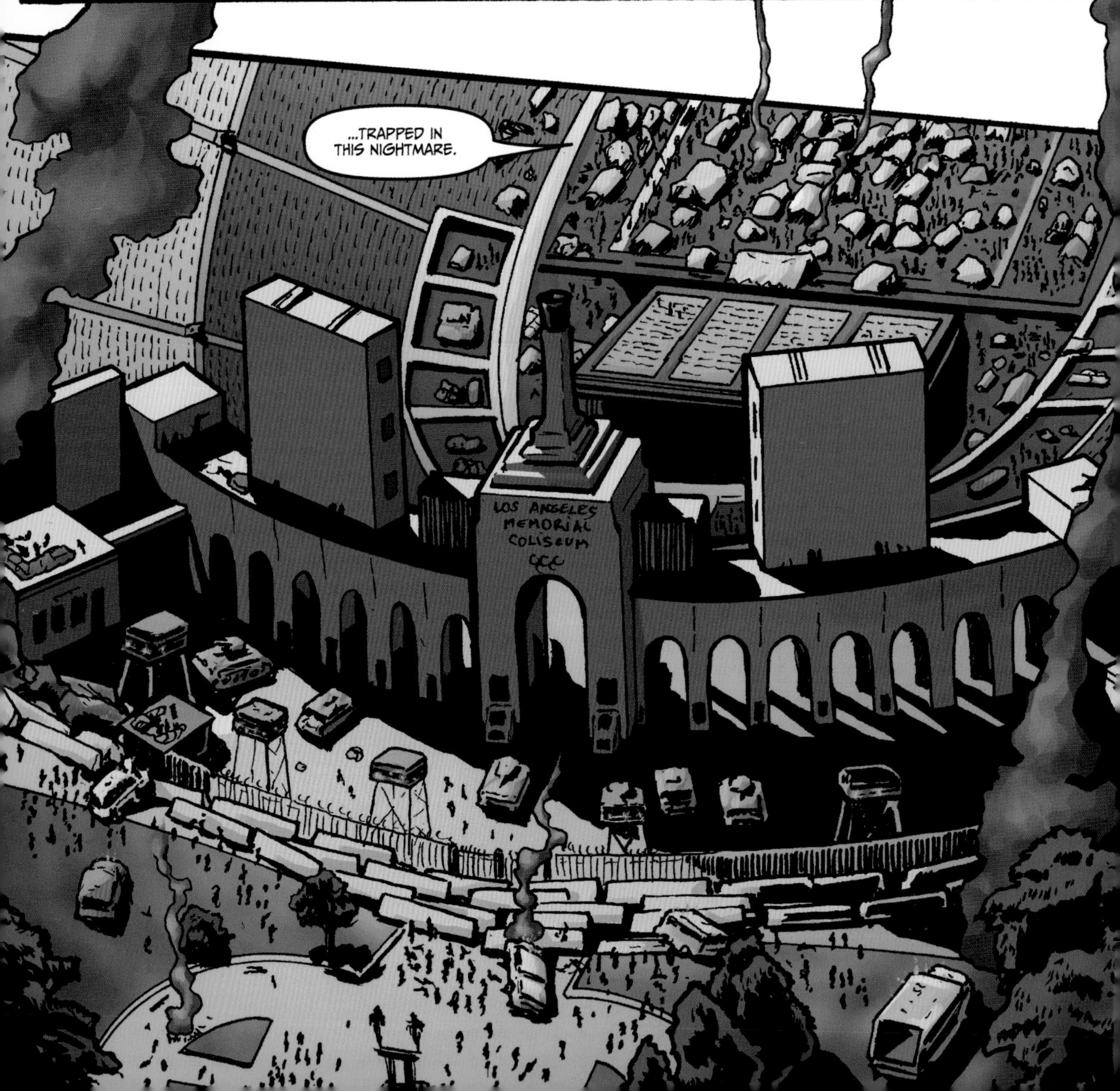
...TRAPPED IN THIS NIGHTMARE.
LOS ANGELES MEMORIAL COLISEUM

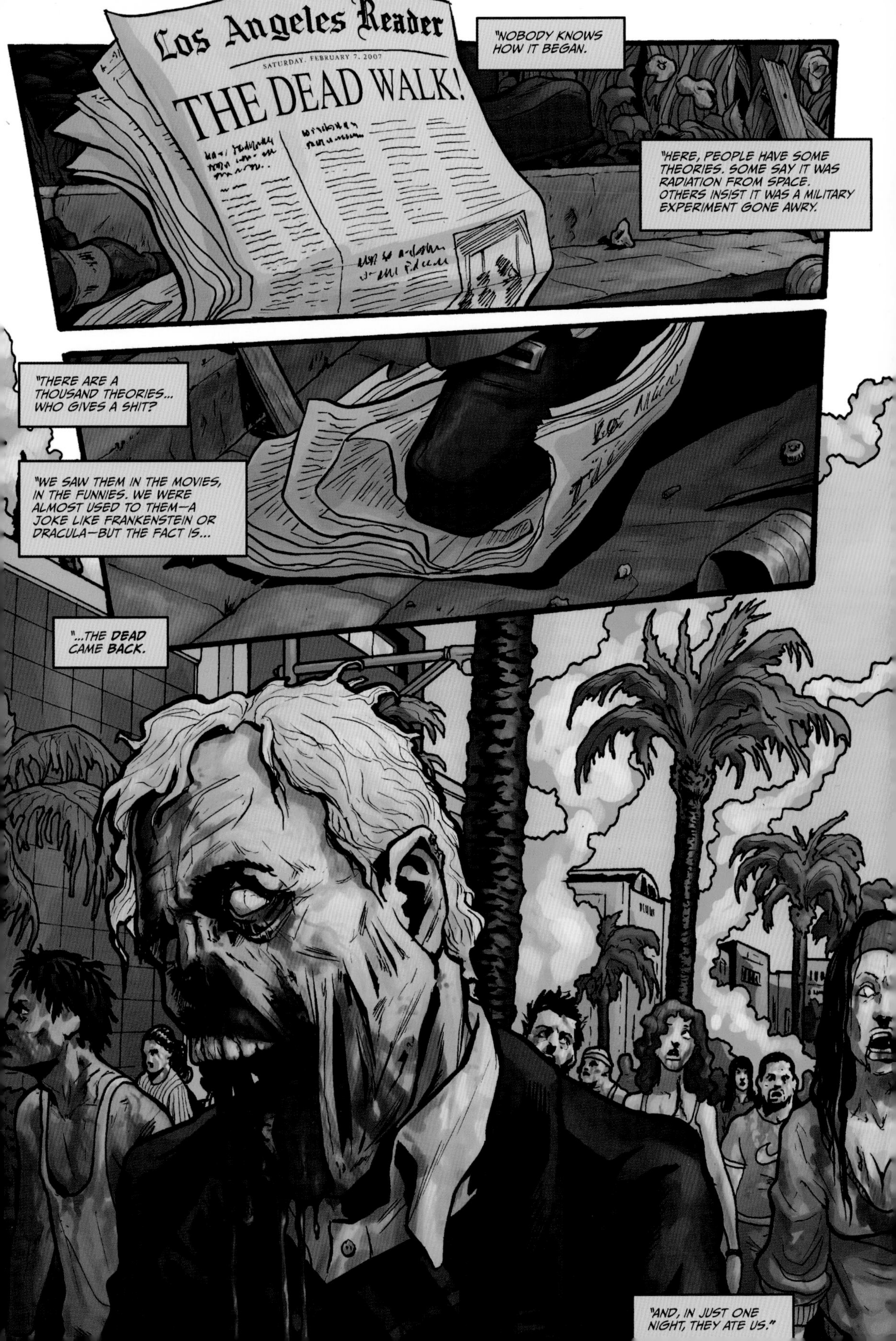
Los Angeles Reader
SATURDAY, FEBRUARY 7, 2007
THE DEAD WALK!
"NOBODY KNOWS HOW IT BEGAN.
"HERE, PEOPLE HAVE SOME THEORIES. SOME SAY IT WAS RADIATION FROM SPACE. OTHERS INSIST IT WAS A MILITARY EXPERIMENT GONE AWRY.
"THERE ARE A THOUSAND THEORIES... WHO GIVES A SHIT?
"WE SAW THEM IN THE MOVIES, IN THE FUNNIES. WE WERE ALMOST USED TO THEM—A JOKE LIKE FRANKENSTEIN OR DRACULA—BUT THE FACT IS...
"...THE DEAD CAME BACK.
"AND, IN JUST ONE NIGHT, THEY ATE US."

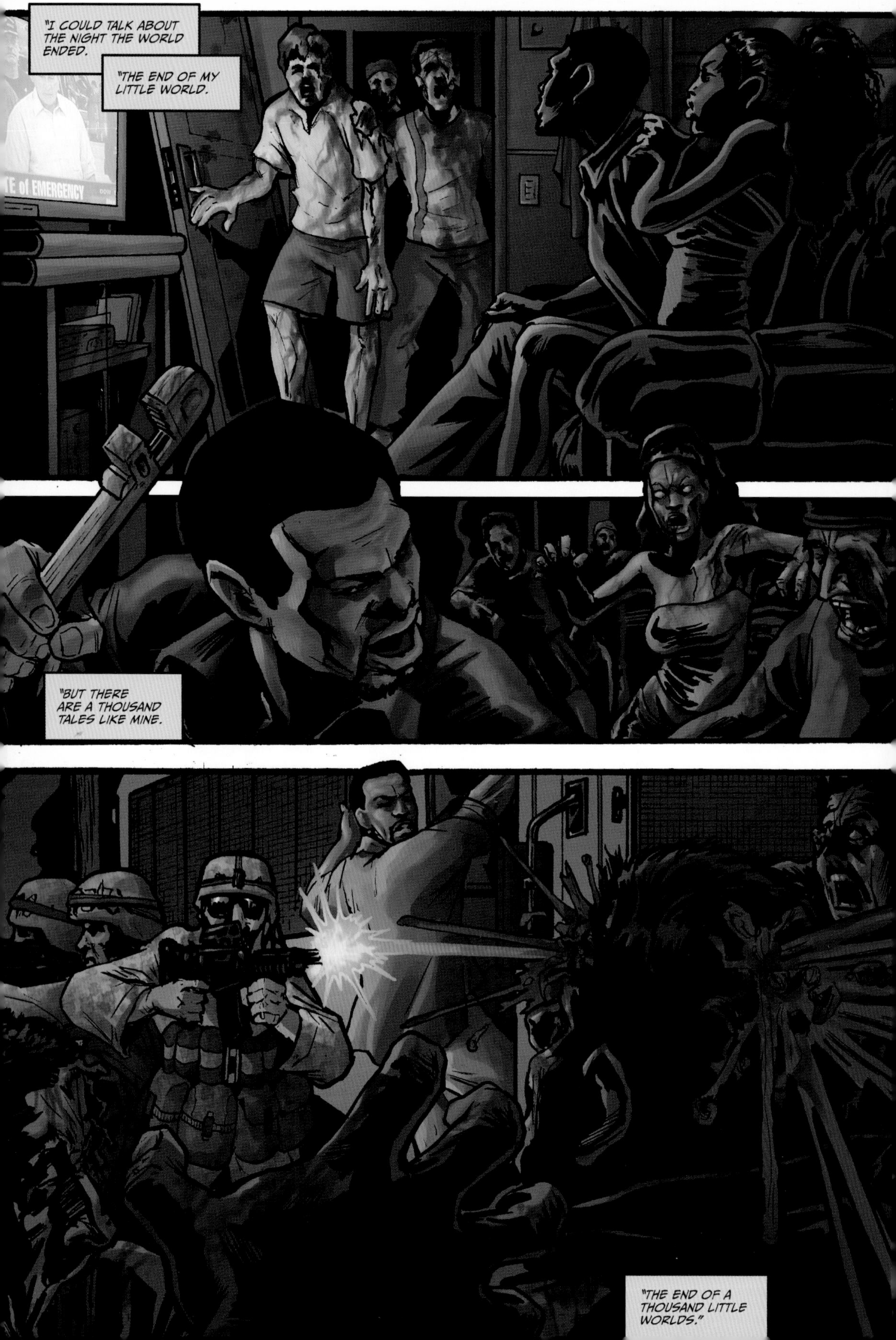
"I COULD TALK ABOUT THE NIGHT THE WORLD ENDED.
"THE END OF MY LITTLE WORLD.
TE of EMERGENCY
"BUT THERE ARE A THOUSAND TALES LIKE MINE.
"THE END OF A THOUSAND LITTLE WORLDS."

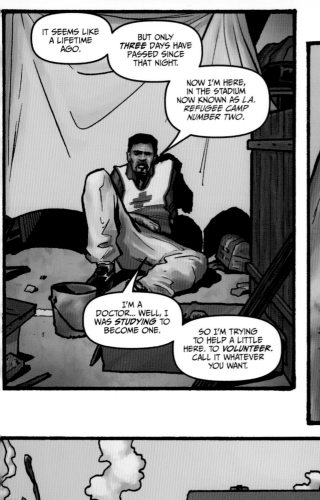

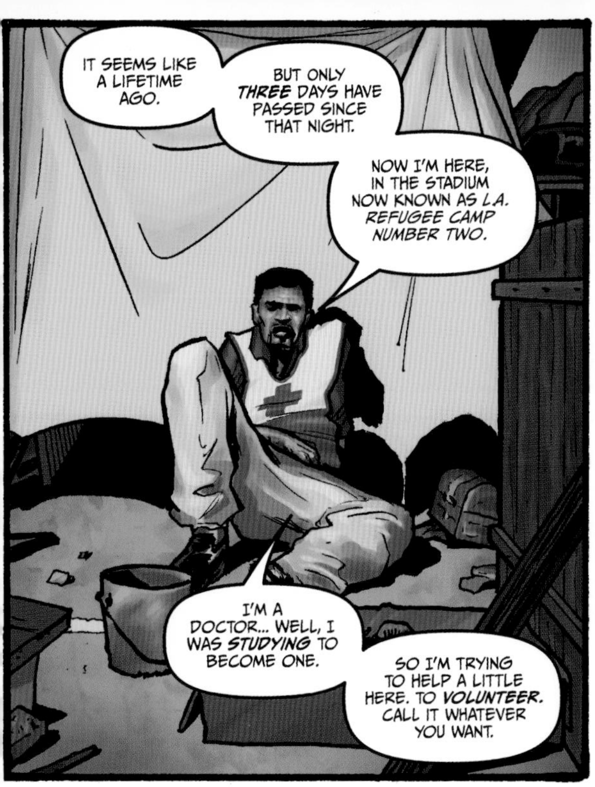
IT SEEMS LIKE A LIFETIME AGO.
BUT ONLY *THREE* DAYS HAVE PASSED SINCE THAT NIGHT.
NOW I'M HERE, IN THE STADIUM NOW KNOWN AS *L.A. REFUGEE CAMP NUMBER TWO.*
I'M A DOCTOR... WELL, I WAS *STUDYING* TO BECOME ONE.
SO I'M TRYING TO HELP A LITTLE HERE. TO *VOLUNTEER.* CALL IT WHATEVER YOU WANT.

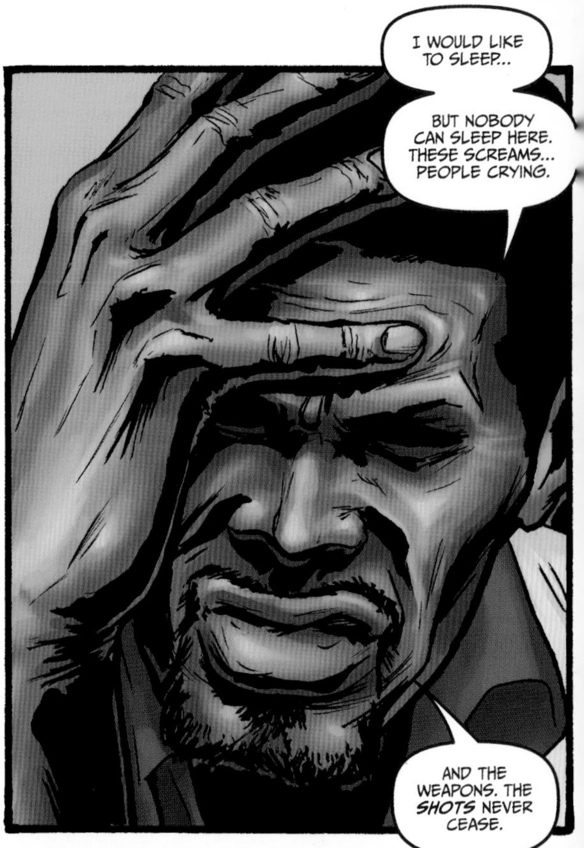
I WOULD LIKE TO SLEEP...
BUT NOBODY CAN SLEEP HERE. THESE SCREAMS... PEOPLE CRYING.
AND THE WEAPONS. THE *SHOTS* NEVER CEASE.

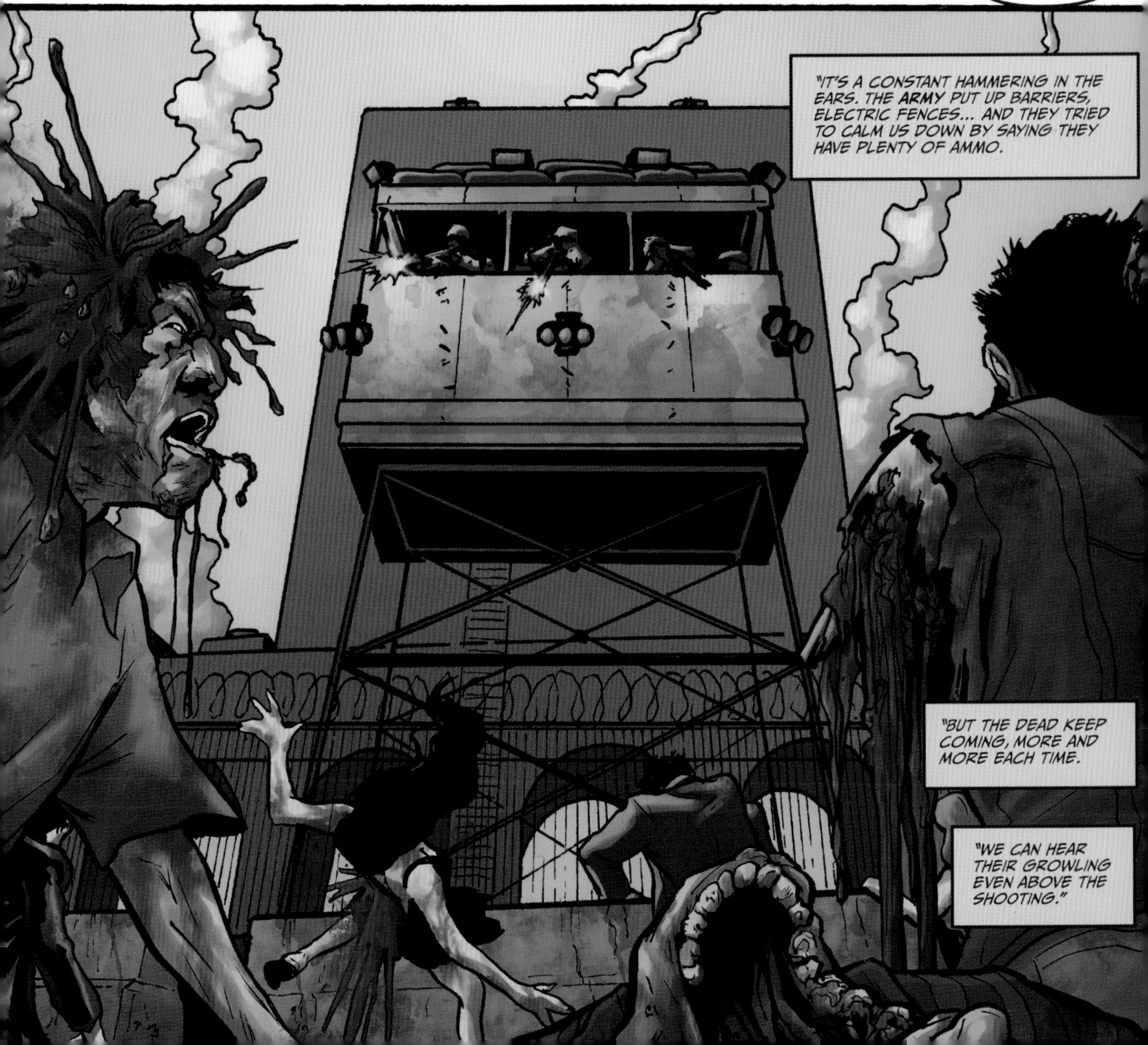
"IT'S A CONSTANT HAMMERING IN THE EARS. THE ***ARMY*** *PUT UP BARRIERS, ELECTRIC FENCES... AND THEY TRIED TO CALM US DOWN BY SAYING THEY HAVE PLENTY OF AMMO.*
"BUT THE DEAD KEEP COMING, MORE AND MORE EACH TIME.
"WE CAN HEAR THEIR GROWLING EVEN ABOVE THE SHOOTING."

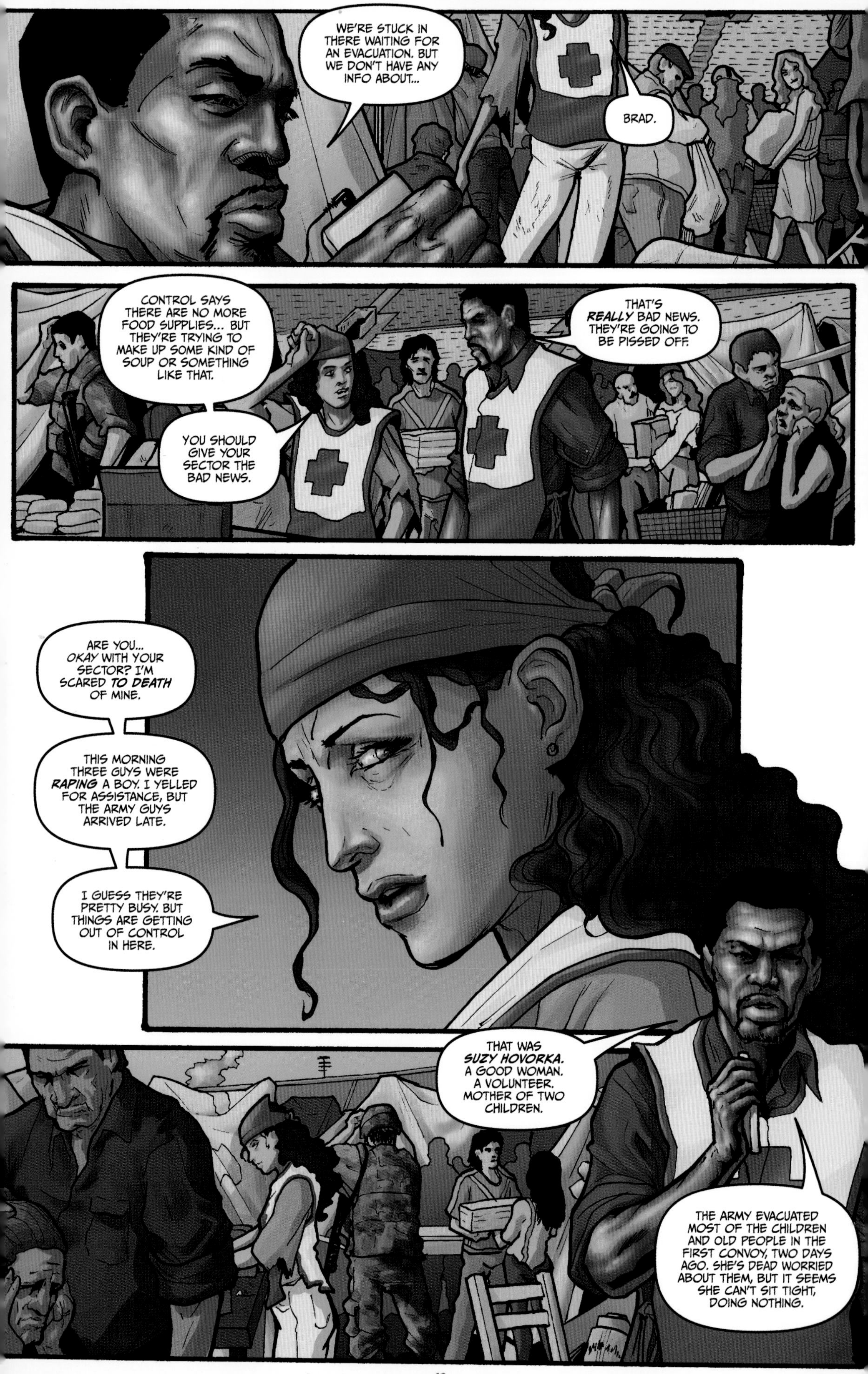
WE'RE STUCK IN THERE WAITING FOR AN EVACUATION. BUT WE DON'T HAVE ANY INFO ABOUT...
BRAD.
CONTROL SAYS THERE ARE NO MORE FOOD SUPPLIES... BUT THEY'RE TRYING TO MAKE UP SOME KIND OF SOUP OR SOMETHING LIKE THAT.
YOU SHOULD GIVE YOUR SECTOR THE BAD NEWS.
THAT'S *REALLY* BAD NEWS. THEY'RE GOING TO BE PISSED OFF.
ARE YOU... *OKAY* WITH YOUR SECTOR? I'M SCARED *TO DEATH* OF MINE.
THIS MORNING THREE GUYS WERE *RAPING* A BOY. I YELLED FOR ASSISTANCE, BUT THE ARMY GUYS ARRIVED LATE.
I GUESS THEY'RE PRETTY BUSY. BUT THINGS ARE GETTING OUT OF CONTROL IN HERE.
THAT WAS *SUZY HOVORKA.* A GOOD WOMAN. A VOLUNTEER. MOTHER OF TWO CHILDREN.
THE ARMY EVACUATED MOST OF THE CHILDREN AND OLD PEOPLE IN THE FIRST CONVOY, TWO DAYS AGO. SHE'S DEAD WORRIED ABOUT THEM, BUT IT SEEMS SHE CAN'T SIT TIGHT, DOING NOTHING.

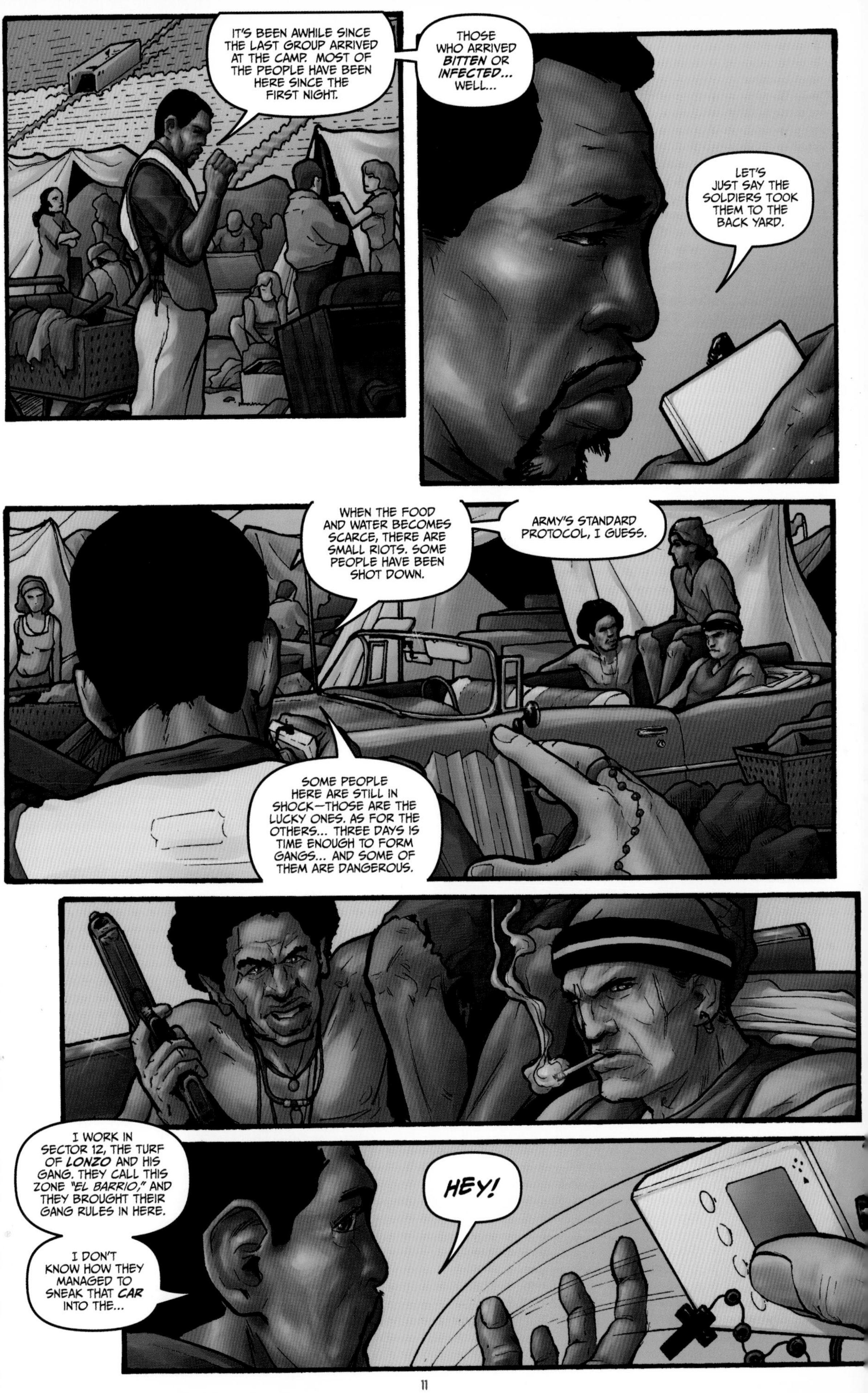
IT'S BEEN AWHILE SINCE THE LAST GROUP ARRIVED AT THE CAMP. MOST OF THE PEOPLE HAVE BEEN HERE SINCE THE FIRST NIGHT.
THOSE WHO ARRIVED *BITTEN* OR *INFECTED...* WELL...
LET'S JUST SAY THE SOLDIERS TOOK THEM TO THE BACK YARD.
WHEN THE FOOD AND WATER BECOMES SCARCE, THERE ARE SMALL RIOTS. SOME PEOPLE HAVE BEEN SHOT DOWN.
ARMY'S STANDARD PROTOCOL, I GUESS.
SOME PEOPLE HERE ARE STILL IN SHOCK—THOSE ARE THE LUCKY ONES. AS FOR THE OTHERS... THREE DAYS IS TIME ENOUGH TO FORM GANGS... AND SOME OF THEM ARE DANGEROUS.
I WORK IN SECTOR 12, THE TURF OF *LONZO* AND HIS GANG. THEY CALL THIS ZONE *"EL BARRIO,"* AND THEY BROUGHT THEIR GANG RULES IN HERE.
I DON'T KNOW HOW THEY MANAGED TO SNEAK THAT *CAR* INTO THE...
HEY!

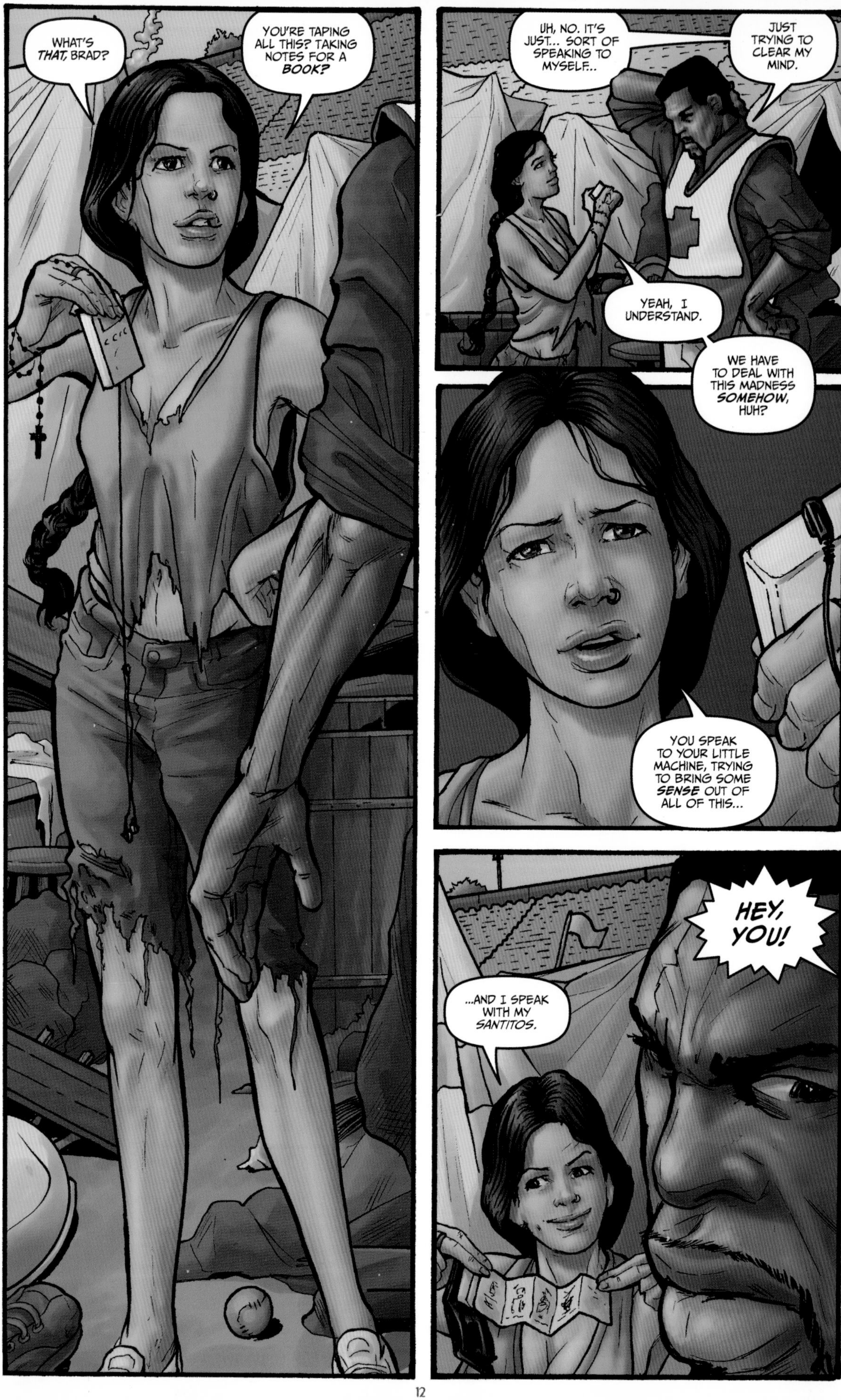
WHAT'S *THAT,* BRAD?
YOU'RE TAPING ALL THIS? TAKING NOTES FOR A *BOOK?*
UH, NO. IT'S JUST... SORT OF SPEAKING TO MYSELF...
JUST TRYING TO CLEAR MY MIND.
YEAH, I UNDERSTAND.
WE HAVE TO DEAL WITH THIS MADNESS *SOMEHOW,* HUH?
YOU SPEAK TO YOUR LITTLE MACHINE, TRYING TO BRING SOME *SENSE* OUT OF ALL OF THIS...
...AND I SPEAK WITH MY *SANTITOS.*
HEY, YOU!

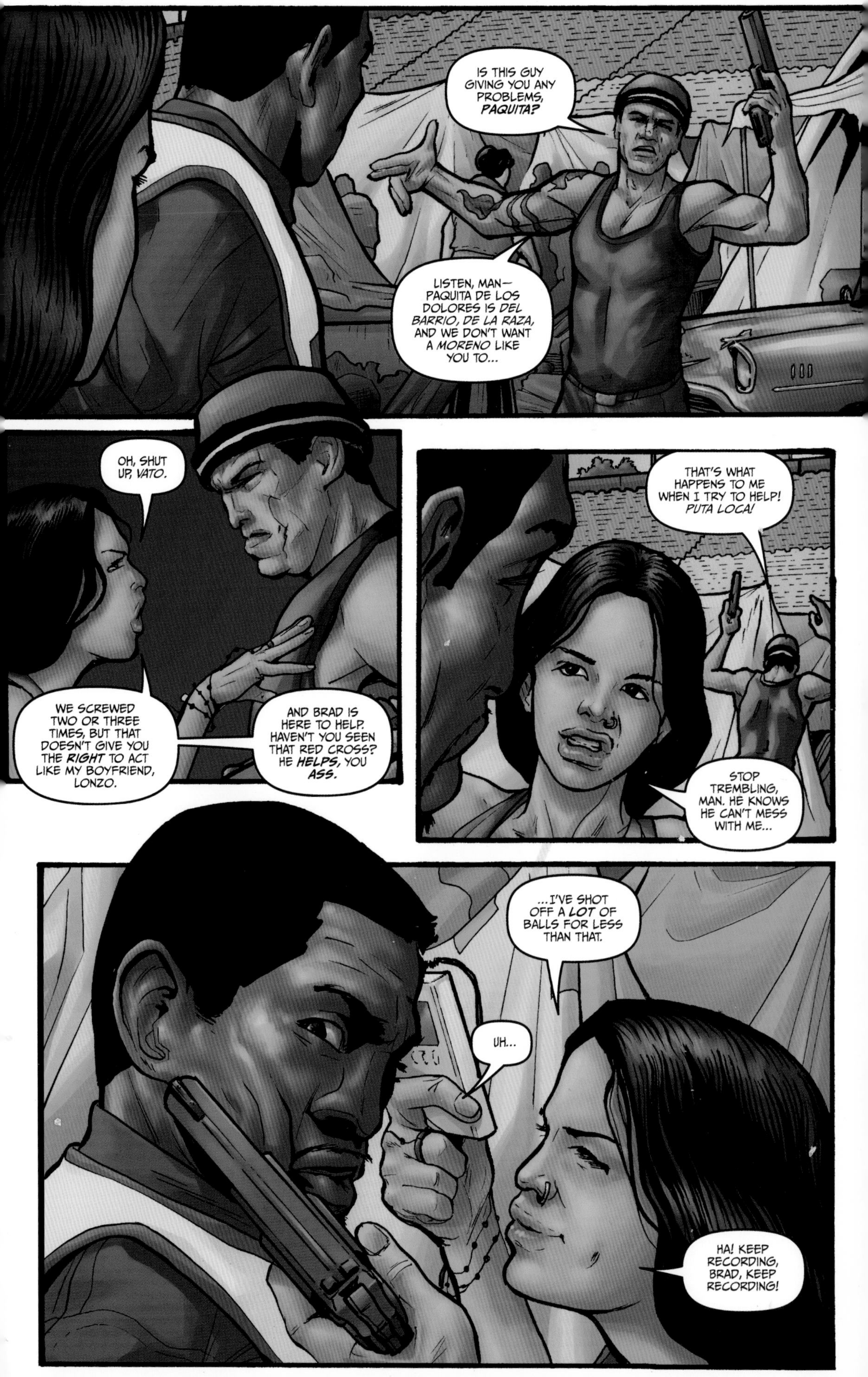
IS THIS GUY GIVING YOU ANY PROBLEMS, *PAQUITA?*
LISTEN, MAN— PAQUITA DE LOS DOLORES IS *DEL BARRIO, DE LA RAZA,* AND WE DON'T WANT A *MORENO* LIKE YOU TO...
OH, SHUT UP, *VATO.*
WE SCREWED TWO OR THREE TIMES, BUT THAT DOESN'T GIVE YOU THE ***RIGHT*** TO ACT LIKE MY BOYFRIEND, LONZO.
AND BRAD IS HERE TO HELP. HAVEN'T YOU SEEN THAT RED CROSS? HE ***HELPS,*** YOU ***ASS.***
THAT'S WHAT HAPPENS TO ME WHEN I TRY TO HELP! *PUTA LOCA!*
STOP TREMBLING, MAN. HE KNOWS HE CAN'T MESS WITH ME...
...I'VE SHOT OFF A ***LOT*** OF BALLS FOR LESS THAN THAT.
UH...
HA! KEEP RECORDING, BRAD, KEEP RECORDING!

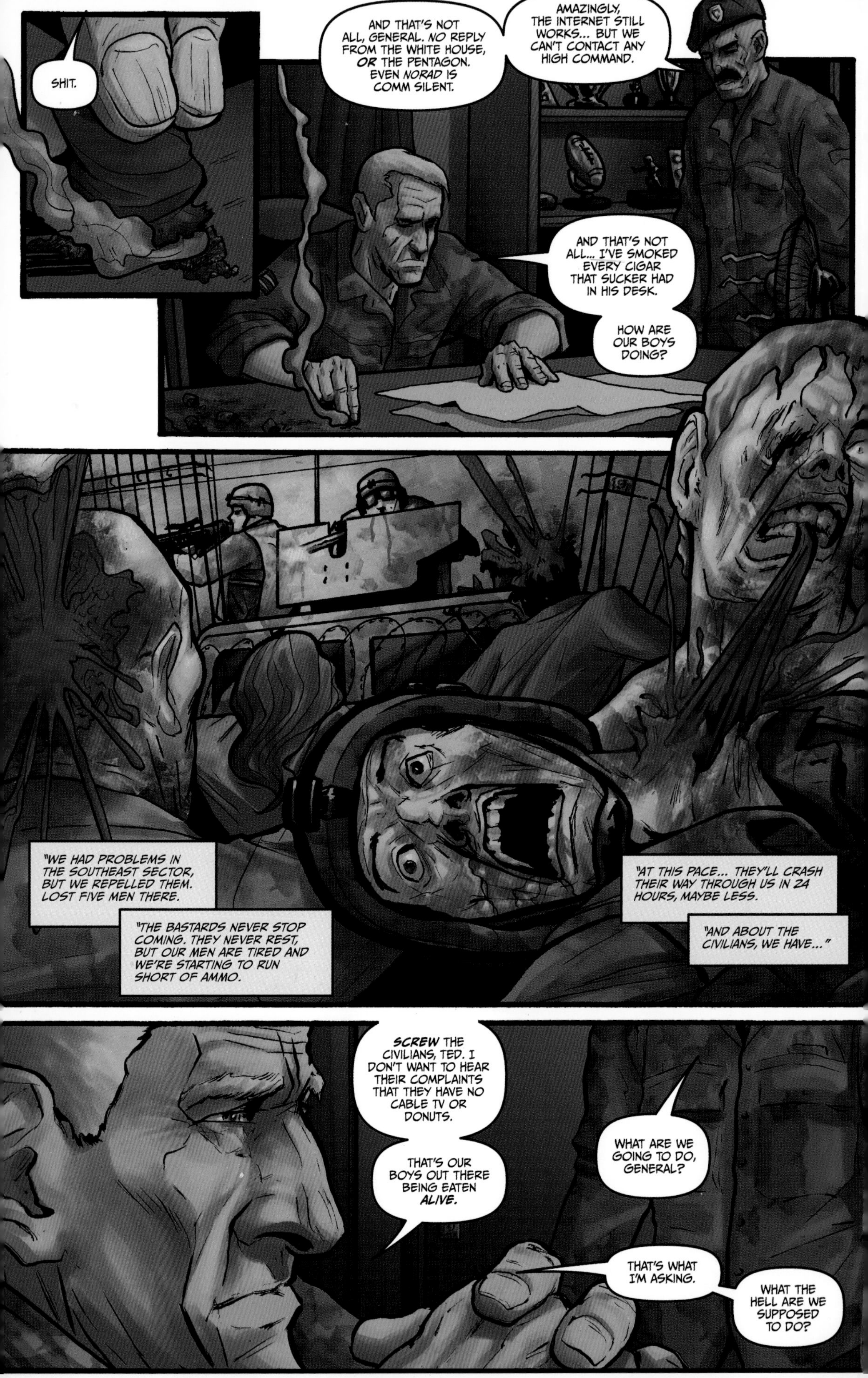

SHIT.
AND THAT'S NOT ALL, GENERAL. *NO* REPLY FROM THE WHITE HOUSE, ***OR*** THE PENTAGON. EVEN *NORAD* IS COMM SILENT.
AMAZINGLY, THE INTERNET STILL WORKS... BUT WE CAN'T CONTACT ANY HIGH COMMAND.
AND THAT'S NOT ALL... I'VE SMOKED EVERY CIGAR THAT SUCKER HAD IN HIS DESK.
HOW ARE OUR BOYS DOING?
"WE HAD PROBLEMS IN THE SOUTHEAST SECTOR, BUT WE REPELLED THEM. LOST FIVE MEN THERE.
"THE BASTARDS NEVER STOP COMING. THEY NEVER REST, BUT OUR MEN ARE TIRED AND WE'RE STARTING TO RUN SHORT OF AMMO.
"AT THIS PACE... THEY'LL CRASH THEIR WAY THROUGH US IN 24 HOURS, MAYBE LESS.
"AND ABOUT THE CIVILIANS, WE HAVE..."
SCREW THE CIVILIANS, TED. I DON'T WANT TO HEAR THEIR COMPLAINTS THAT THEY HAVE NO CABLE TV OR DONUTS.
THAT'S OUR BOYS OUT THERE BEING EATEN ***ALIVE.***
WHAT ARE WE GOING TO DO, GENERAL?
THAT'S WHAT I'M ASKING.
WHAT THE HELL ARE WE SUPPOSED TO DO?

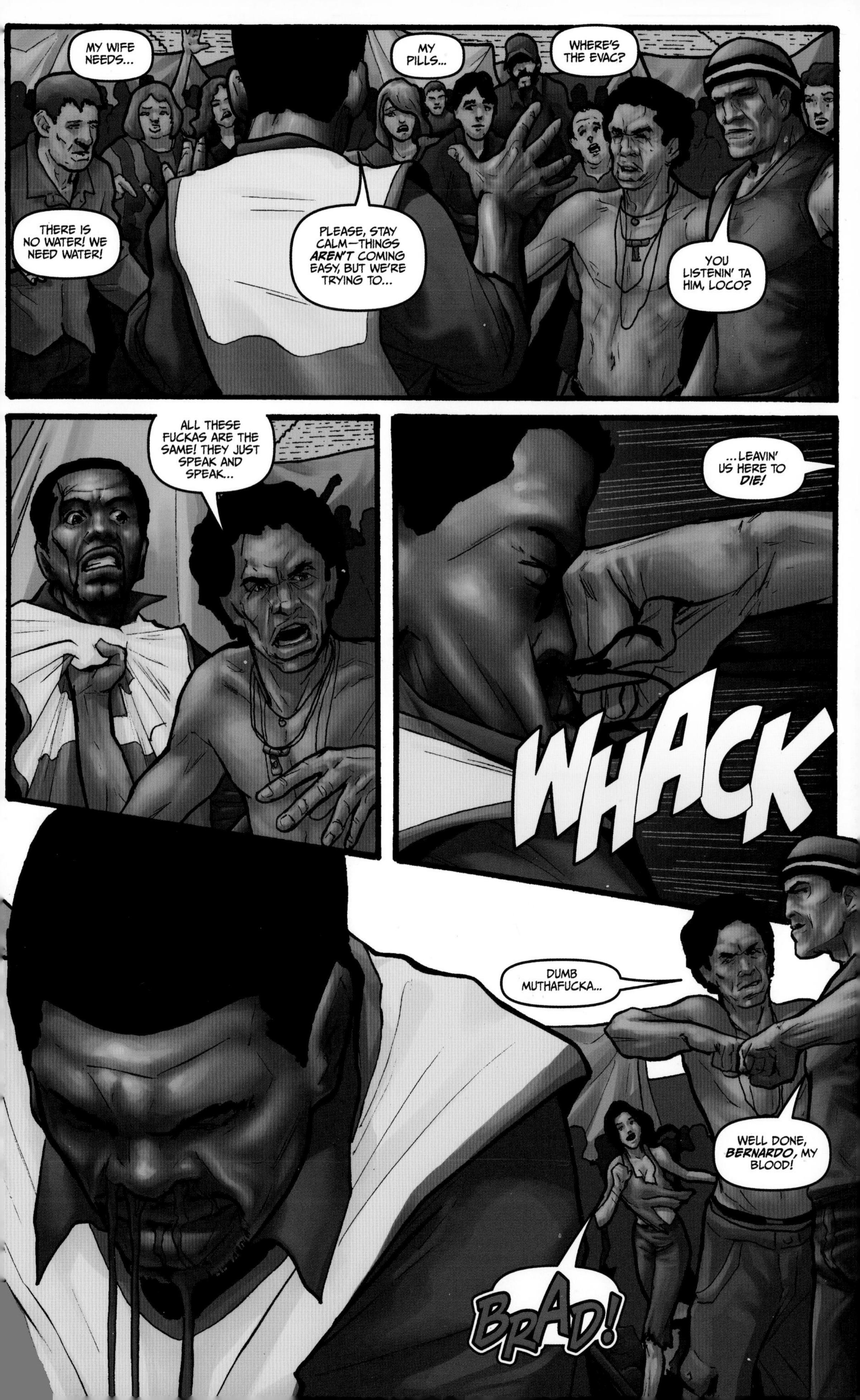
MY WIFE NEEDS...
MY PILLS...
WHERE'S THE EVAC?
THERE IS NO WATER! WE NEED WATER!
PLEASE, STAY CALM—THINGS *AREN'T* COMING EASY, BUT WE'RE TRYING TO...
YOU LISTENIN' TA HIM, LOCO?
ALL THESE FUCKAS ARE THE SAME! THEY JUST SPEAK AND SPEAK...
...LEAVIN' US HERE TO *DIE!*
WHACK
DUMB MUTHAFUCKA...
WELL DONE, *BERNARDO*, MY BLOOD!
BRAD!

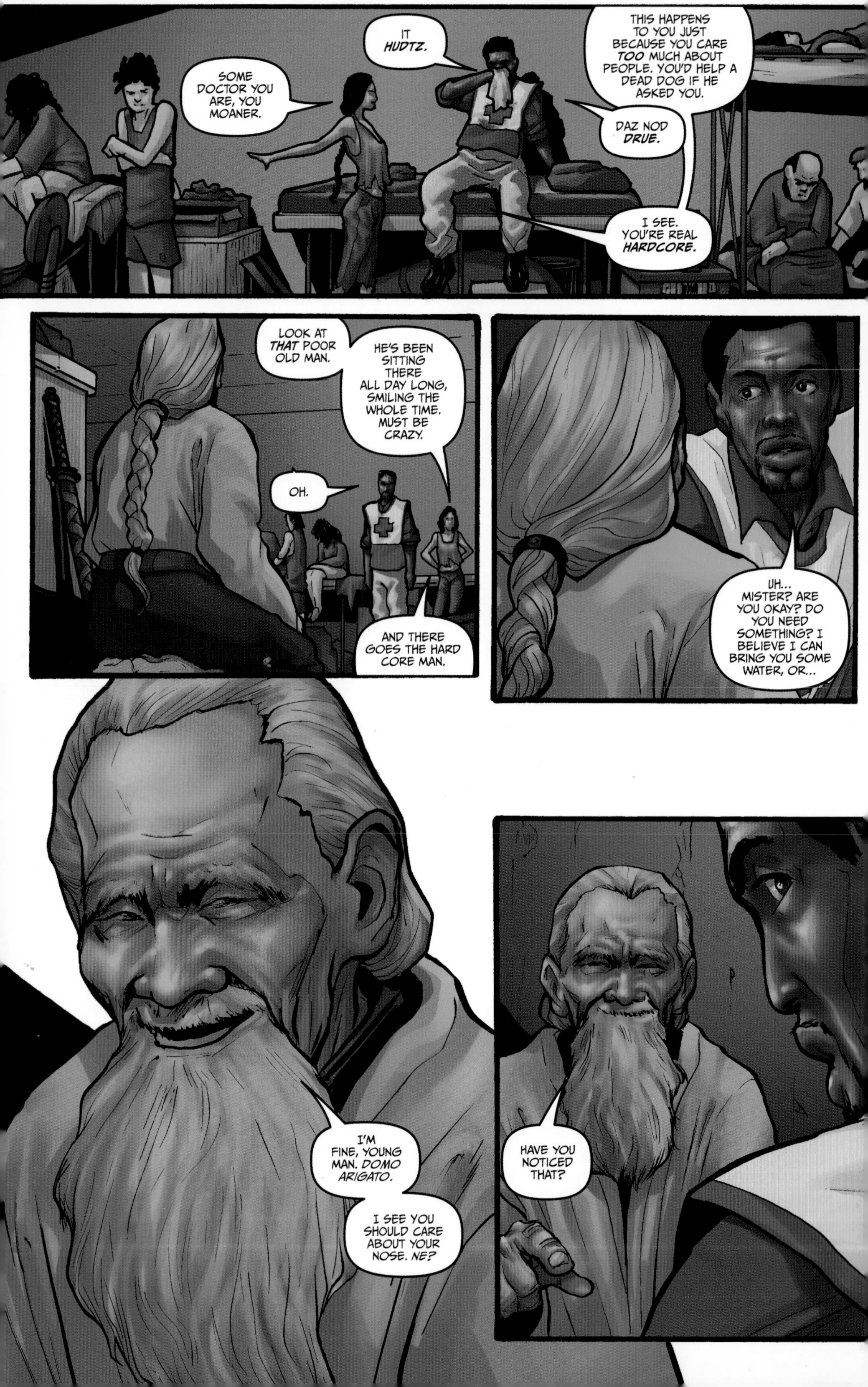
SOME DOCTOR YOU ARE, YOU MOANER.
IT HUDTZ.
THIS HAPPENS TO YOU JUST BECAUSE YOU CARE TOO MUCH ABOUT PEOPLE. YOU'D HELP A DEAD DOG IF HE ASKED YOU.
DAZ NOD DRUE.
I SEE. YOU'RE REAL HARDCORE.
LOOK AT THAT POOR OLD MAN.
HE'S BEEN SITTING THERE ALL DAY LONG, SMILING THE WHOLE TIME. MUST BE CRAZY.
OH.
AND THERE GOES THE HARD CORE MAN.
UH... MISTER? ARE YOU OKAY? DO YOU NEED SOMETHING? I BELIEVE I CAN BRING YOU SOME WATER, OR...
I'M FINE, YOUNG MAN. DOMO ARIGATO.
I SEE YOU SHOULD CARE ABOUT YOUR NOSE. NE?
HAVE YOU NOTICED THAT?

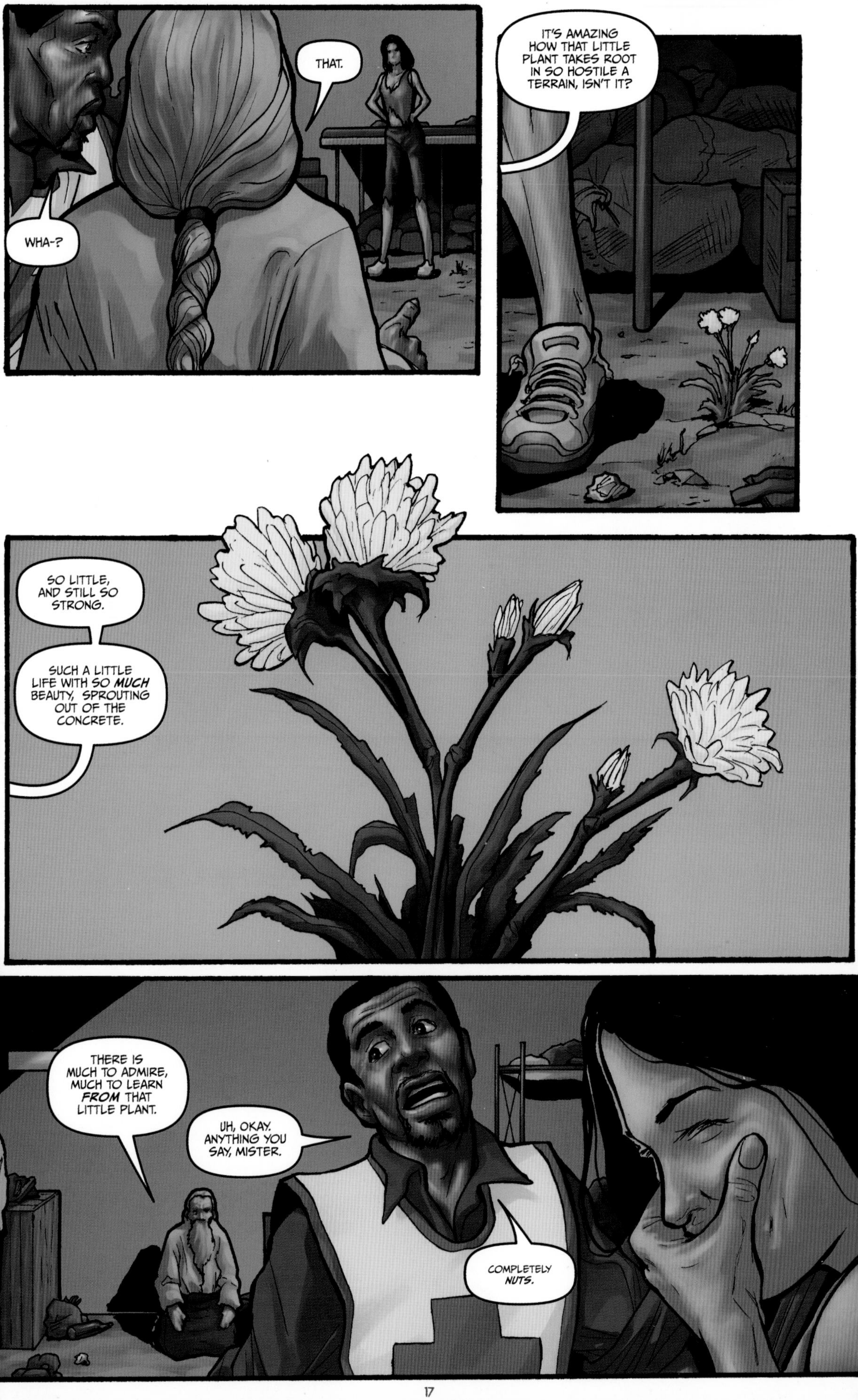
THAT.
WHA-?
IT'S AMAZING HOW THAT LITTLE PLANT TAKES ROOT IN SO HOSTILE A TERRAIN, ISN'T IT?
SO LITTLE, AND STILL SO STRONG.
SUCH A LITTLE LIFE WITH SO *MUCH* BEAUTY, SPROUTING OUT OF THE CONCRETE.
THERE IS MUCH TO ADMIRE, MUCH TO LEARN *FROM* THAT LITTLE PLANT.
UH, OKAY. ANYTHING YOU SAY, MISTER.
COMPLETELY *NUTS*.

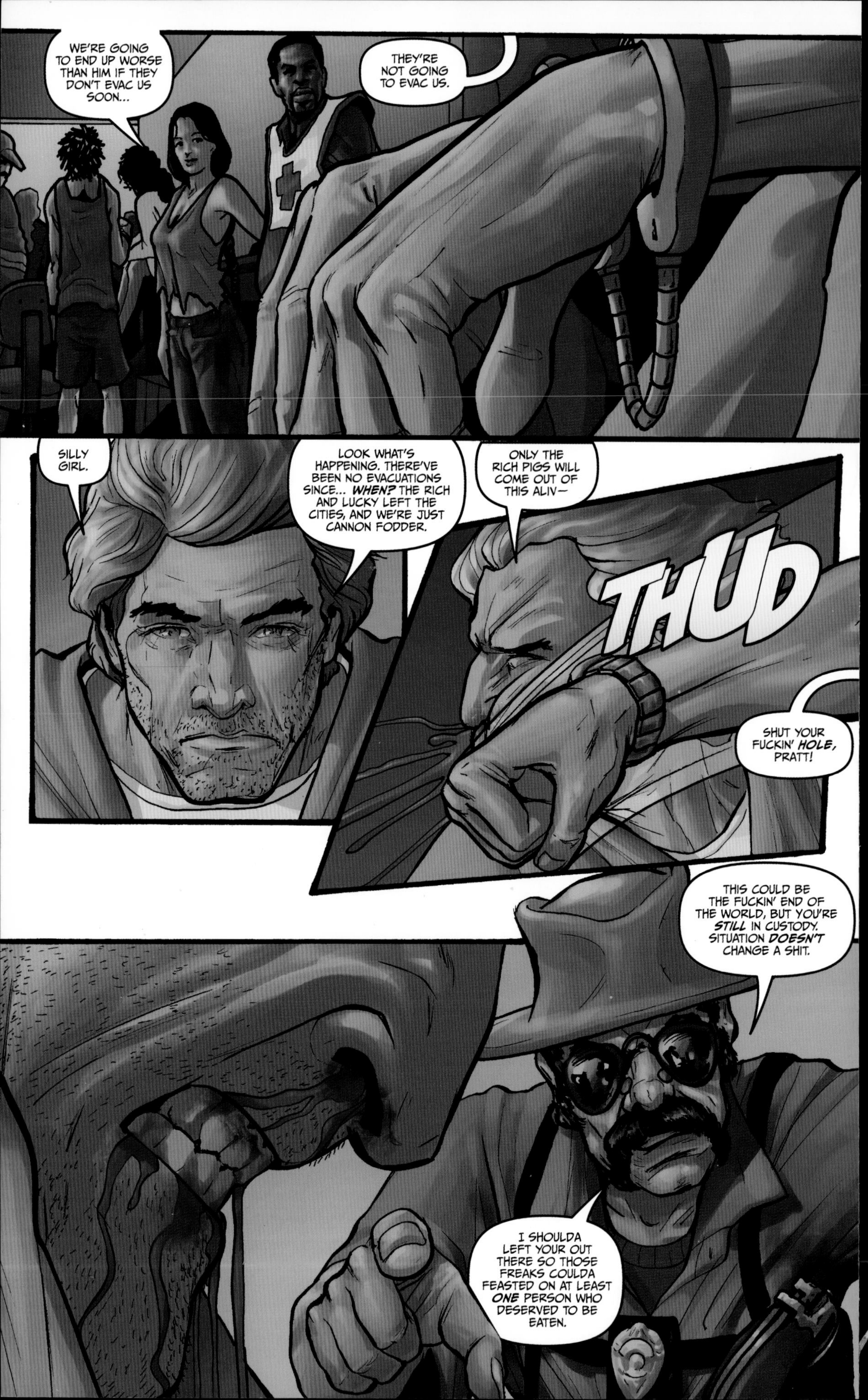

WE'RE GOING TO END UP WORSE THAN HIM IF THEY DON'T EVAC US SOON...
THEY'RE NOT GOING TO EVAC US.
SILLY GIRL.
LOOK WHAT'S HAPPENING. THERE'VE BEEN NO EVACUATIONS SINCE... WHEN? THE RICH AND LUCKY LEFT THE CITIES, AND WE'RE JUST CANNON FODDER.
ONLY THE RICH PIGS WILL COME OUT OF THIS ALIV—
THUD
SHUT YOUR FUCKIN' HOLE, PRATT!
THIS COULD BE THE FUCKIN' END OF THE WORLD, BUT YOU'RE STILL IN CUSTODY. SITUATION DOESN'T CHANGE A SHIT.
I SHOULDA LEFT YOUR OUT THERE SO THOSE FREAKS COULDA FEASTED ON AT LEAST ONE PERSON WHO DESERVED TO BE EATEN.

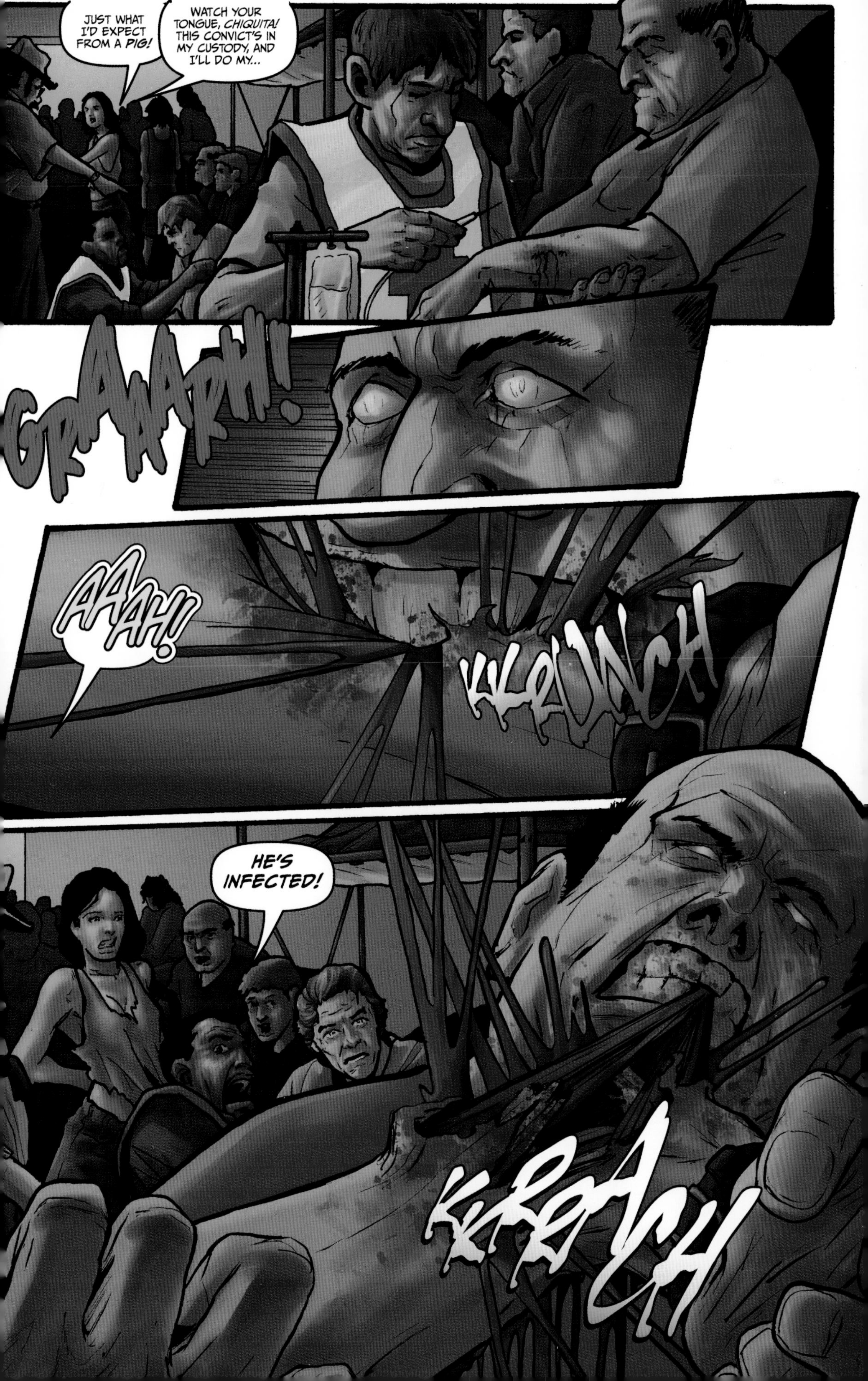
JUST WHAT I'D EXPECT FROM A *PIG*!
WATCH YOUR TONGUE, *CHIQUITA!* THIS CONVICT'S IN MY CUSTODY, AND I'LL DO MY...
GRAAARH!
AAAAH!
KKRUNCH
HE'S INFECTED!
KKREACH

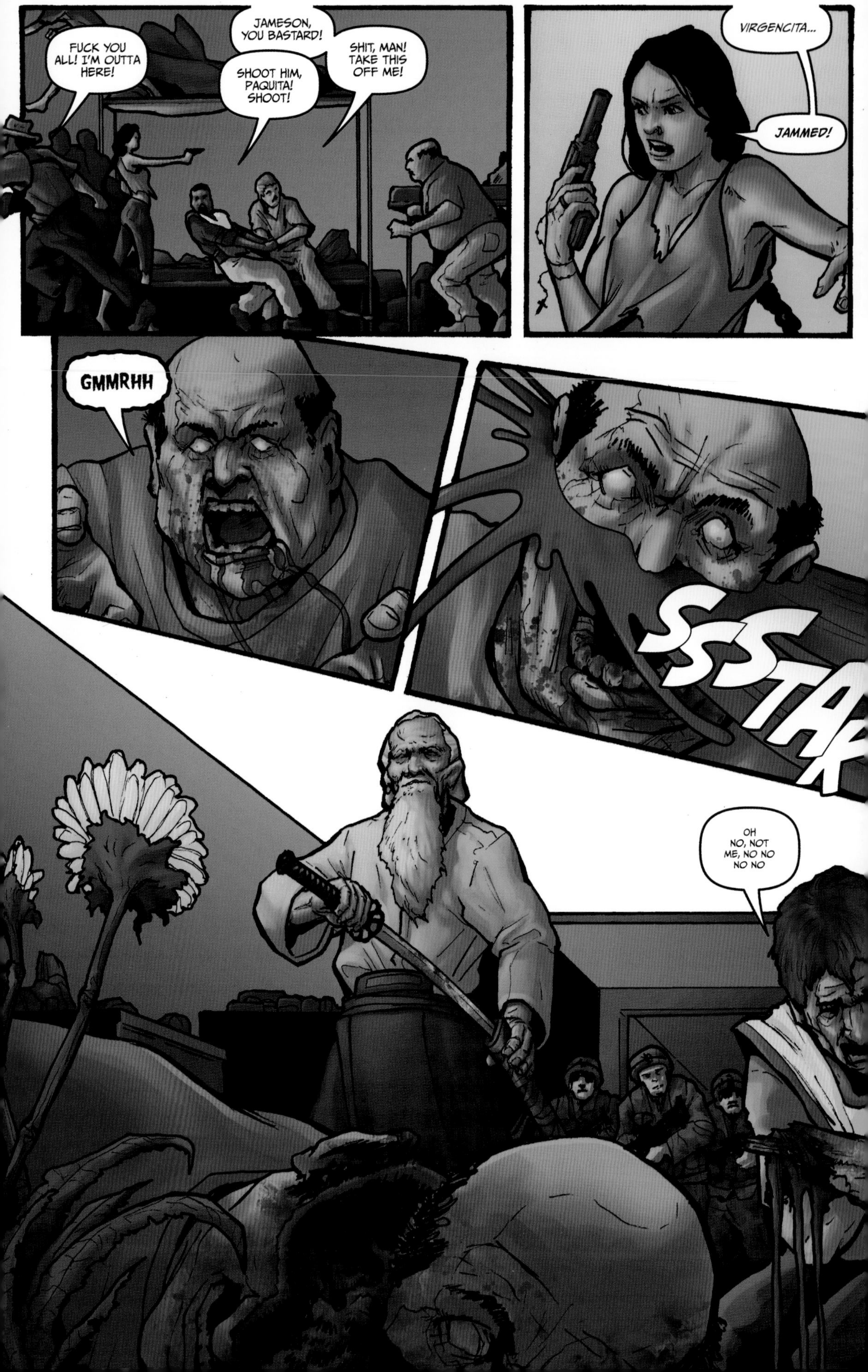
FUCK YOU ALL! I'M OUTTA HERE!
JAMESON, YOU BASTARD!
SHOOT HIM, PAQUITA! SHOOT!
SHIT, MAN! TAKE THIS OFF ME!
VIRGENCITA...
JAMMED!
GMMRHH
SSTAK
OH NO, NOT ME, NO NO NO NO

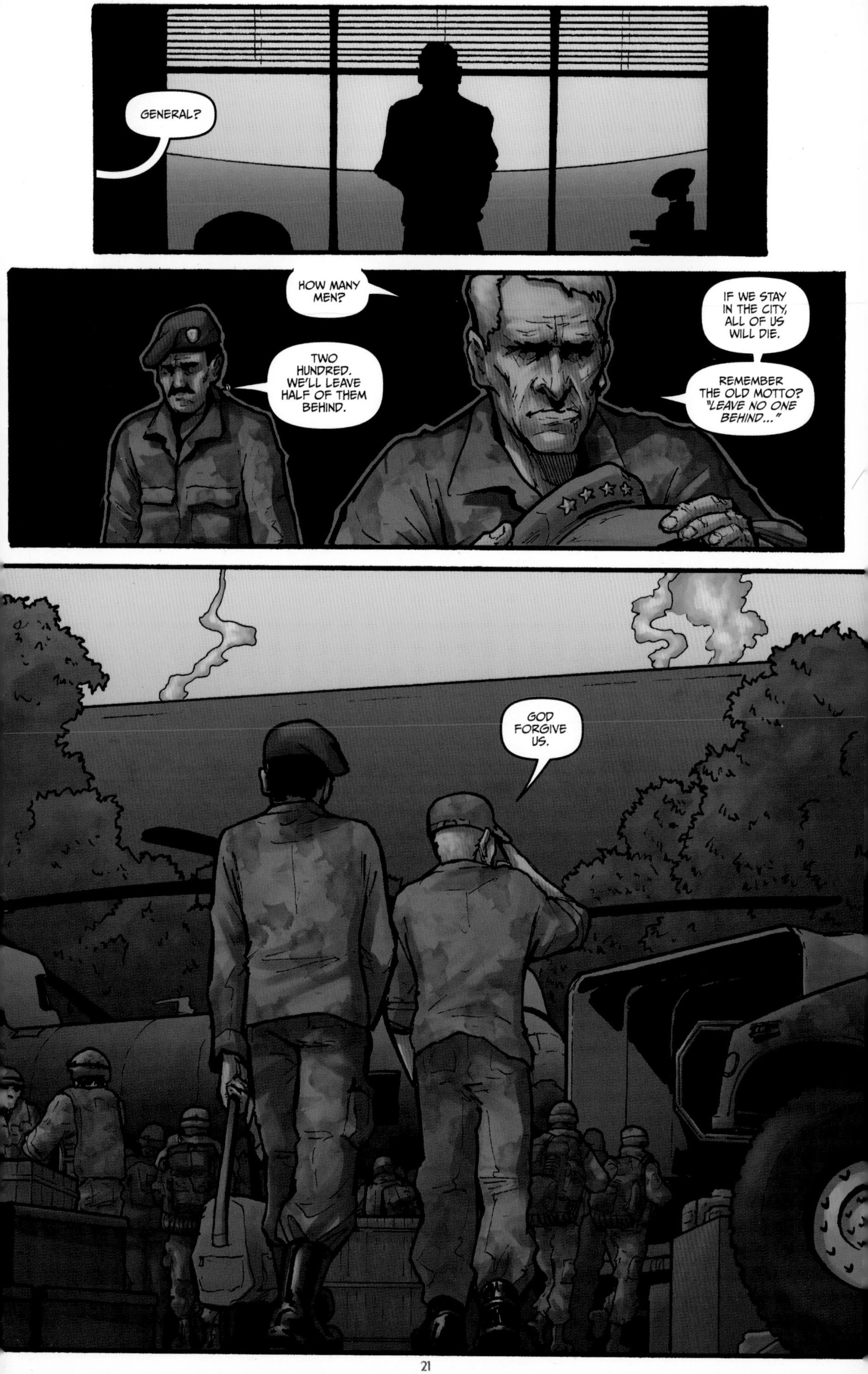
GENERAL?
HOW MANY MEN?
TWO HUNDRED. WE'LL LEAVE HALF OF THEM BEHIND.
IF WE STAY IN THE CITY, ALL OF US WILL DIE.
REMEMBER THE OLD MOTTO? "LEAVE NO ONE BEHIND..."
GOD FORGIVE US.

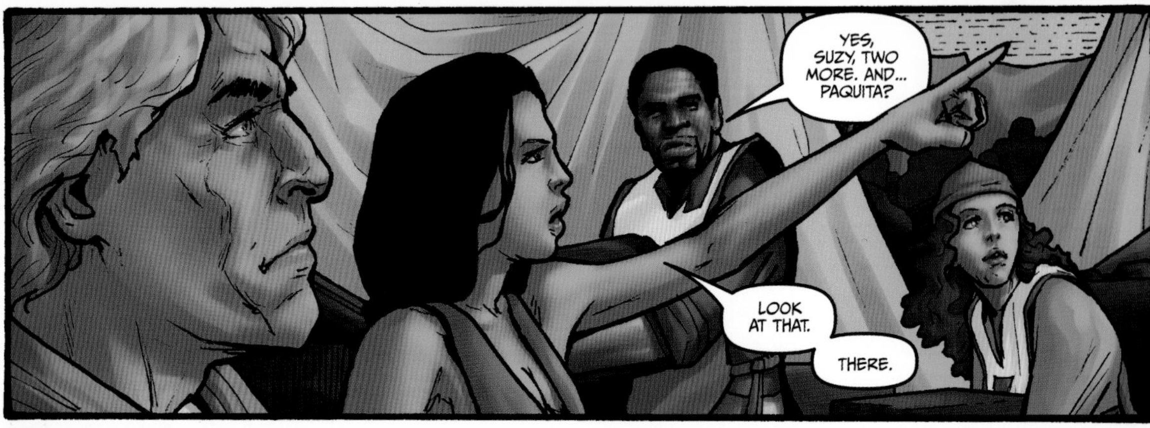
YES, SUZY, TWO MORE. AND... PAQUITA?
LOOK AT THAT.
THERE.

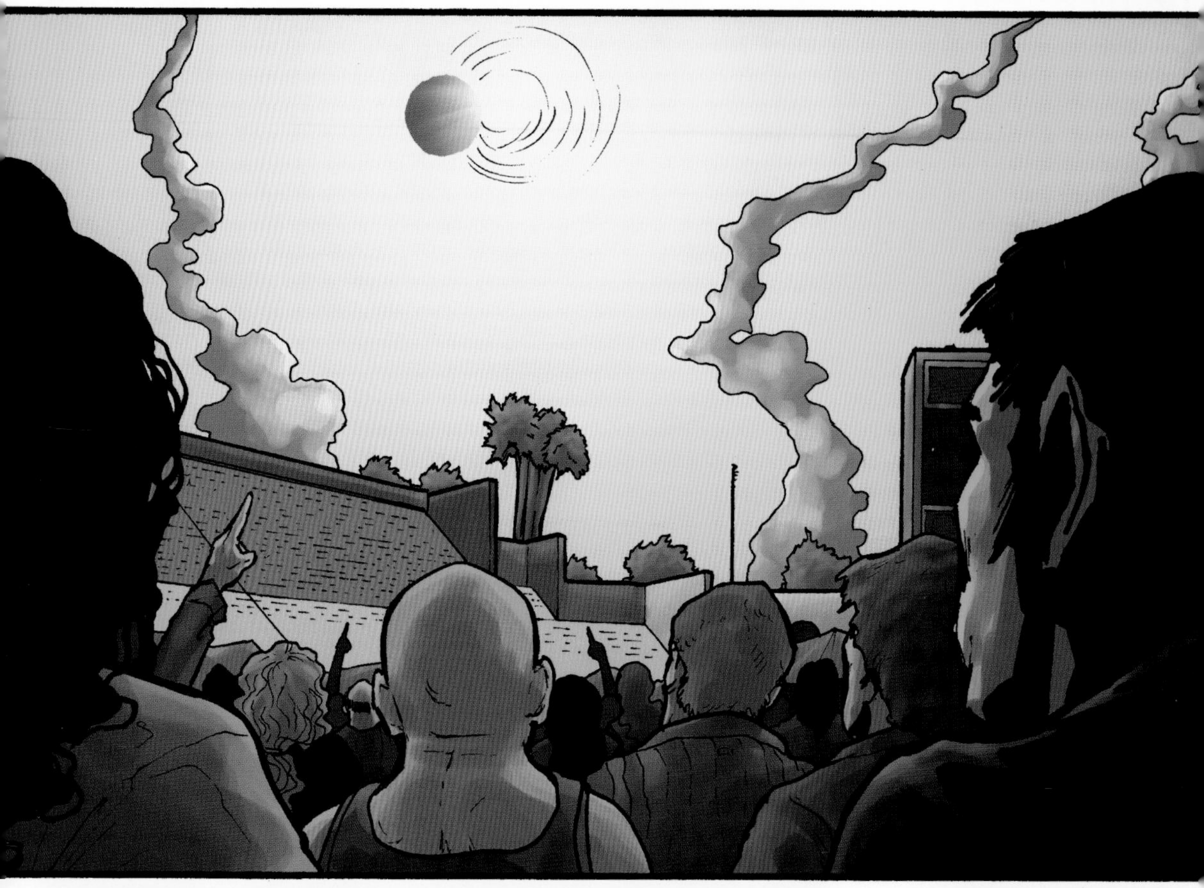

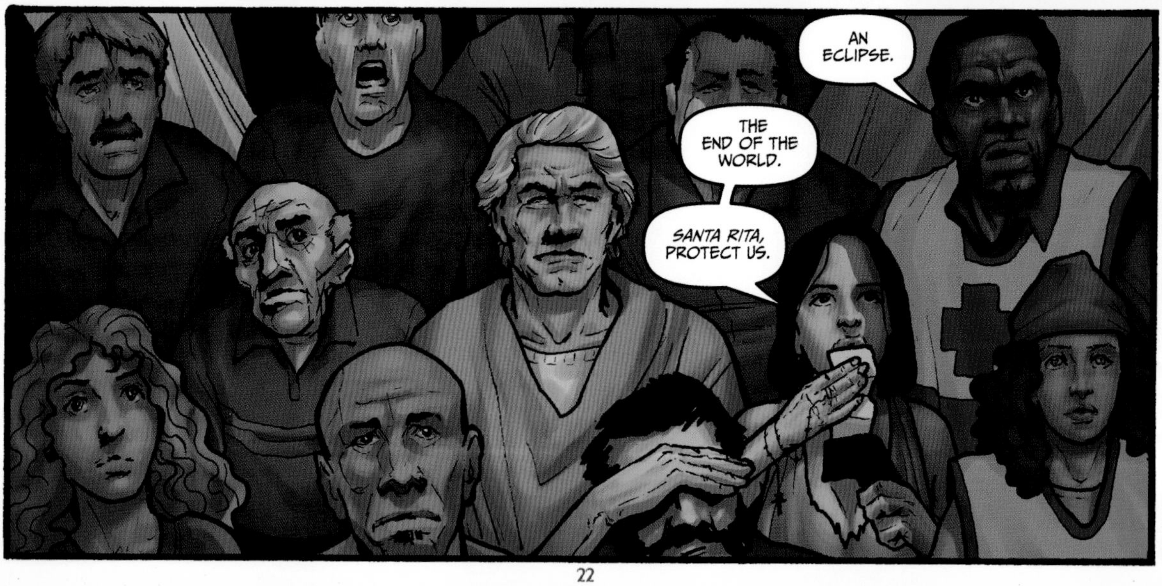
AN ECLIPSE.
THE END OF THE WORLD.
SANTA RITA, PROTECT US.

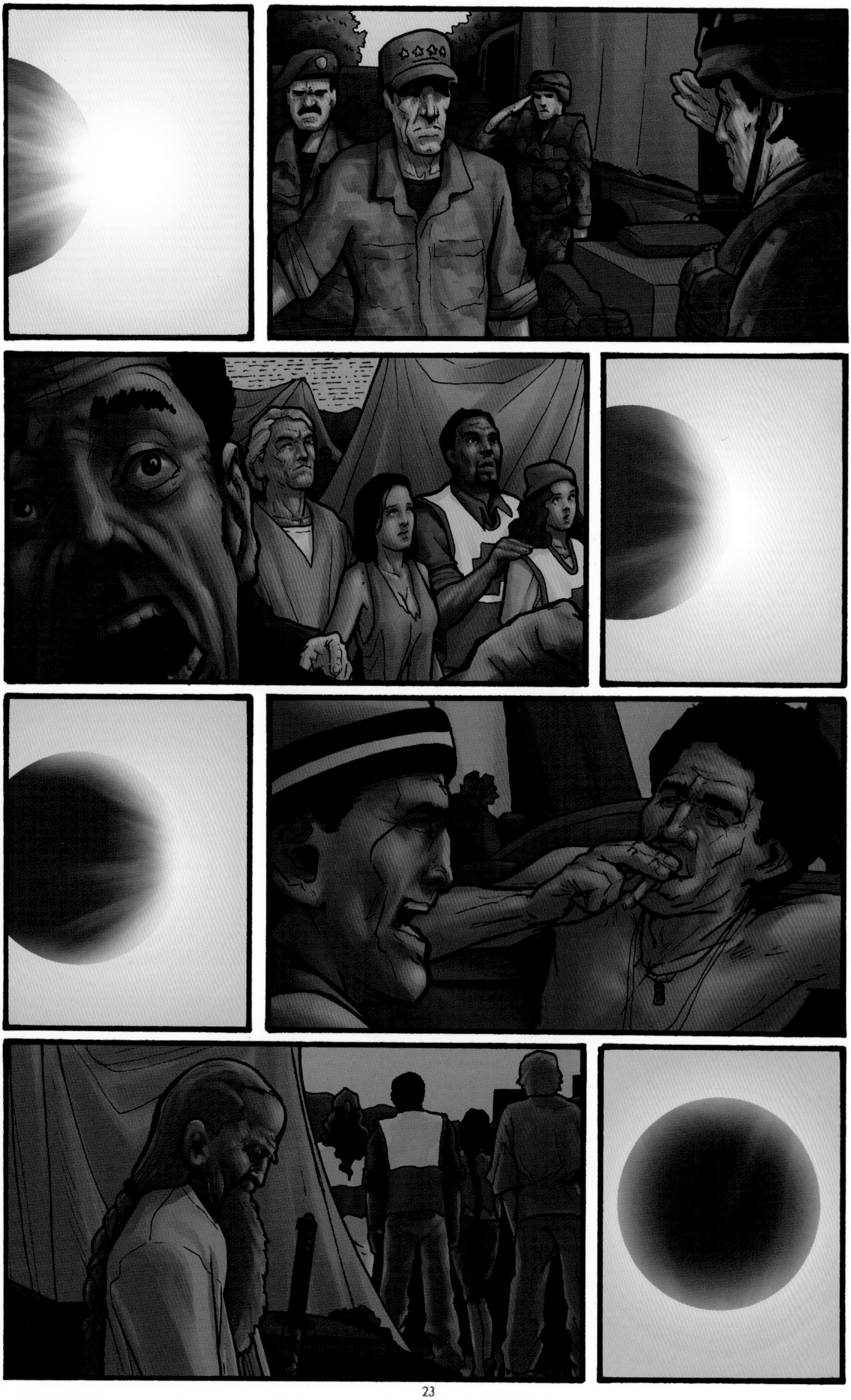

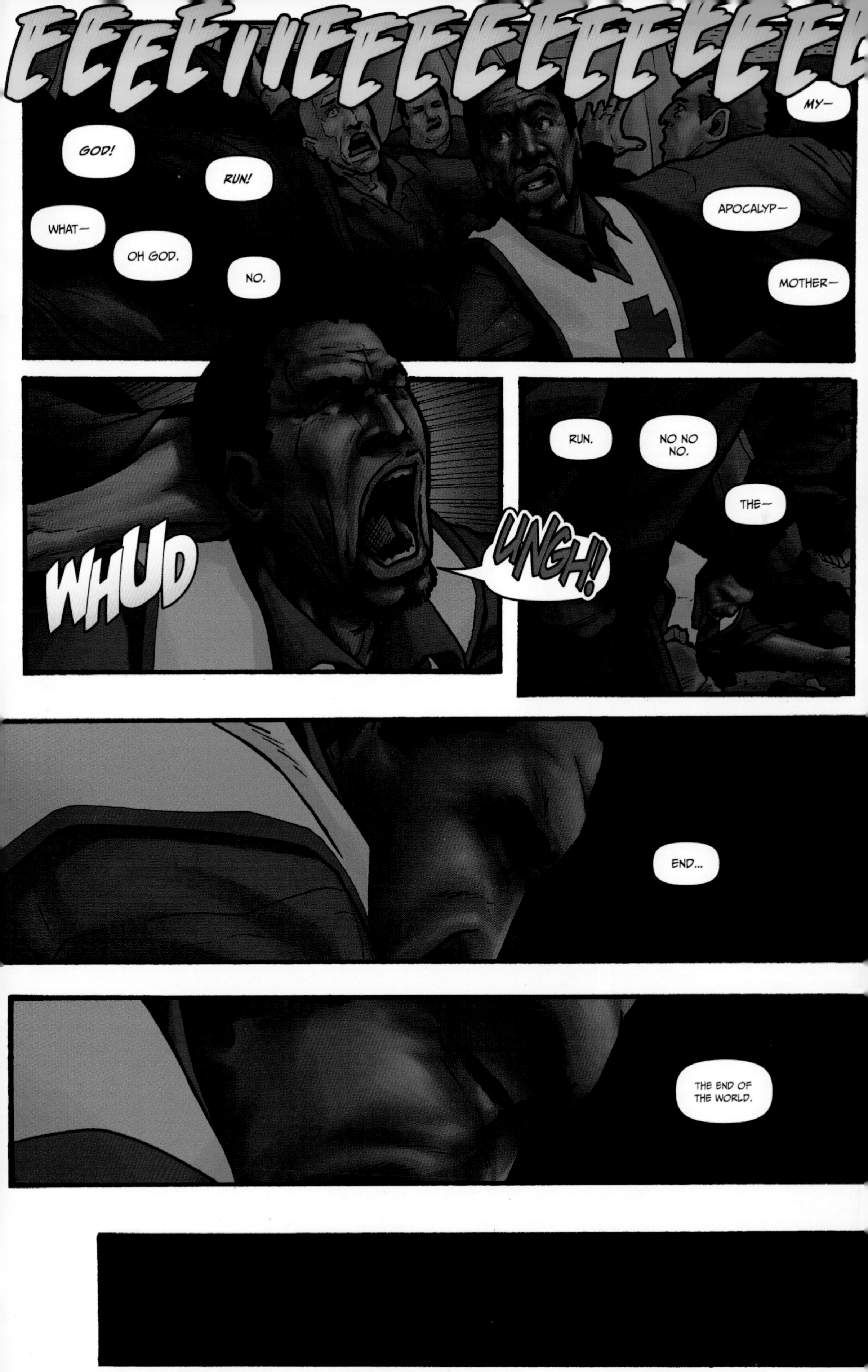
EEEEIIEEEEEEEEEEEE
GOD!
RUN!
WHAT—
OH GOD.
NO.
MY—
APOCALYP—
MOTHER—
WHUD
UNGH!
RUN.
NO NO NO.
THE—
END...
THE END OF THE WORLD.

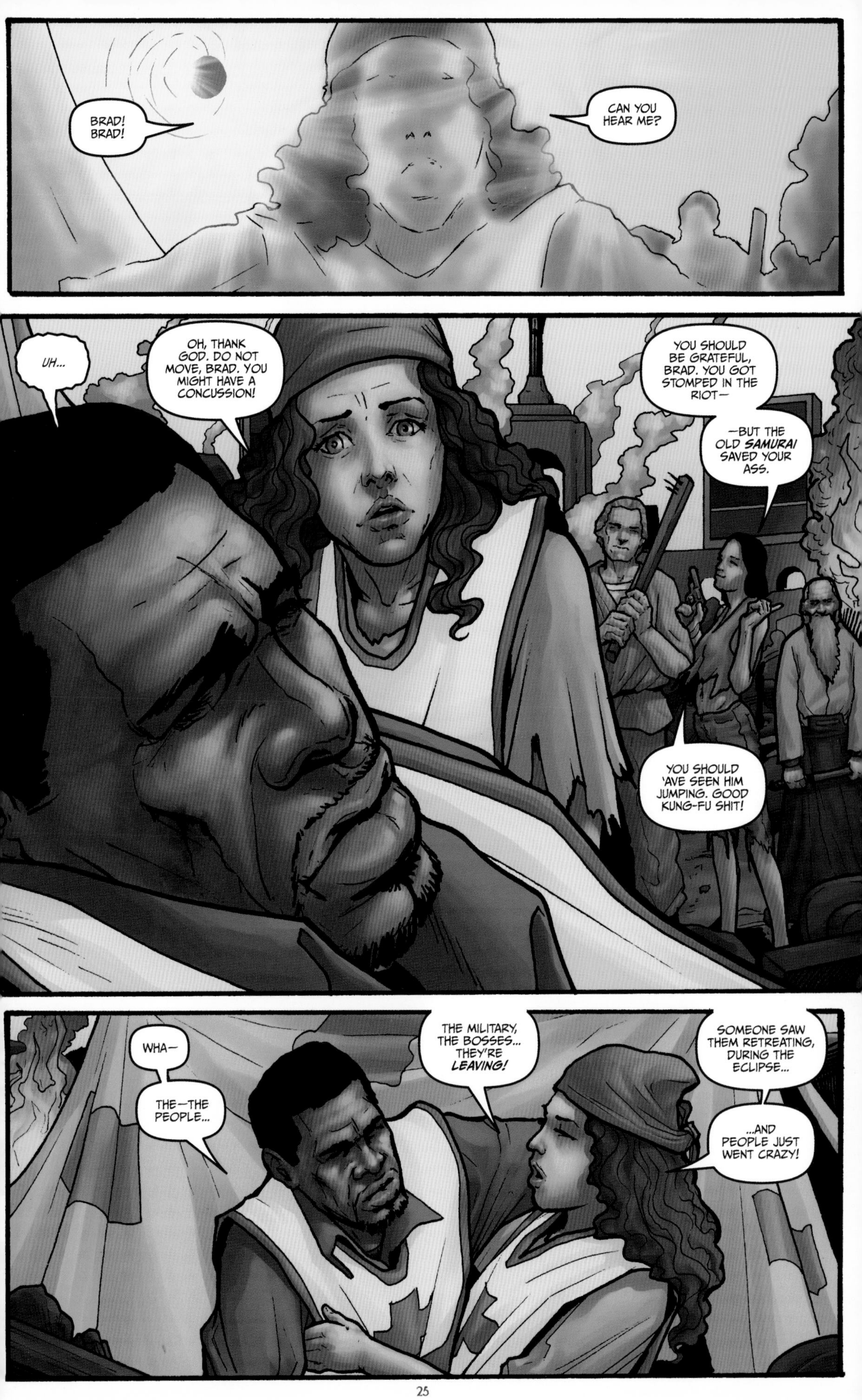
BRAD! BRAD!
CAN YOU HEAR ME?
UH...
OH, THANK GOD. DO NOT MOVE, BRAD. YOU MIGHT HAVE A CONCUSSION!
YOU SHOULD BE GRATEFUL, BRAD. YOU GOT STOMPED IN THE RIOT—
—BUT THE OLD SAMURAI SAVED YOUR ASS.
YOU SHOULD 'AVE SEEN HIM JUMPING. GOOD KUNG-FU SHIT!
WHA—
THE—THE PEOPLE...
THE MILITARY, THE BOSSES... THEY'RE LEAVING!
SOMEONE SAW THEM RETREATING, DURING THE ECLIPSE...
...AND PEOPLE JUST WENT CRAZY!

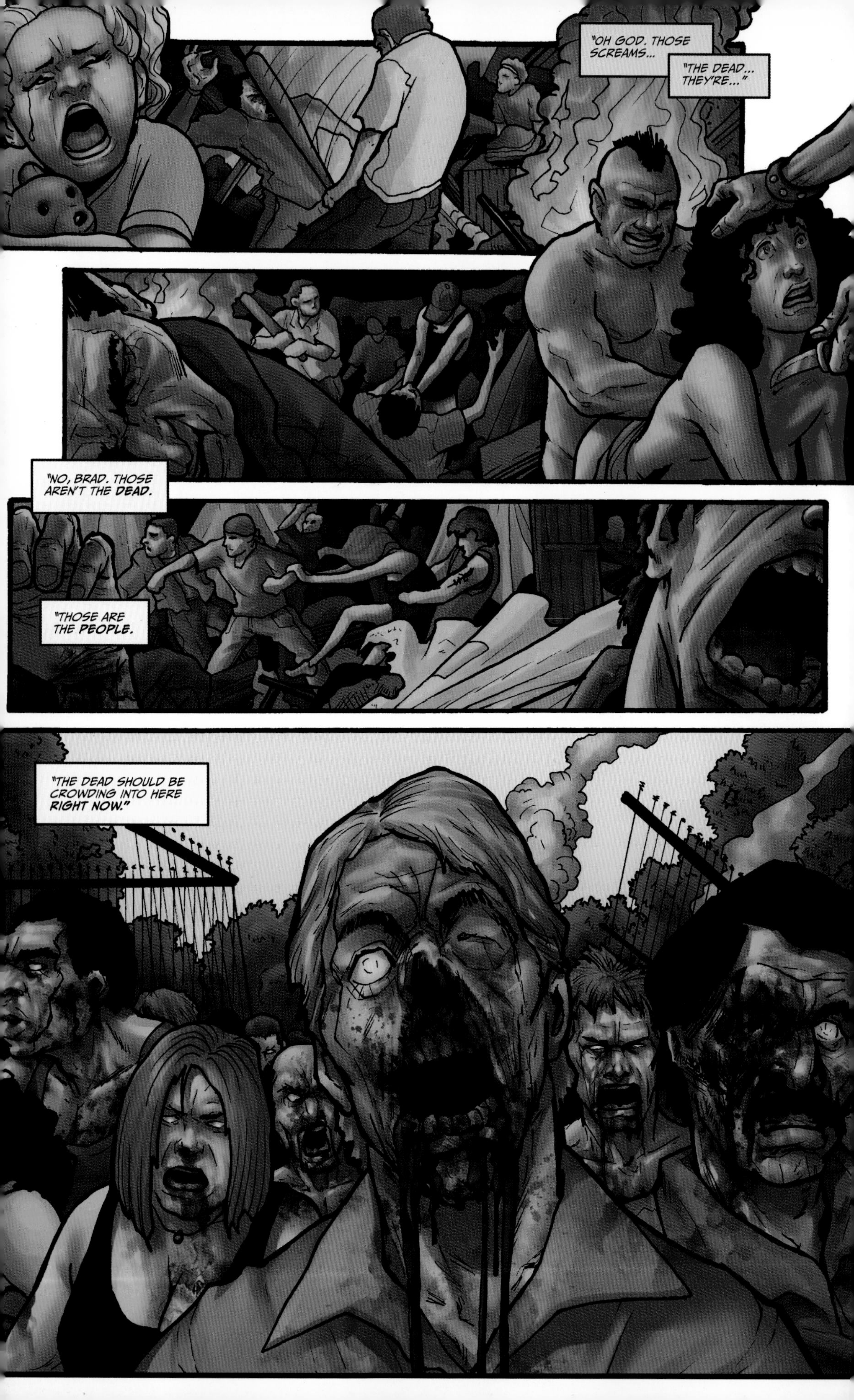
"OH GOD. THOSE SCREAMS...
"THE DEAD... THEY'RE..."
"NO, BRAD. THOSE AREN'T THE DEAD.
"THOSE ARE THE PEOPLE.
"THE DEAD SHOULD BE CROWDING INTO HERE RIGHT NOW."

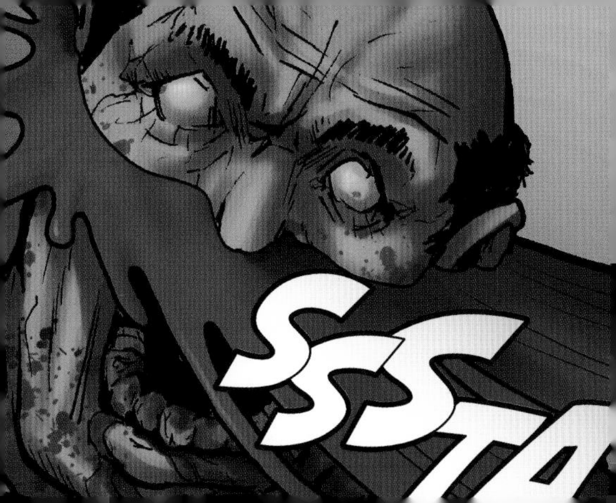
SSTA

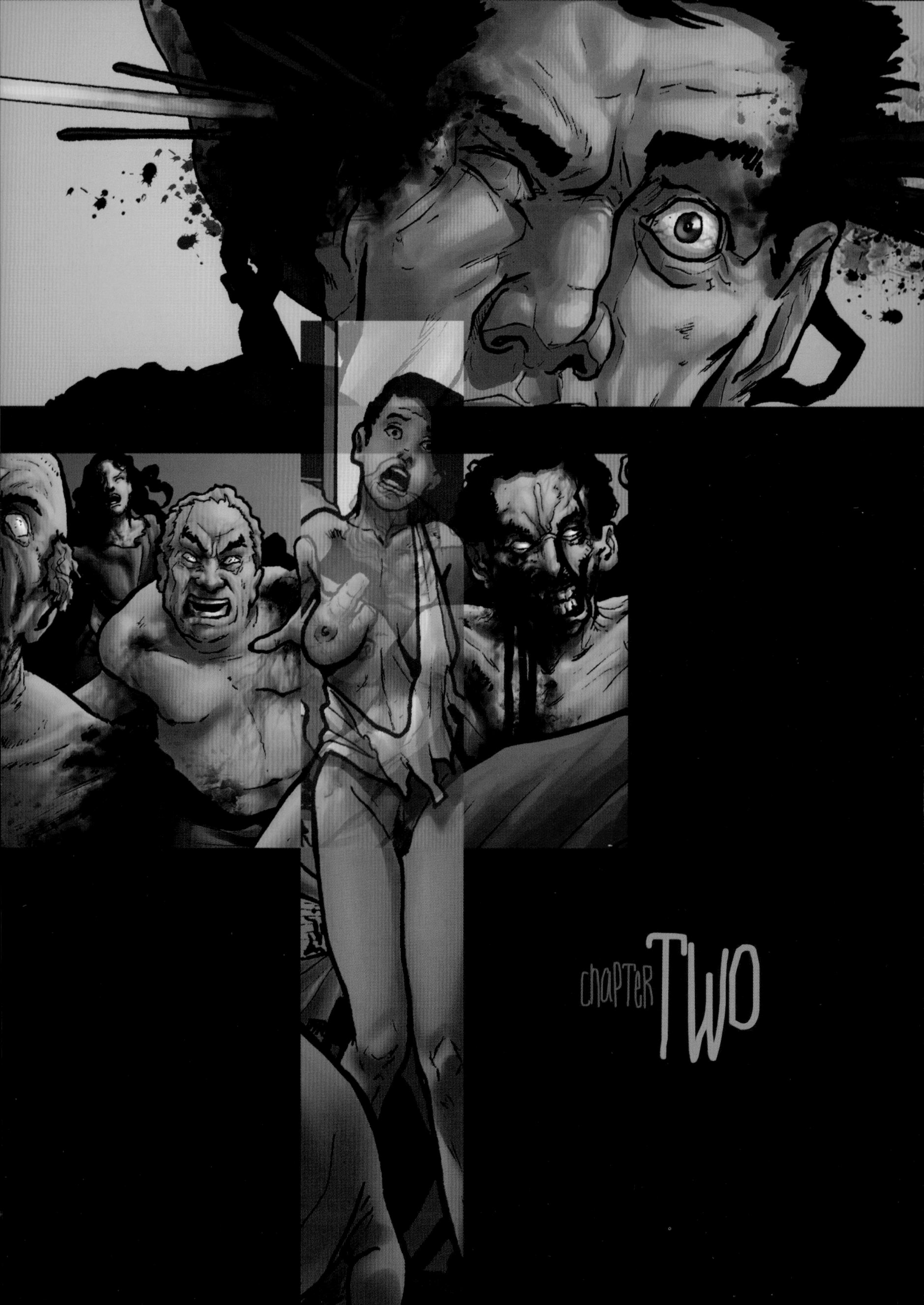
chapter TWO

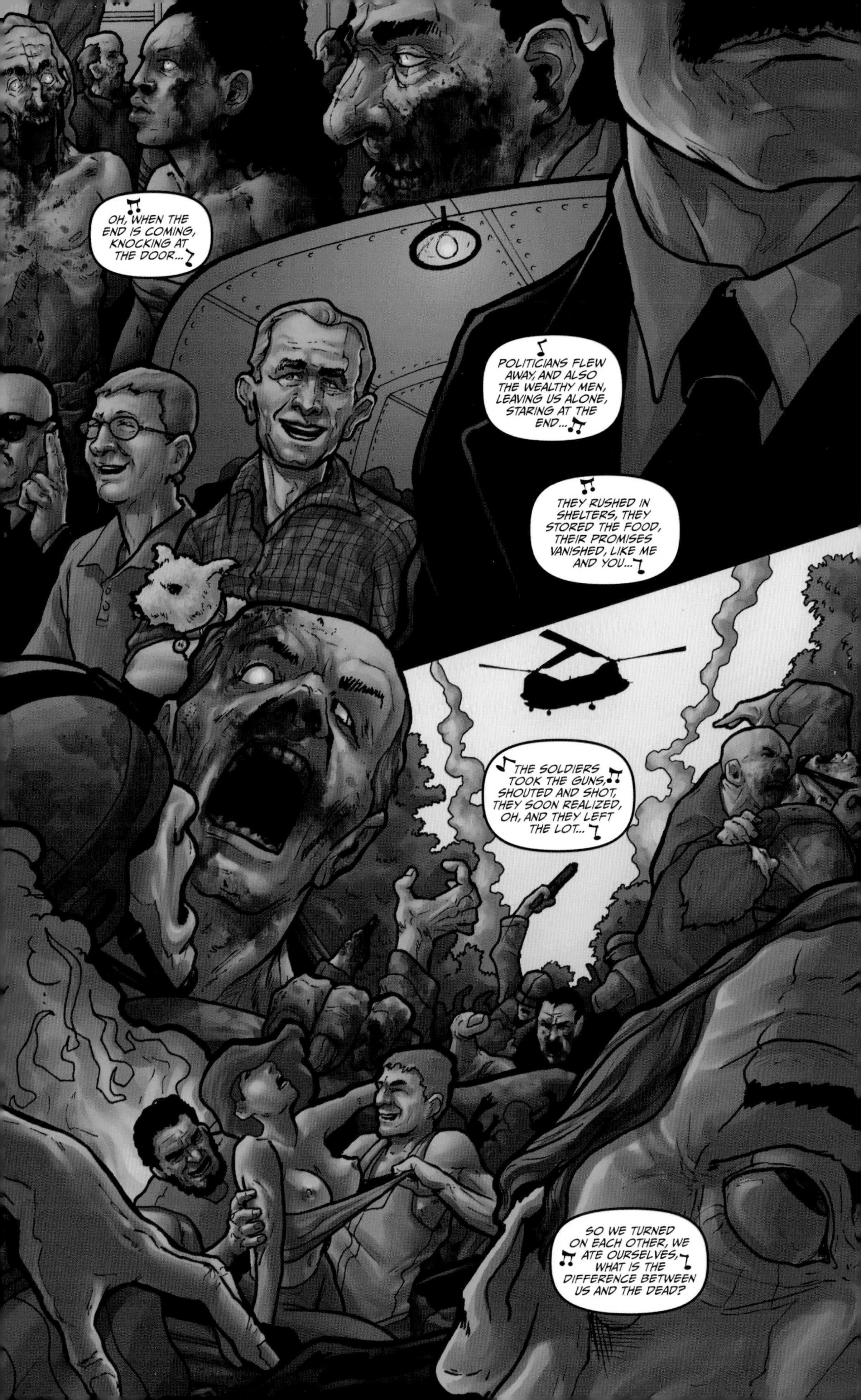
OH, WHEN THE END IS COMING, KNOCKING AT THE DOOR...
POLITICIANS FLEW AWAY, AND ALSO THE WEALTHY MEN, LEAVING US ALONE, STARING AT THE END...
THEY RUSHED IN SHELTERS, THEY STORED THE FOOD, THEIR PROMISES VANISHED, LIKE ME AND YOU...
THE SOLDIERS TOOK THE GUNS, SHOUTED AND SHOT, THEY SOON REALIZED, OH, AND THEY LEFT THE LOT...
SO WE TURNED ON EACH OTHER, WE ATE OURSELVES, WHAT IS THE DIFFERENCE BETWEEN US AND THE DEAD?

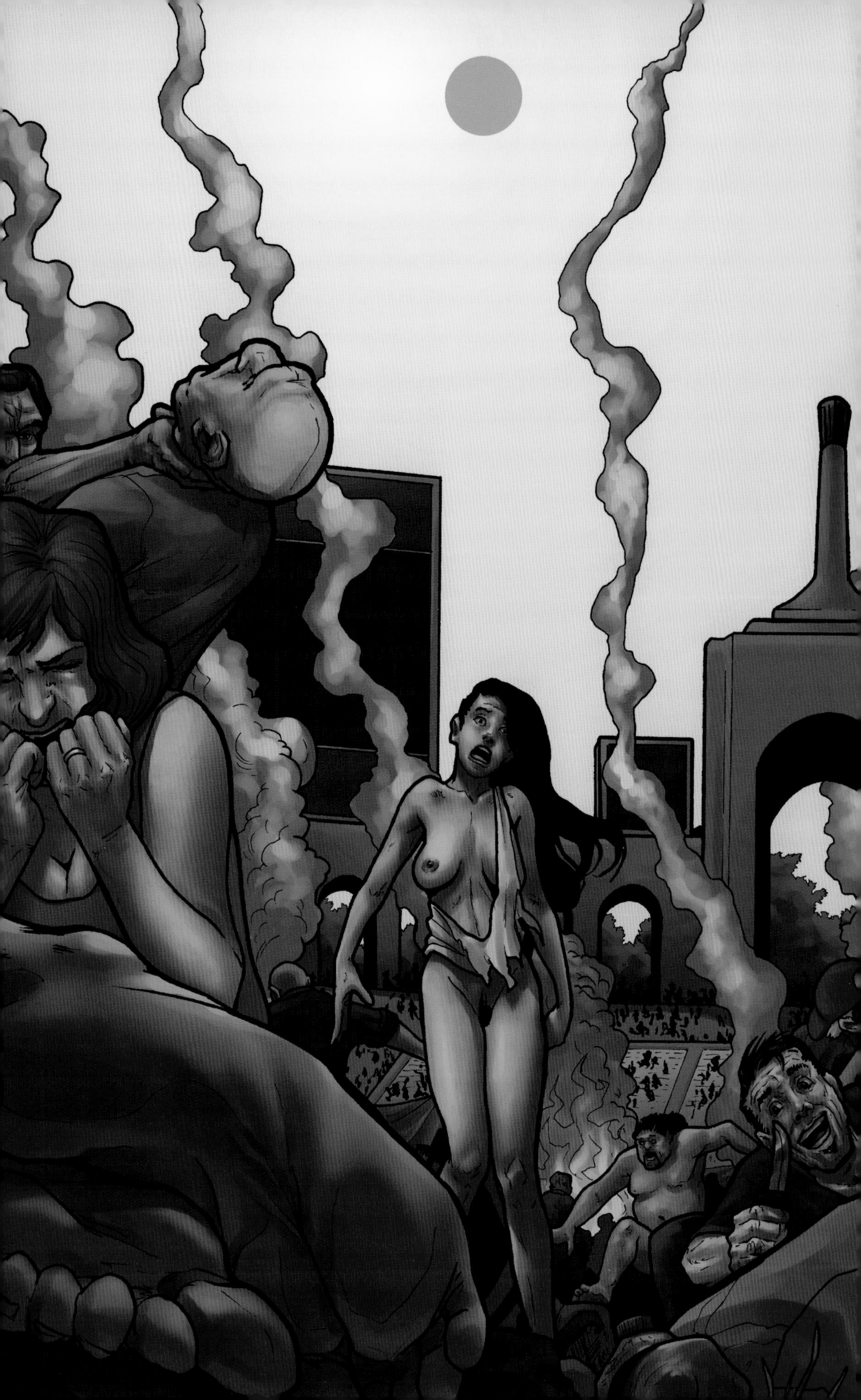

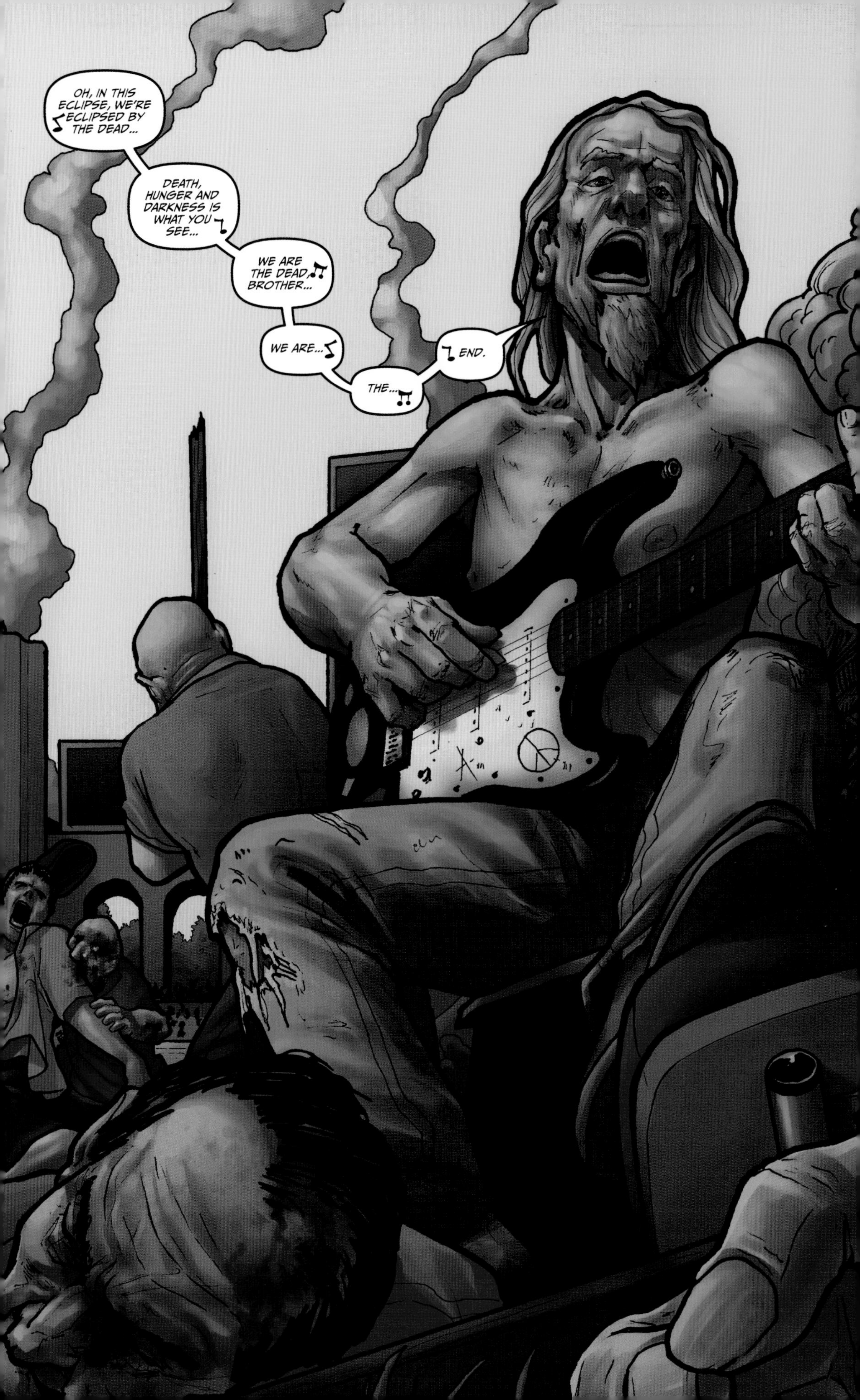
OH, IN THIS ECLIPSE, WE'RE ECLIPSED BY THE DEAD...
DEATH, HUNGER AND DARKNESS IS WHAT YOU SEE...
WE ARE THE DEAD, BROTHER...
WE ARE...
THE...
END.

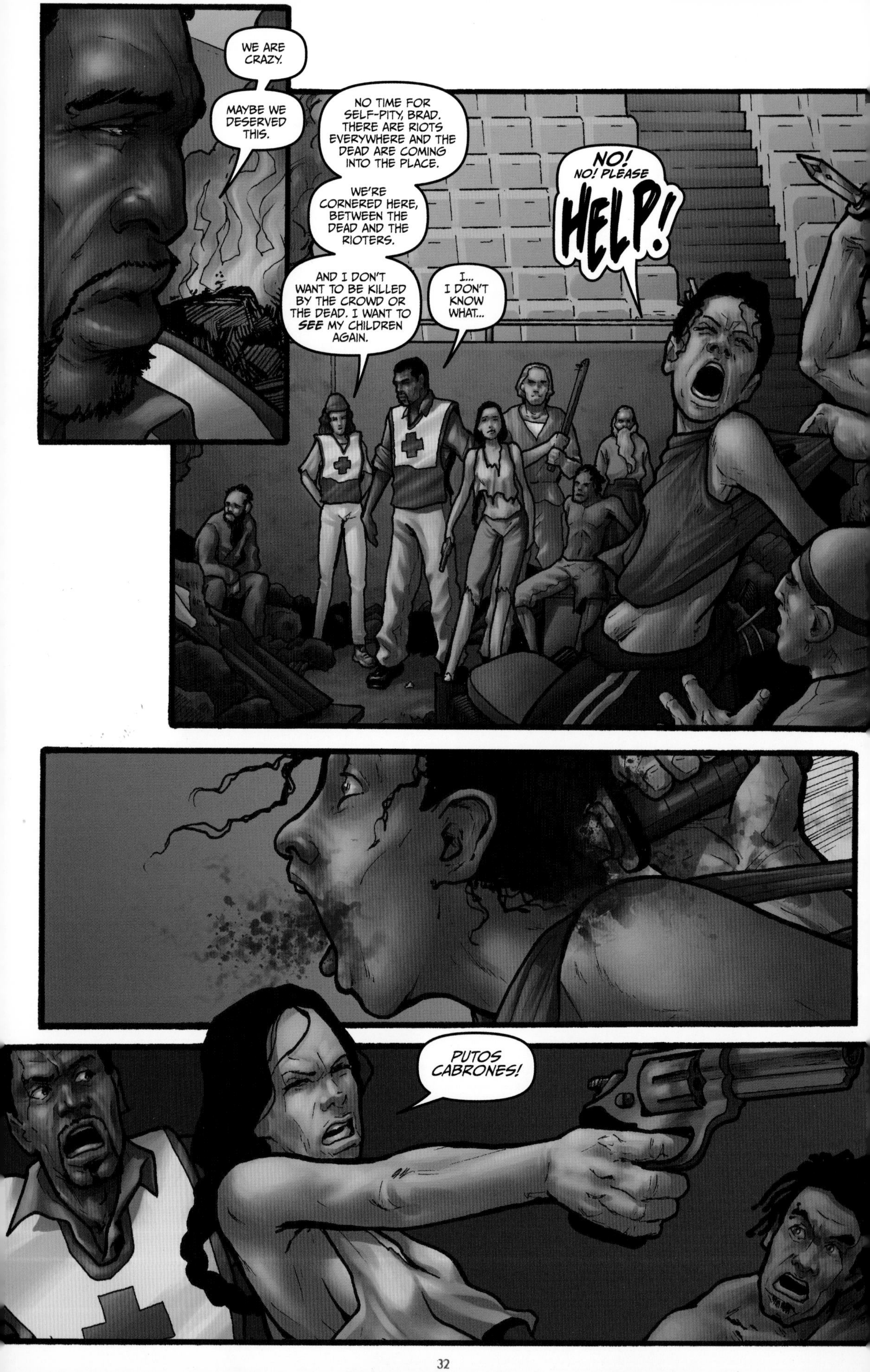
WE ARE CRAZY.
MAYBE WE DESERVED THIS.
NO TIME FOR SELF-PITY, BRAD. THERE ARE RIOTS EVERYWHERE AND THE DEAD ARE COMING INTO THE PLACE.
WE'RE CORNERED HERE, BETWEEN THE DEAD AND THE RIOTERS.
AND I DON'T WANT TO BE KILLED BY THE CROWD OR THE DEAD. I WANT TO SEE MY CHILDREN AGAIN.
I... I DON'T KNOW WHAT...
NO! NO! PLEASE HELP!
PUTOS CABRONES!

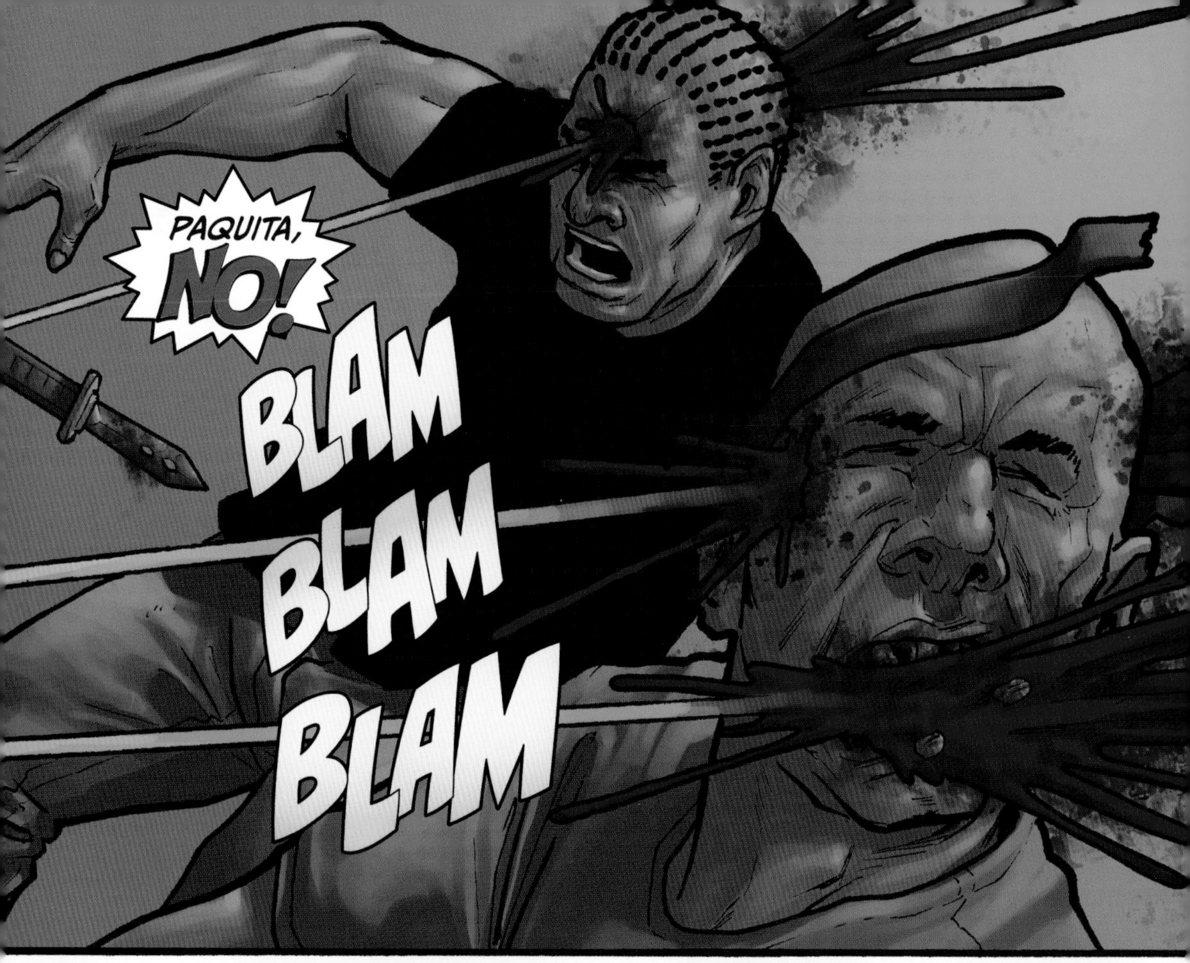
PAQUITA, NO!
BLAM
BLAM
BLAM

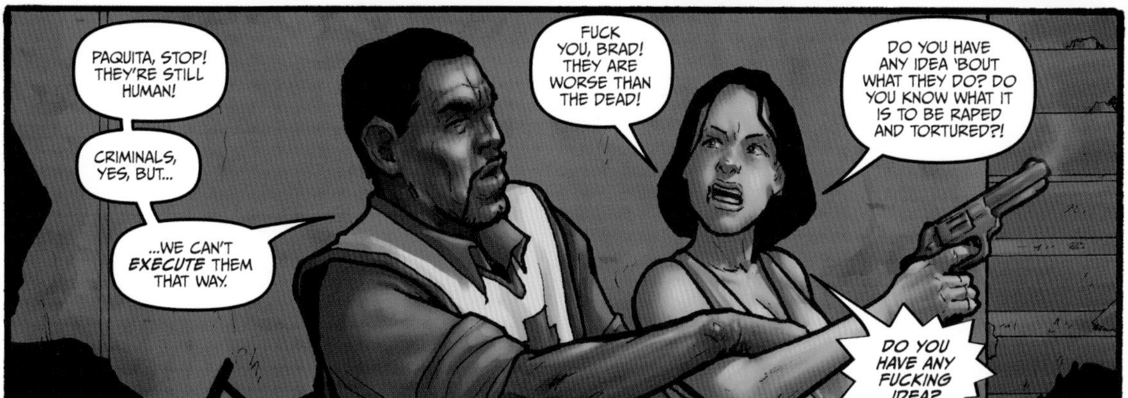
PAQUITA, STOP! THEY'RE STILL HUMAN!
CRIMINALS, YES, BUT...
...WE CAN'T *EXECUTE* THEM THAT WAY.
FUCK YOU, BRAD! THEY ARE WORSE THAN THE DEAD!
DO YOU HAVE ANY IDEA 'BOUT WHAT THEY DO? DO YOU KNOW WHAT IT IS TO BE RAPED AND TORTURED?!
DO YOU HAVE ANY FUCKING IDEA?

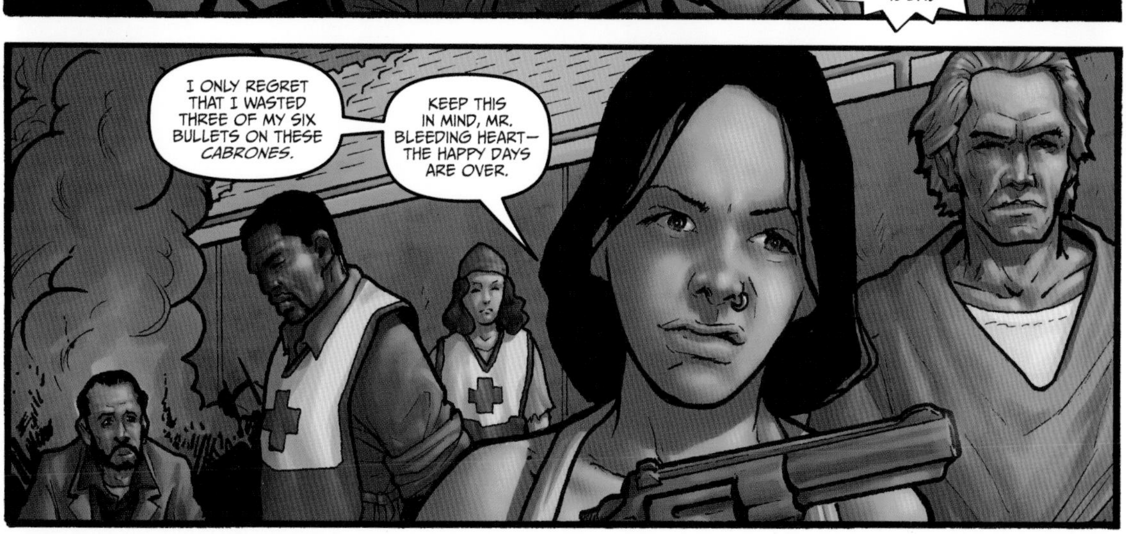
I ONLY REGRET THAT I WASTED THREE OF MY SIX BULLETS ON THESE *CABRONES.*
KEEP THIS IN MIND, MR. BLEEDING HEART— THE HAPPY DAYS ARE OVER.

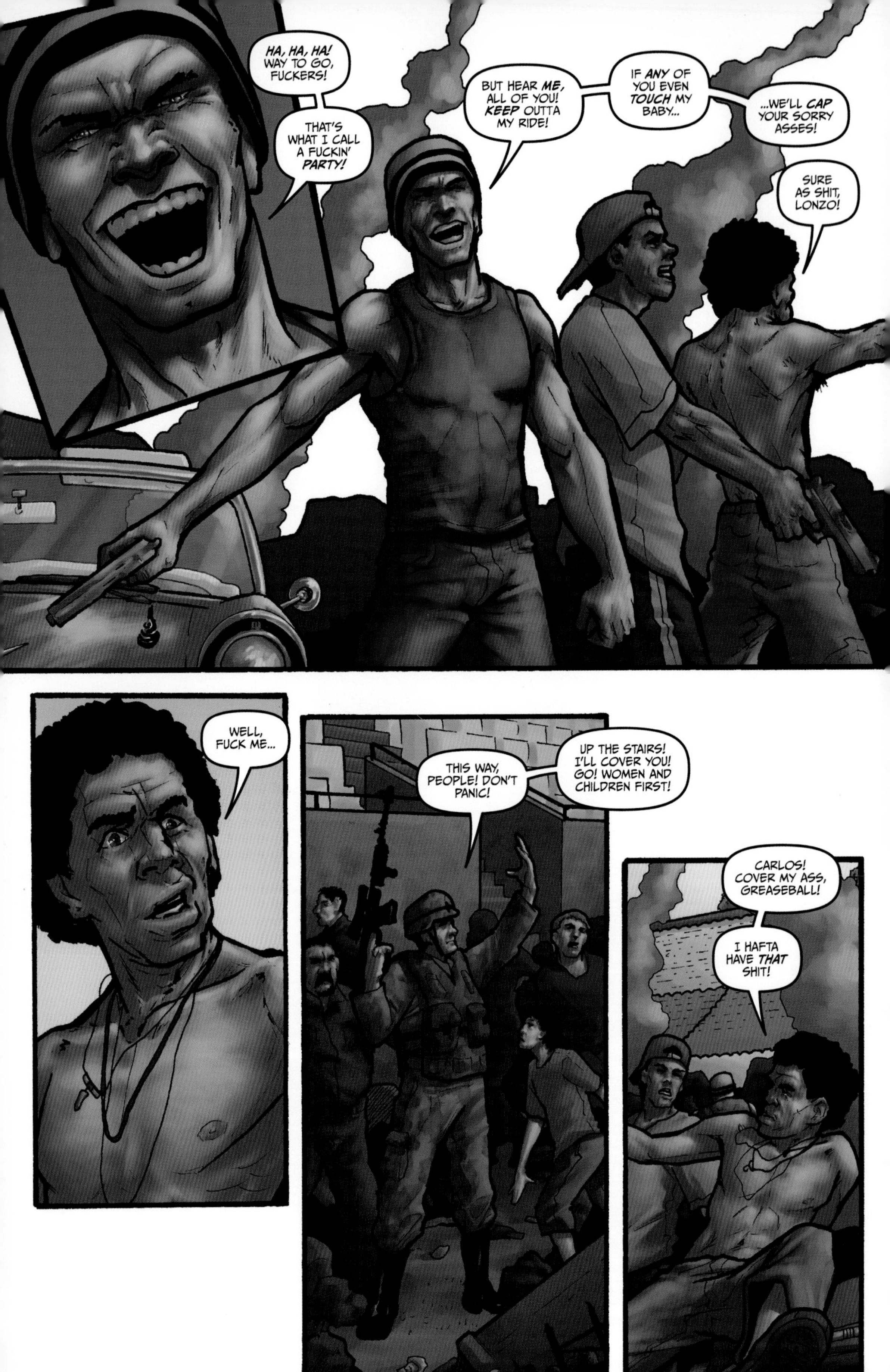
HA, HA, HA! WAY TO GO, FUCKERS!
THAT'S WHAT I CALL A FUCKIN' PARTY!
BUT HEAR ME, ALL OF YOU! KEEP OUTTA MY RIDE!
IF ANY OF YOU EVEN TOUCH MY BABY...
...WE'LL CAP YOUR SORRY ASSES!
SURE AS SHIT, LONZO!
WELL, FUCK ME...
THIS WAY, PEOPLE! DON'T PANIC!
UP THE STAIRS! I'LL COVER YOU! GO! WOMEN AND CHILDREN FIRST!
CARLOS! COVER MY ASS, GREASEBALL!
I HAFTA HAVE THAT SHIT!

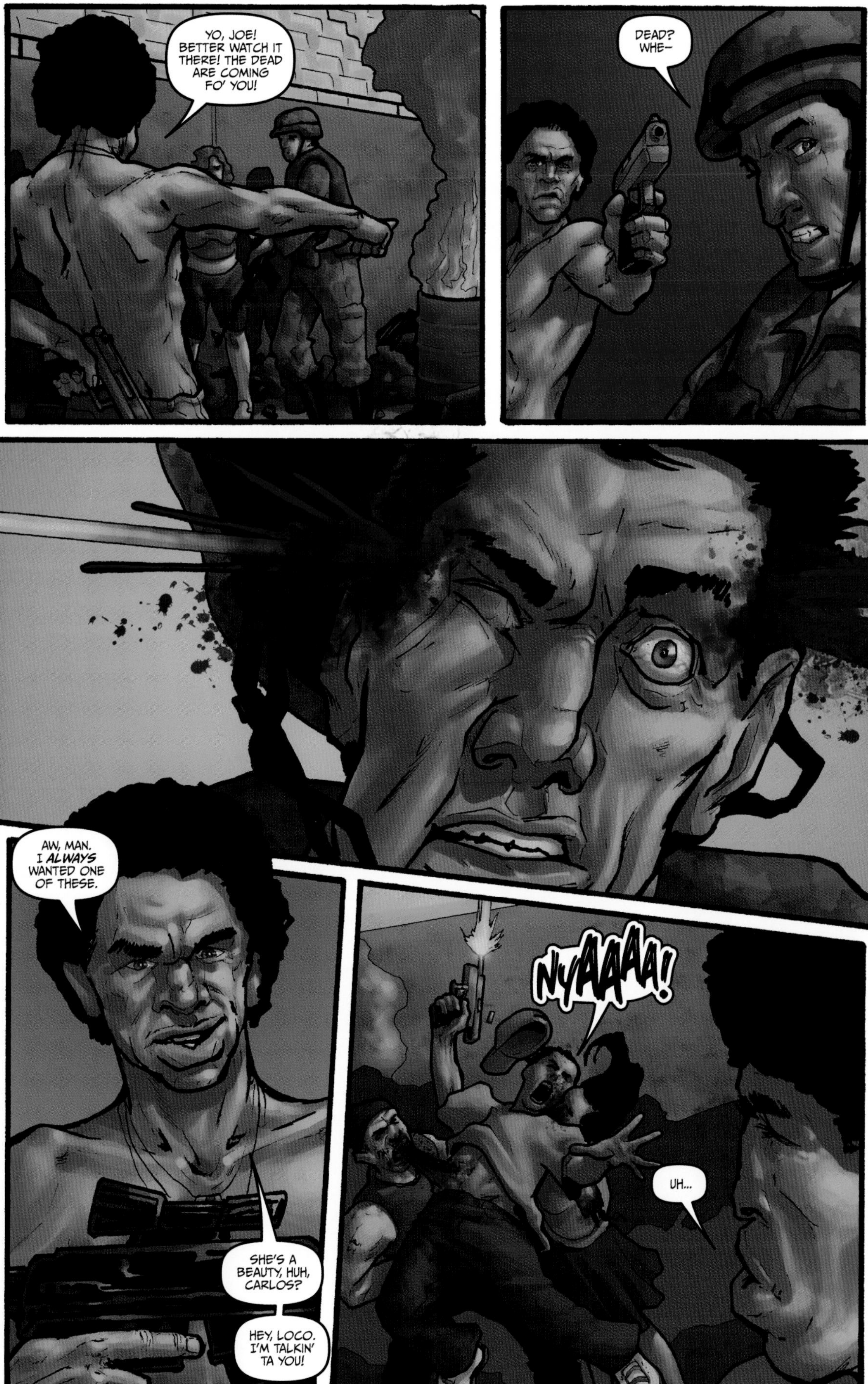
YO, JOE! BETTER WATCH IT THERE! THE DEAD ARE COMING FO' YOU!
DEAD? WHE-
AW, MAN. I *ALWAYS* WANTED ONE OF THESE.
SHE'S A BEAUTY, HUH, CARLOS?
HEY, LOCO. I'M TALKIN' TA YOU!
NyAAAA!
UH...

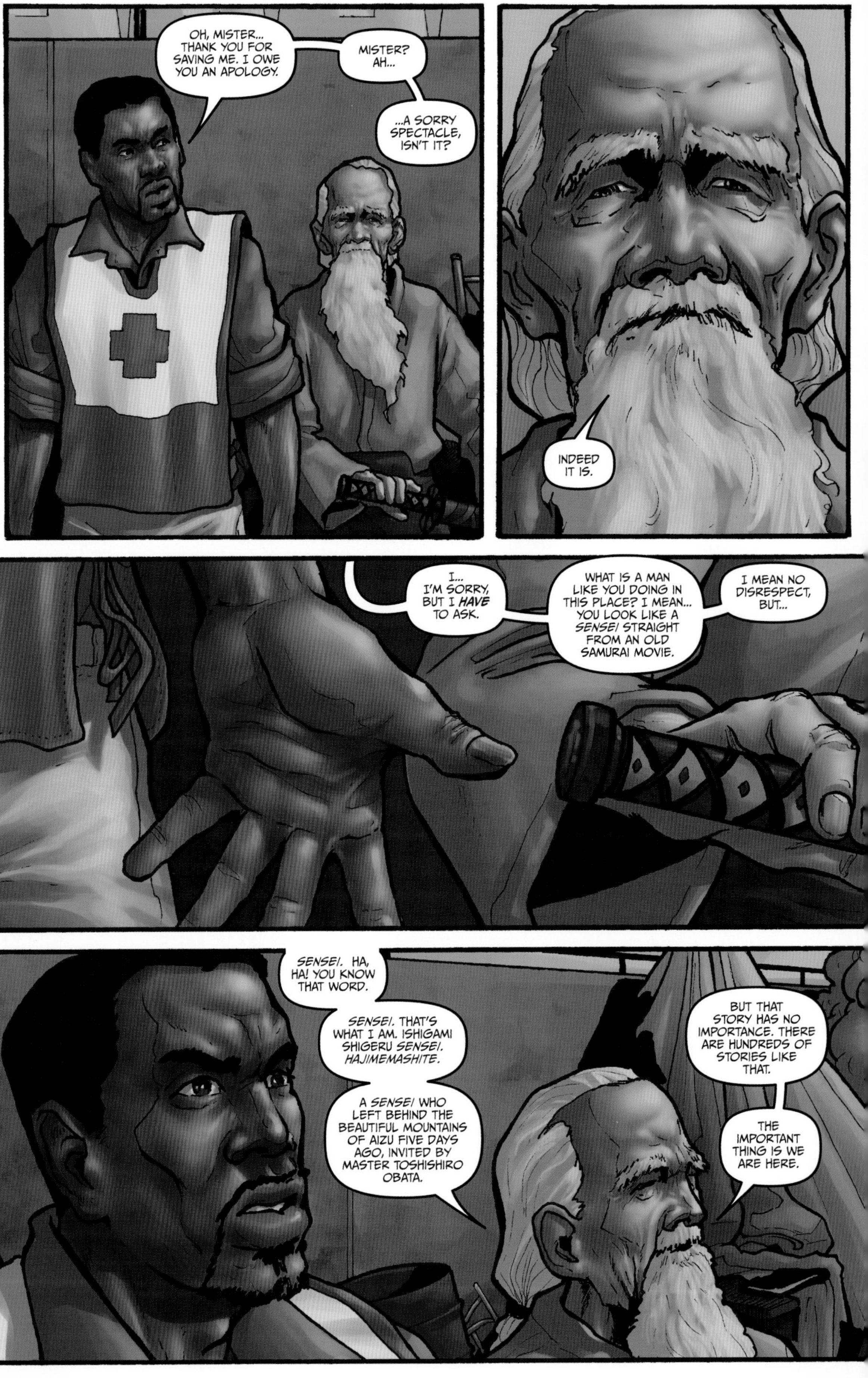
OH, MISTER... THANK YOU FOR SAVING ME. I OWE YOU AN APOLOGY.
MISTER? AH...
...A SORRY SPECTACLE, ISN'T IT?
INDEED IT IS.
I... I'M SORRY, BUT I *HAVE* TO ASK.
WHAT IS A MAN LIKE YOU DOING IN THIS PLACE? I MEAN... YOU LOOK LIKE A *SENSEI* STRAIGHT FROM AN OLD SAMURAI MOVIE.
I MEAN NO DISRESPECT, BUT...
SENSEI. HA, HA! YOU KNOW THAT WORD.
SENSEI. THAT'S WHAT I AM. ISHIGAMI SHIGERU *SENSEI*. *HAJIMEMASHITE*.
A *SENSEI* WHO LEFT BEHIND THE BEAUTIFUL MOUNTAINS OF AIZU FIVE DAYS AGO, INVITED BY MASTER TOSHISHIRO OBATA.
BUT THAT STORY HAS NO IMPORTANCE. THERE ARE HUNDREDS OF STORIES LIKE THAT.
THE IMPORTANT THING IS WE ARE HERE.

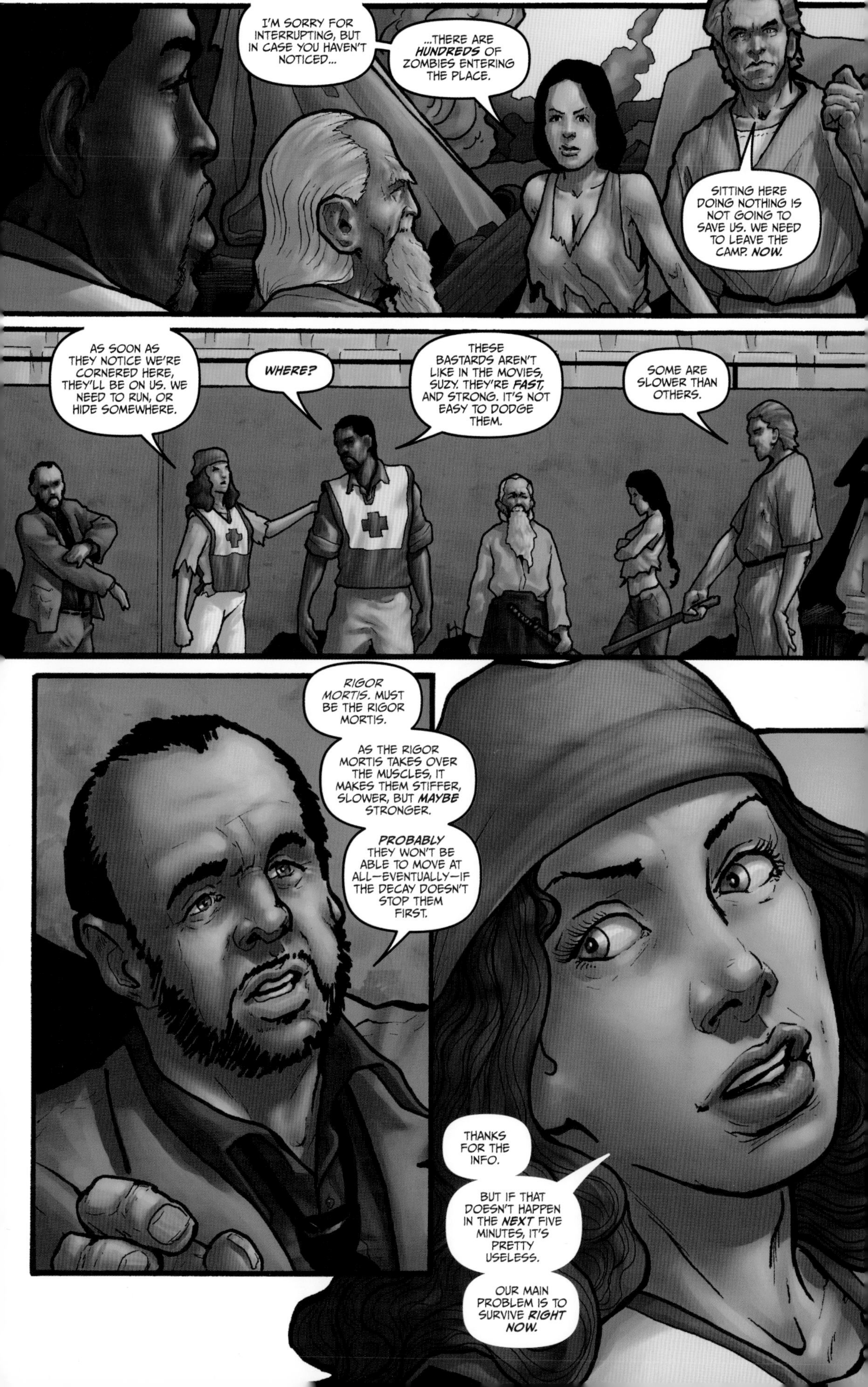
I'M SORRY FOR INTERRUPTING, BUT IN CASE YOU HAVEN'T NOTICED...
...THERE ARE *HUNDREDS* OF ZOMBIES ENTERING THE PLACE.
SITTING HERE DOING NOTHING IS NOT GOING TO SAVE US. WE NEED TO LEAVE THE CAMP. *NOW.*
AS SOON AS THEY NOTICE WE'RE CORNERED HERE, THEY'LL BE ON US. WE NEED TO RUN, OR HIDE SOMEWHERE.
WHERE?
THESE BASTARDS AREN'T LIKE IN THE MOVIES, SUZY. THEY'RE *FAST,* AND STRONG. IT'S NOT EASY TO DODGE THEM.
SOME ARE SLOWER THAN OTHERS.
RIGOR MORTIS. MUST BE THE RIGOR MORTIS.
AS THE RIGOR MORTIS TAKES OVER THE MUSCLES, IT MAKES THEM STIFFER, SLOWER, BUT *MAYBE* STRONGER.
PROBABLY THEY WON'T BE ABLE TO MOVE AT ALL—EVENTUALLY—IF THE DECAY DOESN'T STOP THEM FIRST.
THANKS FOR THE INFO.
BUT IF THAT DOESN'T HAPPEN IN THE *NEXT* FIVE MINUTES, IT'S PRETTY USELESS.
OUR MAIN PROBLEM IS TO SURVIVE *RIGHT NOW.*

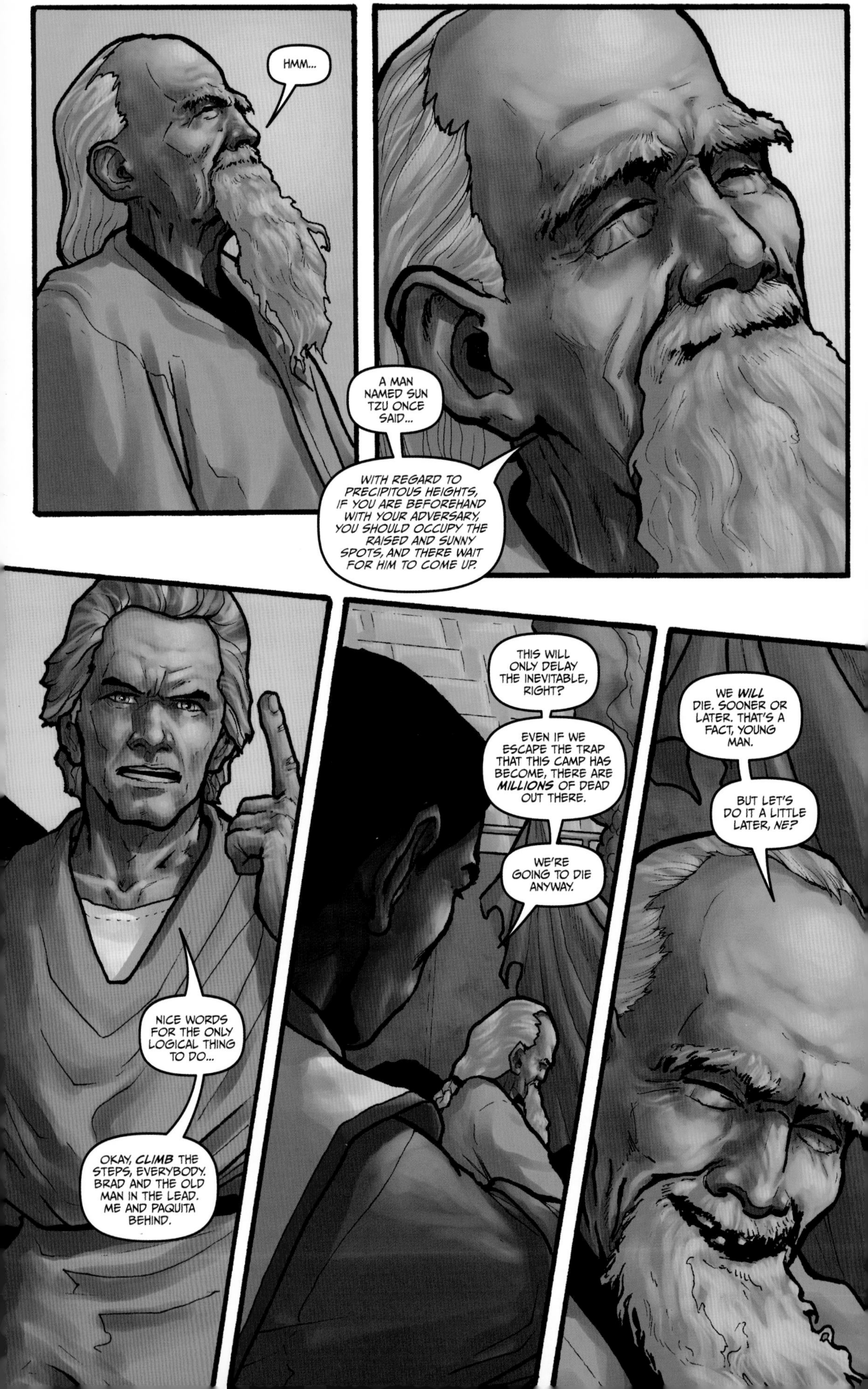
HMM...
A MAN NAMED SUN TZU ONCE SAID...
WITH REGARD TO PRECIPITOUS HEIGHTS, IF YOU ARE BEFOREHAND WITH YOUR ADVERSARY, YOU SHOULD OCCUPY THE RAISED AND SUNNY SPOTS, AND THERE WAIT FOR HIM TO COME UP.
NICE WORDS FOR THE ONLY LOGICAL THING TO DO...
OKAY, CLIMB THE STEPS, EVERYBODY. BRAD AND THE OLD MAN IN THE LEAD. ME AND PAQUITA BEHIND.
THIS WILL ONLY DELAY THE INEVITABLE, RIGHT?
EVEN IF WE ESCAPE THE TRAP THAT THIS CAMP HAS BECOME, THERE ARE MILLIONS OF DEAD OUT THERE.
WE'RE GOING TO DIE ANYWAY.
WE WILL DIE. SOONER OR LATER. THAT'S A FACT, YOUNG MAN.
BUT LET'S DO IT A LITTLE LATER, NE?

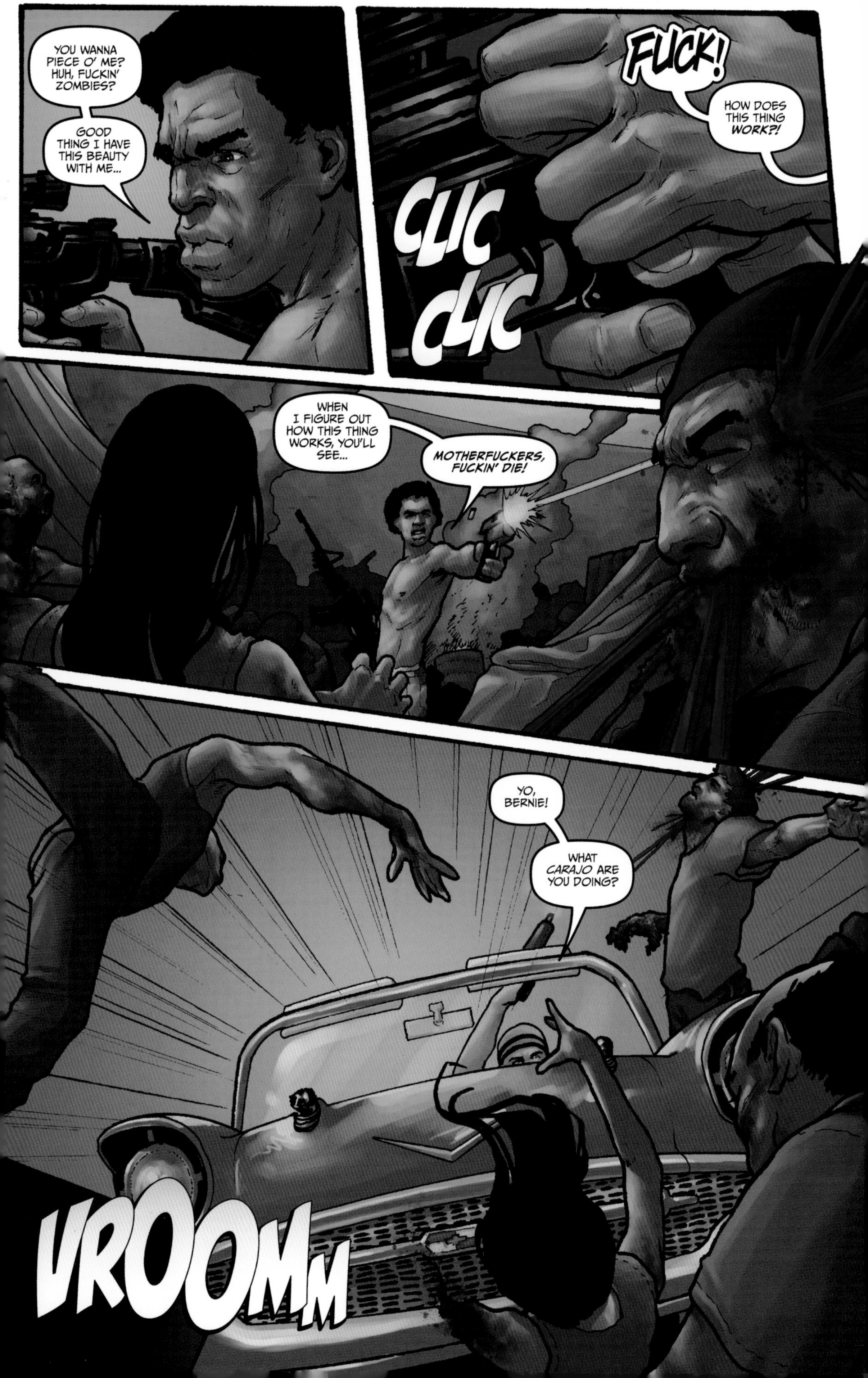
YOU WANNA PIECE O' ME? HUH, FUCKIN' ZOMBIES?
GOOD THING I HAVE THIS BEAUTY WITH ME...
FUCK!
HOW DOES THIS THING WORK?!
CLIC
CLIC
WHEN I FIGURE OUT HOW THIS THING WORKS, YOU'LL SEE...
MOTHERFUCKERS, FUCKIN' DIE!
YO, BERNIE!
WHAT CARAJO ARE YOU DOING?
VROOMM

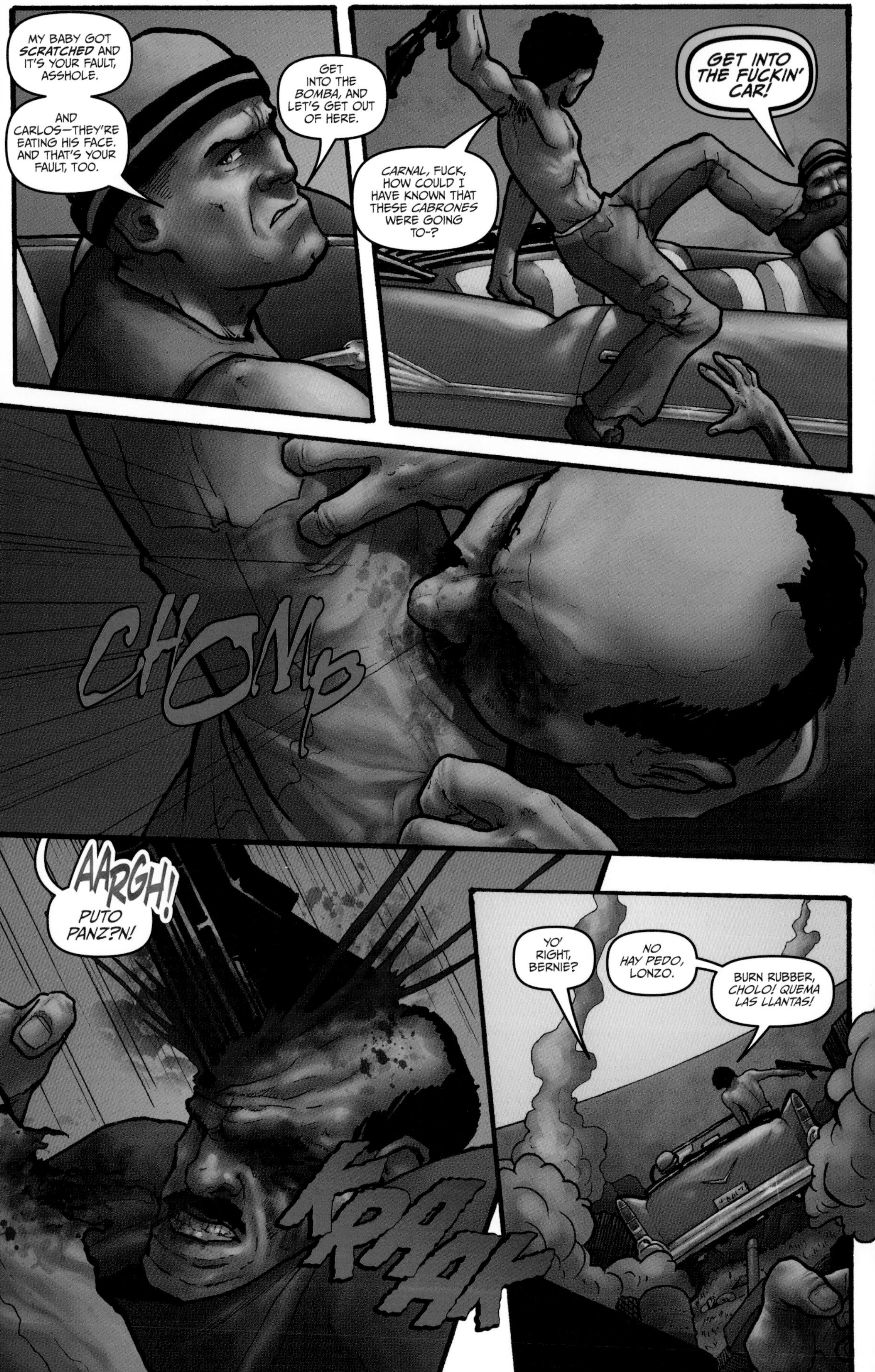
MY BABY GOT *SCRATCHED* AND IT'S YOUR FAULT, ASSHOLE.
AND CARLOS—THEY'RE EATING HIS FACE. AND THAT'S YOUR FAULT, TOO.
GET INTO THE *BOMBA*, AND LET'S GET OUT OF HERE.
CARNAL, FUCK, HOW COULD I HAVE KNOWN THAT THESE *CABRONES* WERE GOING TO-?
GET INTO THE FUCKIN' CAR!
CHOMP
AARGH! *PUTO PANZ?N!*
KRAK
YO' RIGHT, BERNIE?
NO *HAY PEDO*, LONZO.
BURN RUBBER, *CHOLO! QUEMA LAS LLANTAS!*

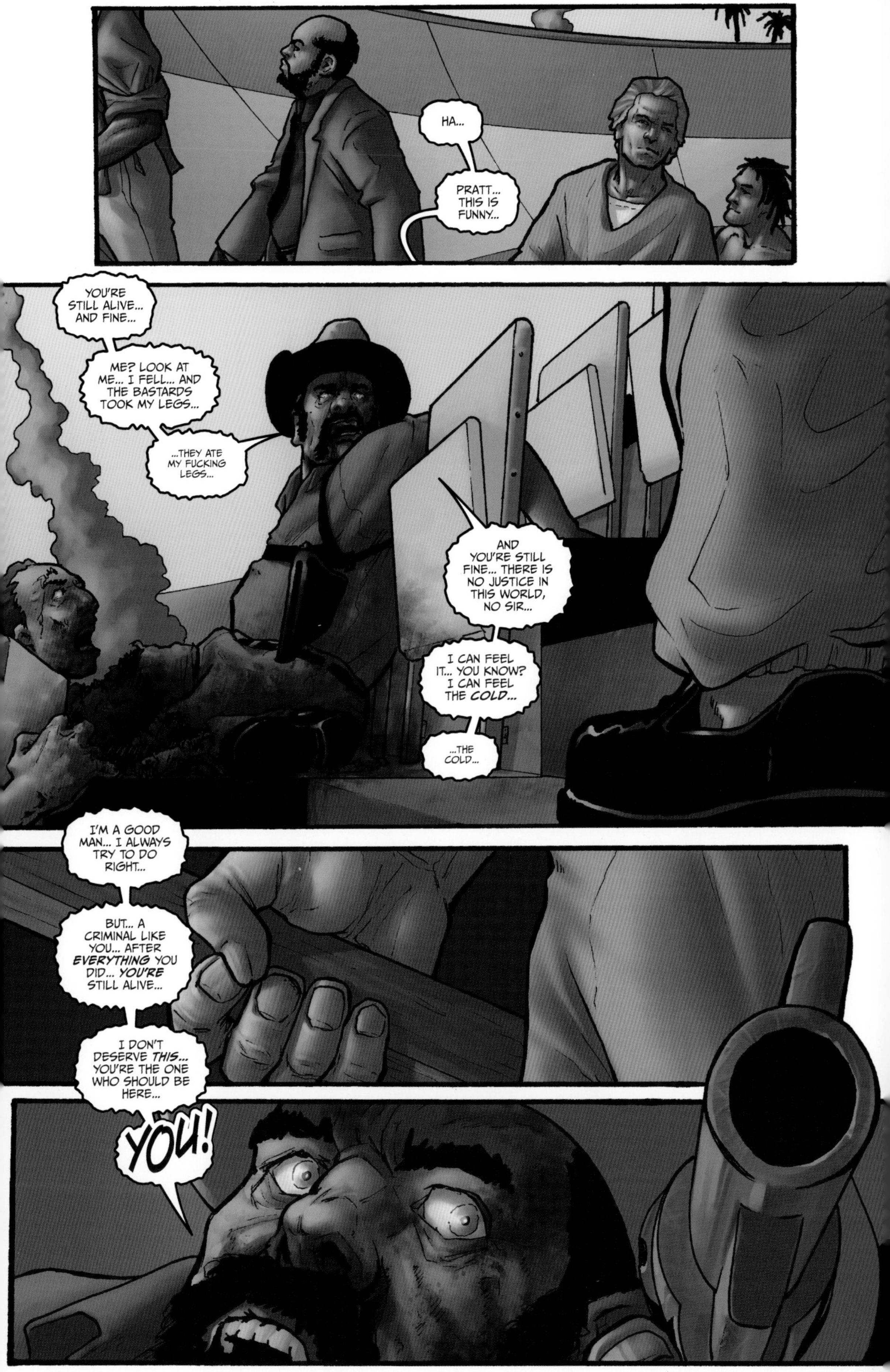
HA...
PRATT... THIS IS FUNNY...
YOU'RE STILL ALIVE... AND FINE...
ME? LOOK AT ME... I FELL... AND THE BASTARDS TOOK MY LEGS...
...THEY ATE MY FUCKING LEGS...
AND YOU'RE STILL FINE... THERE IS NO JUSTICE IN THIS WORLD, NO SIR...
I CAN FEEL IT... YOU KNOW? I CAN FEEL THE *COLD...*
...THE COLD...
I'M A GOOD MAN... I ALWAYS TRY TO DO RIGHT...
BUT... A CRIMINAL LIKE YOU... AFTER *EVERYTHING* YOU DID... *YOU'RE* STILL ALIVE...
I DON'T DESERVE *THIS...* YOU'RE THE ONE WHO SHOULD BE HERE...
YOU!

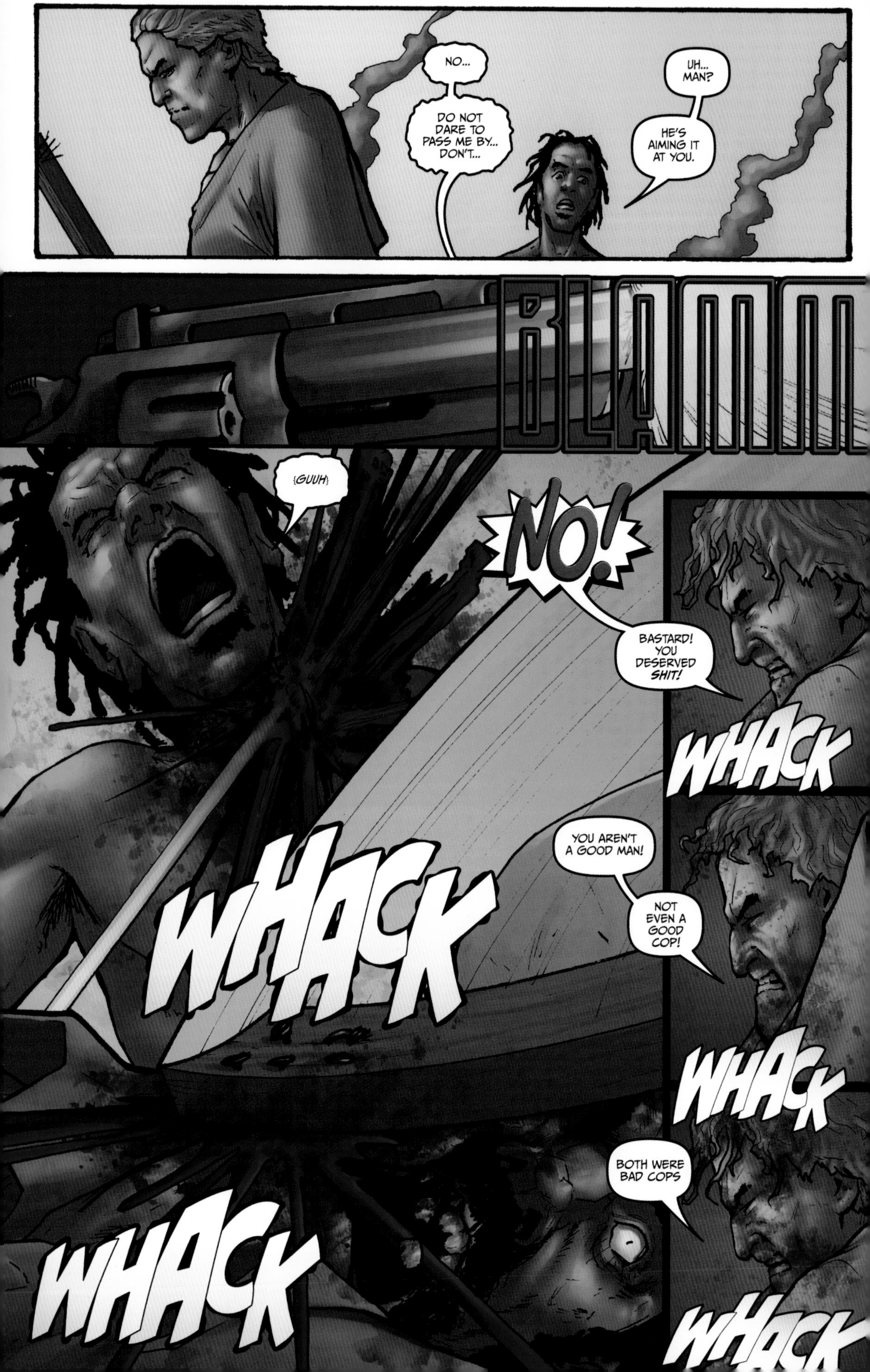
NO...
DO NOT DARE TO PASS ME BY... DON'T...
UH... MAN?
HE'S AIMING IT AT YOU.
BLAMM
{GUUH}
NO!
BASTARD! YOU DESERVED SHIT!
WHACK
WHACK
YOU AREN'T A GOOD MAN!
NOT EVEN A GOOD COP!
WHACK
BOTH WERE BAD COPS
WHACK
WHACK

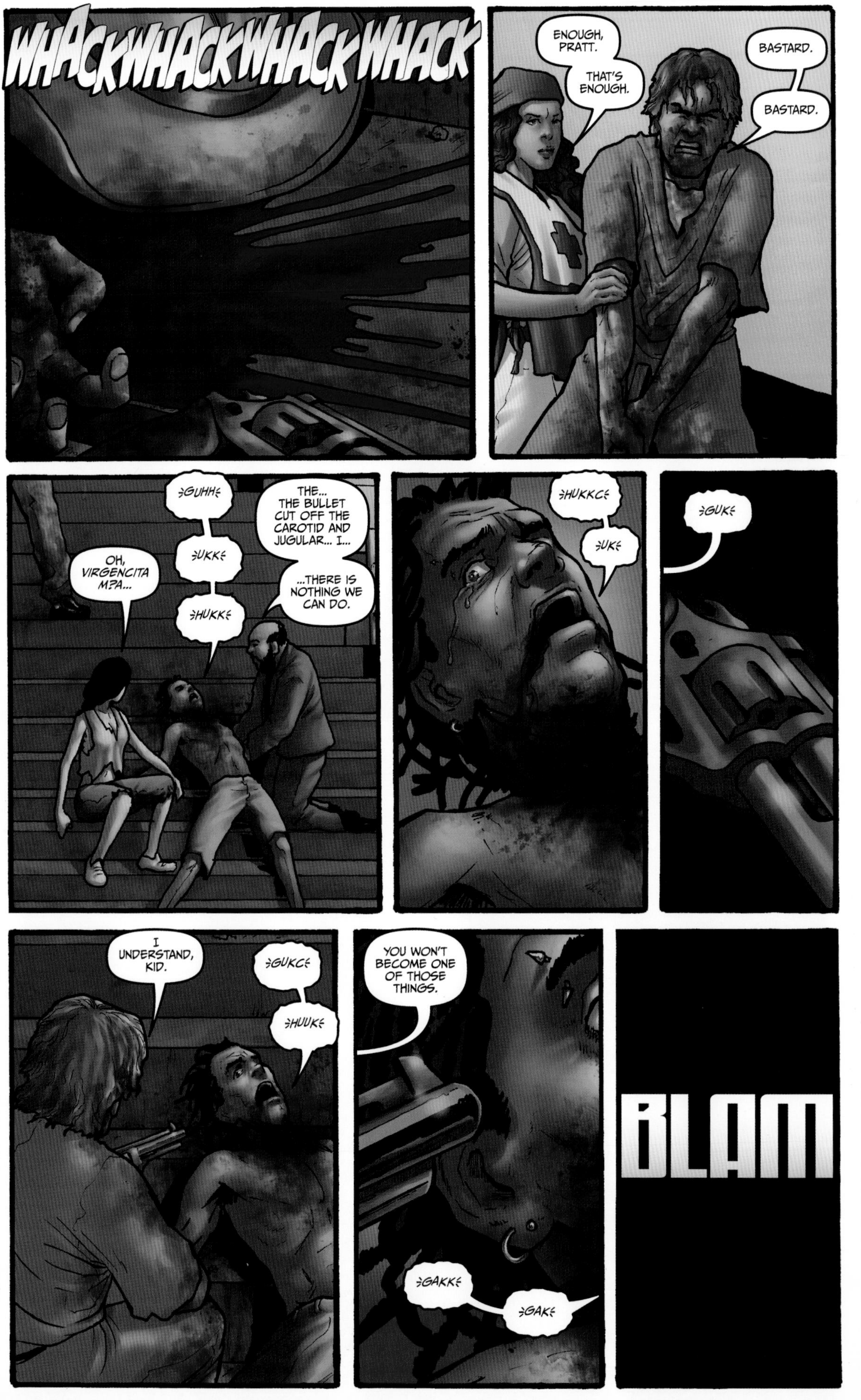
WHACK WHACK WHACK WHACK
ENOUGH, PRATT.
THAT'S ENOUGH.
BASTARD.
BASTARD.
OH, VIRGENCITA M?A...
GUHH
UKK
HUKK
THE... THE BULLET CUT OFF THE CAROTID AND JUGULAR... I...
...THERE IS NOTHING WE CAN DO.
HUKKC
UK
GUK
I UNDERSTAND, KID.
GUKC
HUUK
YOU WON'T BECOME ONE OF THOSE THINGS.
GAKK
GAK
BLAM

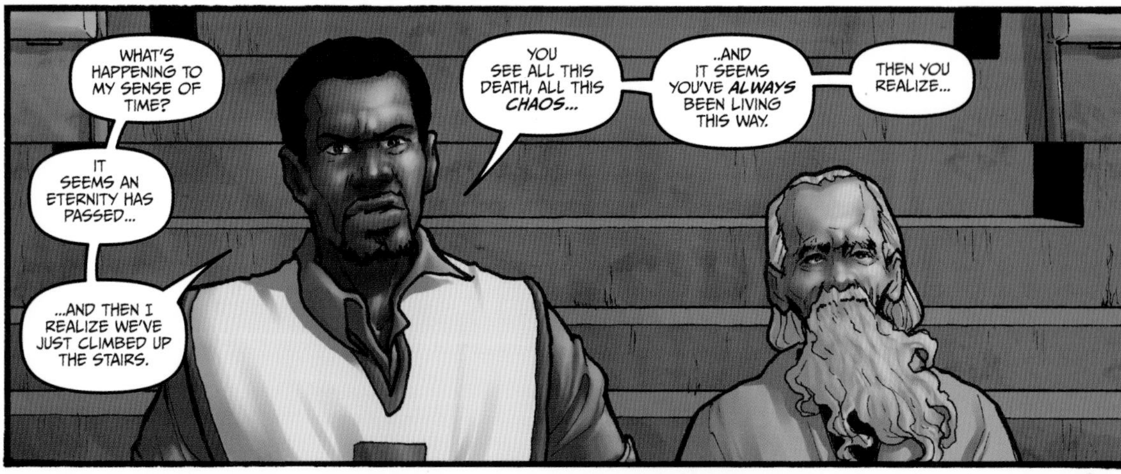
WHAT'S HAPPENING TO MY SENSE OF TIME?
IT SEEMS AN ETERNITY HAS PASSED...
...AND THEN I REALIZE WE'VE JUST CLIMBED UP THE STAIRS.
YOU SEE ALL THIS DEATH, ALL THIS CHAOS...
..AND IT SEEMS YOU'VE ALWAYS BEEN LIVING THIS WAY.
THEN YOU REALIZE...

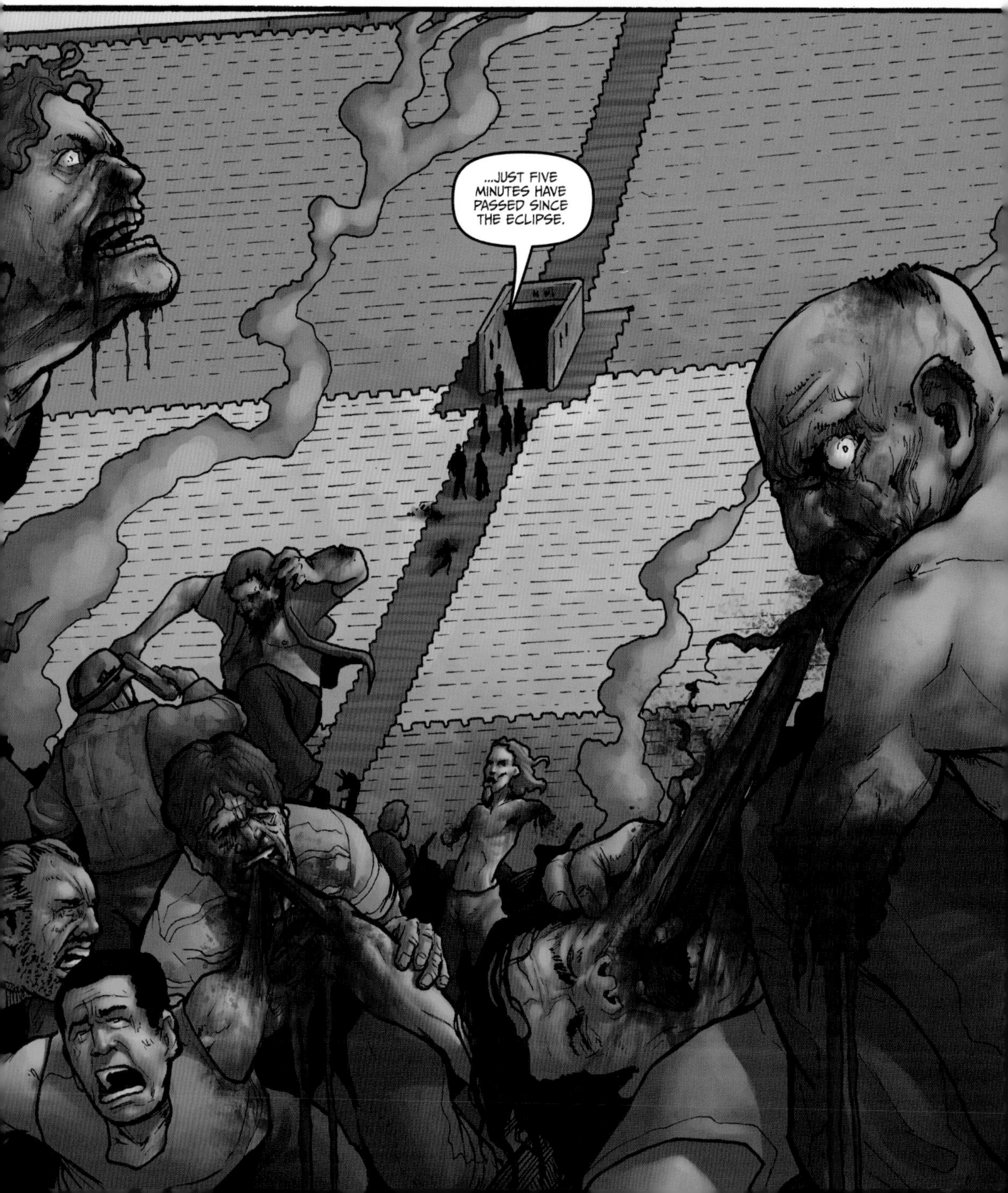
...JUST FIVE MINUTES HAVE PASSED SINCE THE ECLIPSE.

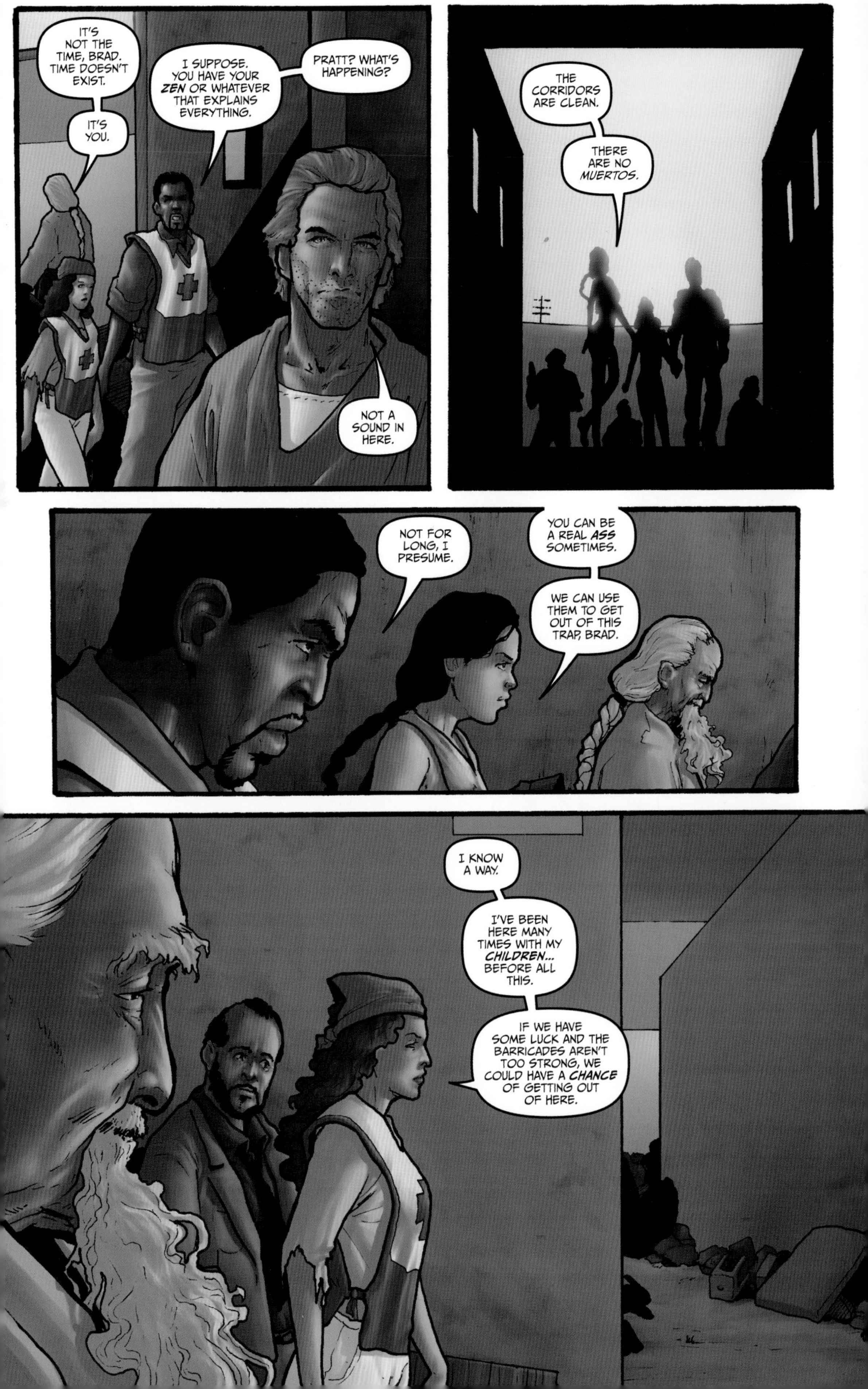
IT'S NOT THE TIME, BRAD. TIME DOESN'T EXIST.
IT'S YOU.
I SUPPOSE. YOU HAVE YOUR ZEN OR WHATEVER THAT EXPLAINS EVERYTHING.
PRATT? WHAT'S HAPPENING?
NOT A SOUND IN HERE.
THE CORRIDORS ARE CLEAN.
THERE ARE NO MUERTOS.
NOT FOR LONG, I PRESUME.
YOU CAN BE A REAL ASS SOMETIMES.
WE CAN USE THEM TO GET OUT OF THIS TRAP, BRAD.
I KNOW A WAY.
I'VE BEEN HERE MANY TIMES WITH MY CHILDREN... BEFORE ALL THIS.
IF WE HAVE SOME LUCK AND THE BARRICADES AREN'T TOO STRONG, WE COULD HAVE A CHANCE OF GETTING OUT OF HERE.

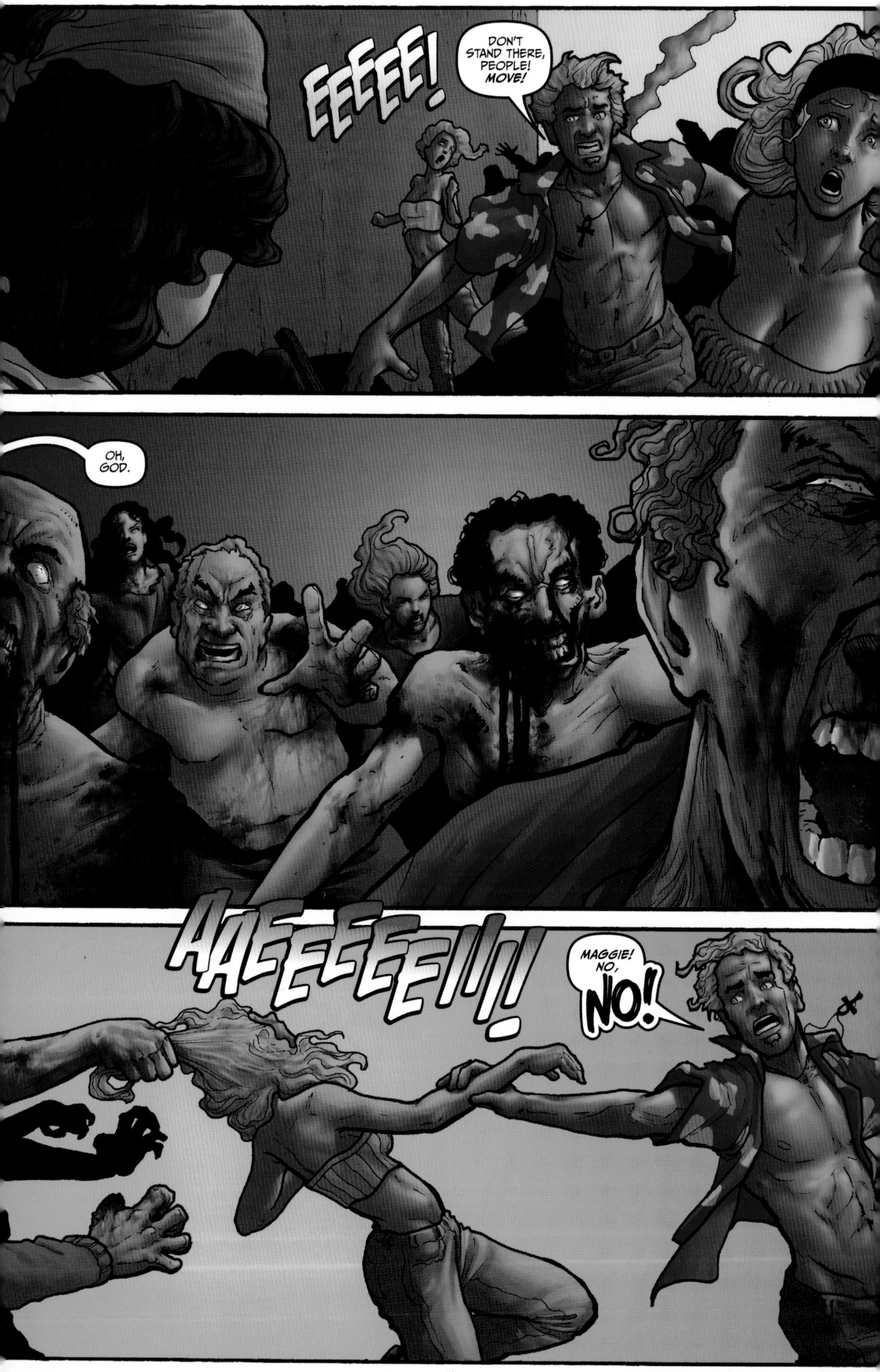
EEEEE!
DON'T STAND THERE, PEOPLE! MOVE!
OH, GOD.
AAEEEEEIII!!
MAGGIE! NO, NO!

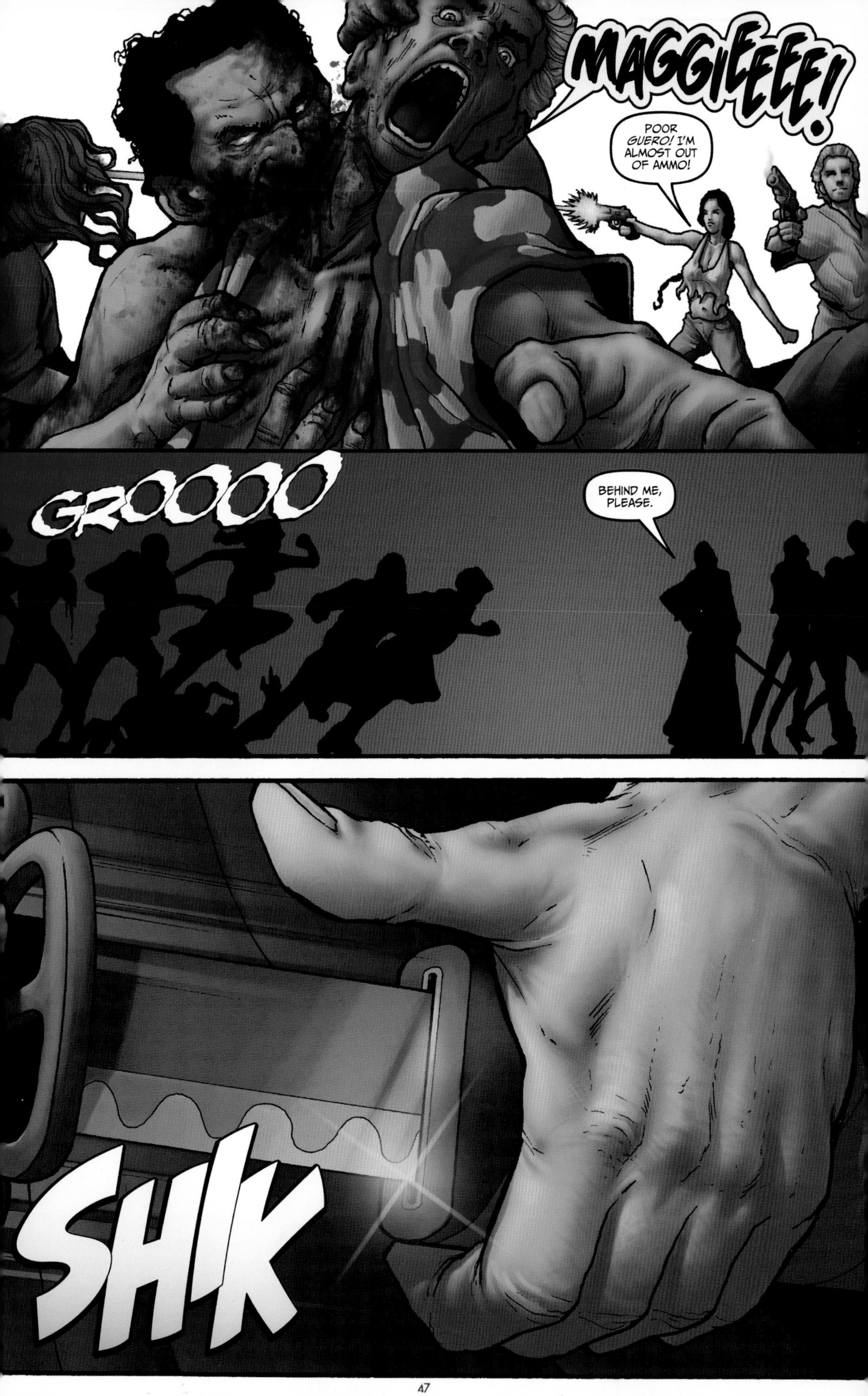
MAGGIEEEE!
POOR GUERO! I'M ALMOST OUT OF AMMO!
GROOOO
BEHIND ME, PLEASE.
SHIK

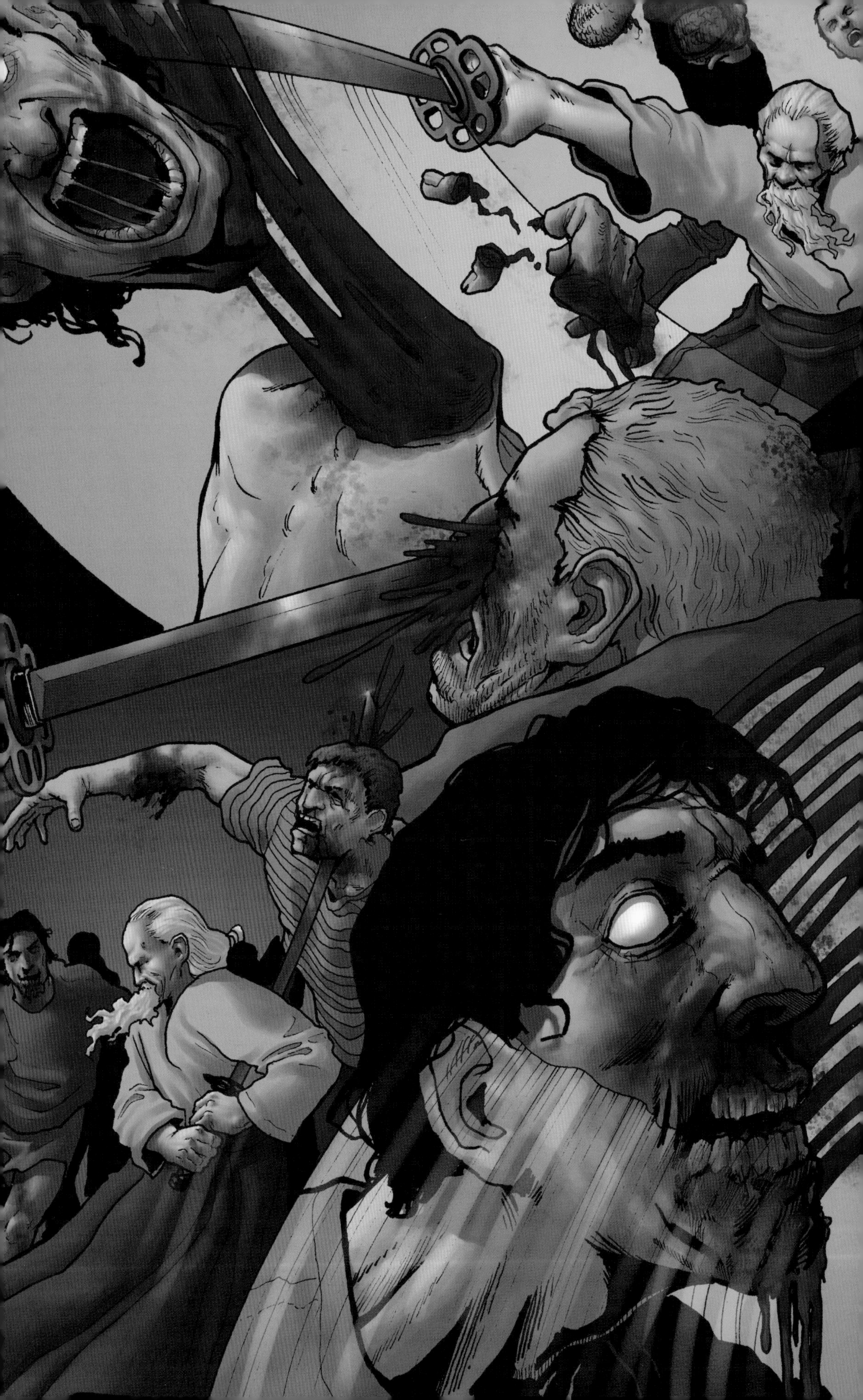

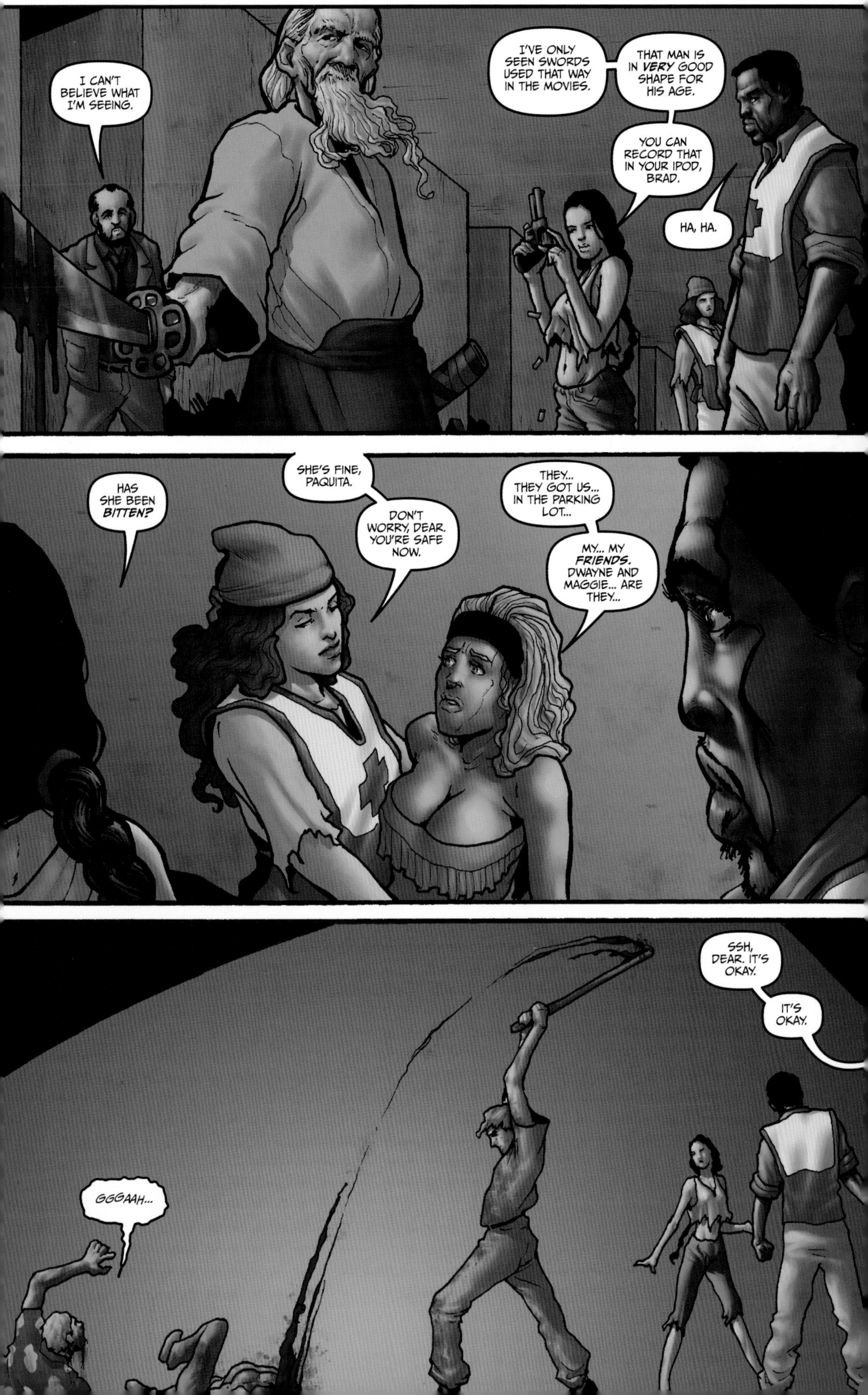
I CAN'T BELIEVE WHAT I'M SEEING.
I'VE ONLY SEEN SWORDS USED THAT WAY IN THE MOVIES.
THAT MAN IS IN VERY GOOD SHAPE FOR HIS AGE.
YOU CAN RECORD THAT IN YOUR IPOD, BRAD.
HA, HA.
HAS SHE BEEN BITTEN?
SHE'S FINE, PAQUITA.
DON'T WORRY, DEAR. YOU'RE SAFE NOW.
THEY... THEY GOT US... IN THE PARKING LOT...
MY... MY FRIENDS. DWAYNE AND MAGGIE... ARE THEY...
SSH, DEAR. IT'S OKAY.
IT'S OKAY.
GGGAAH...

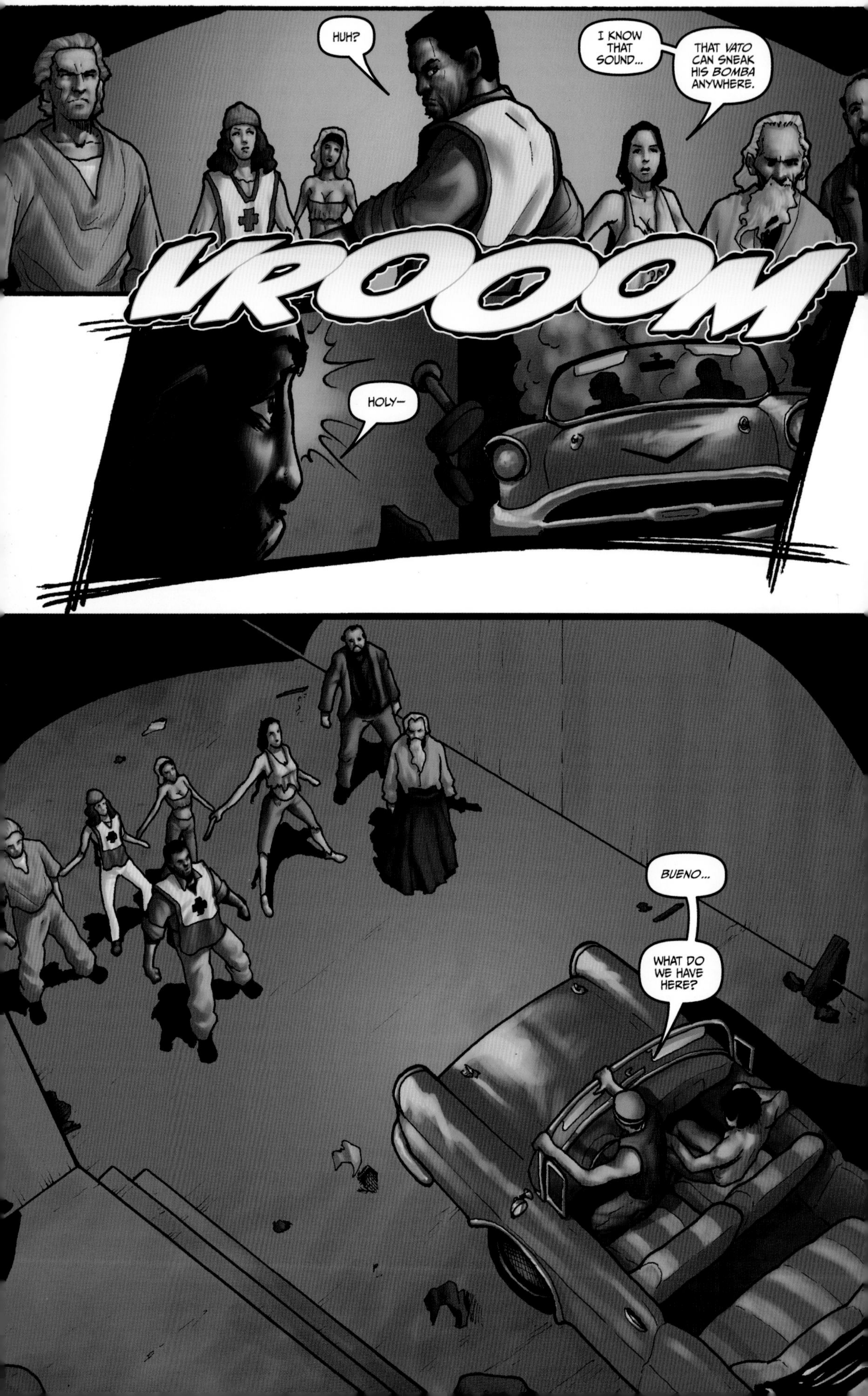
HUH?
I KNOW THAT SOUND...
THAT VATO CAN SNEAK HIS BOMBA ANYWHERE.
VROOOM
HOLY—
BUENO...
WHAT DO WE HAVE HERE?

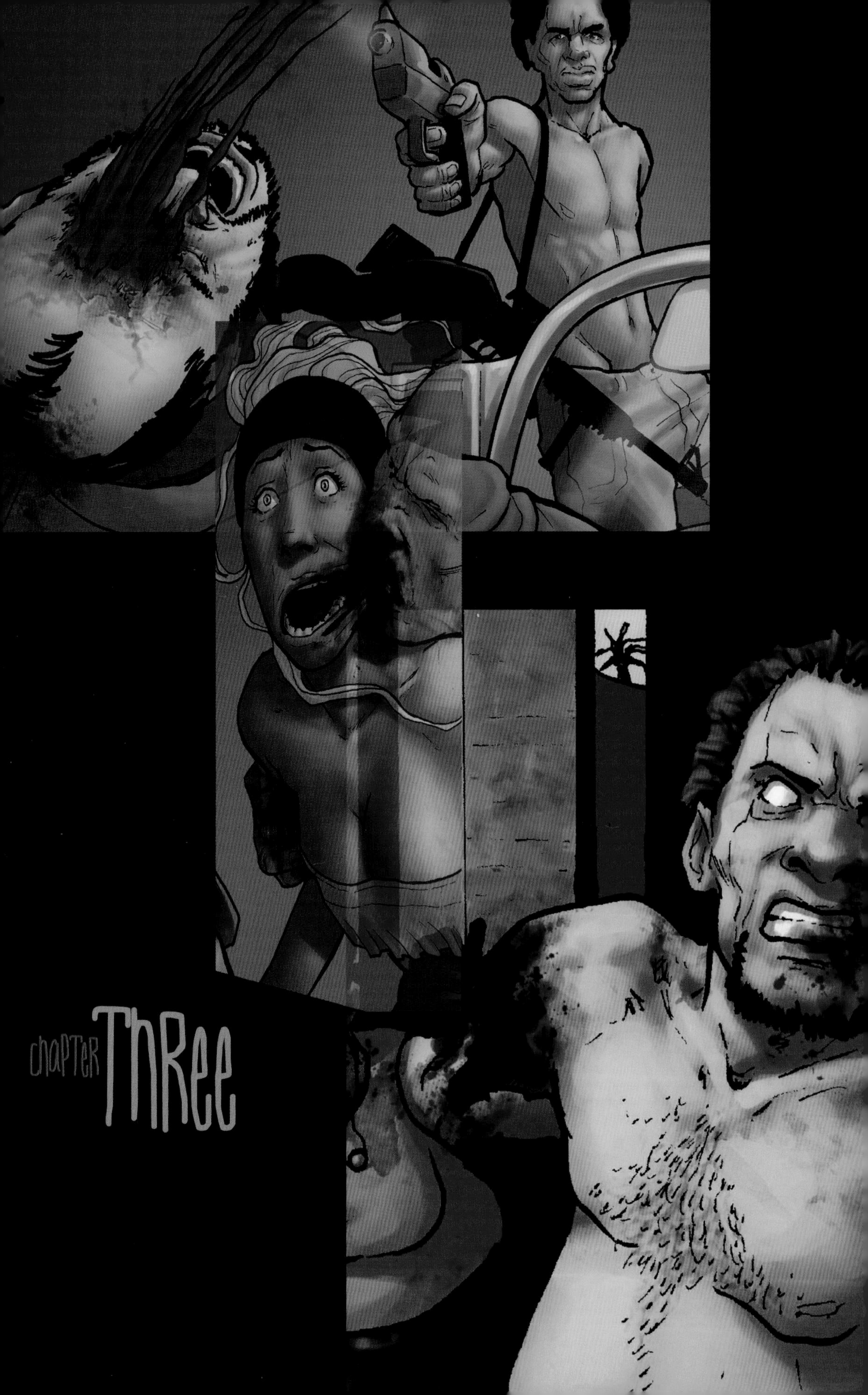
chapter Three

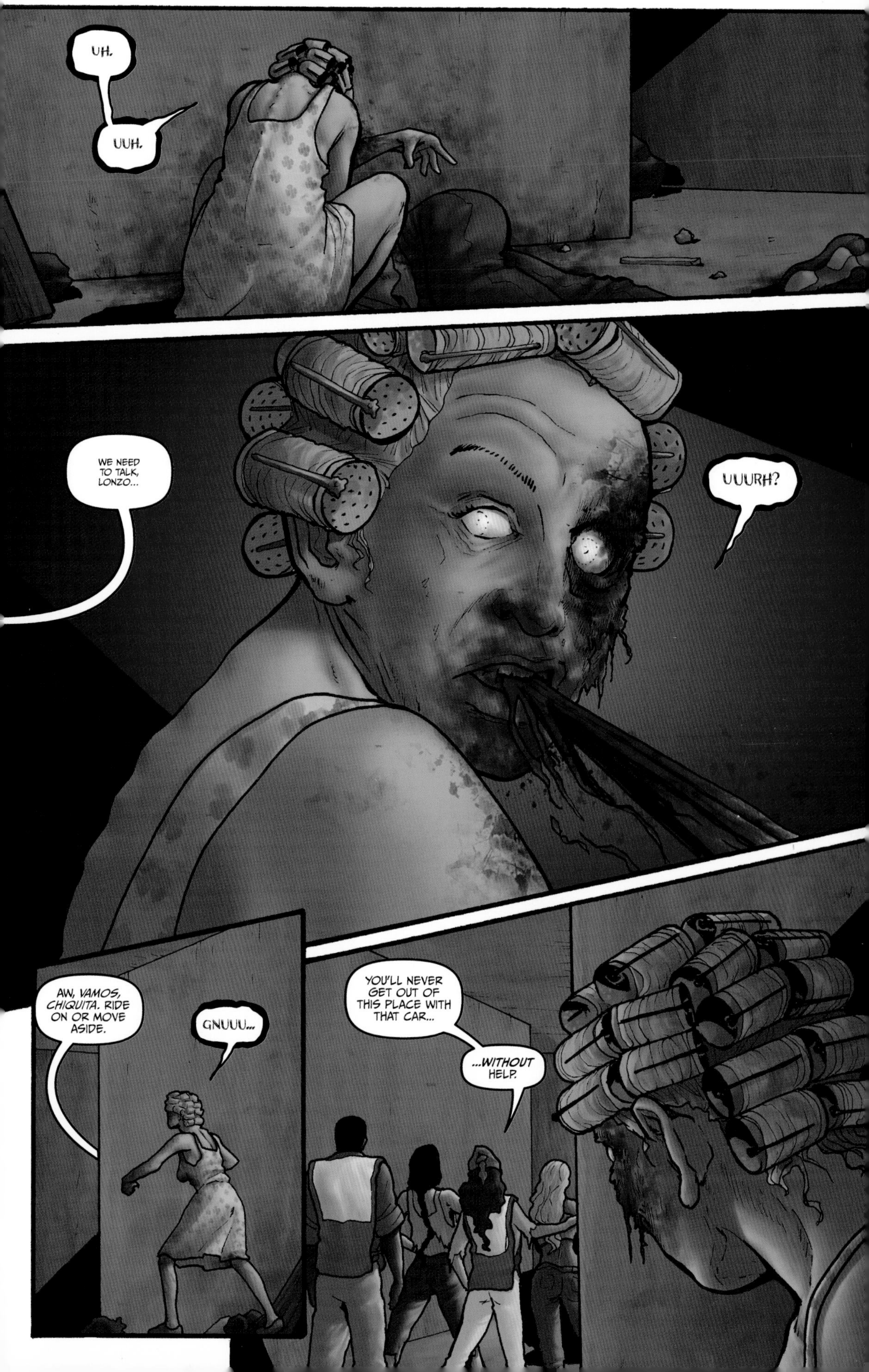
UH.
UUH.
WE NEED TO TALK, LONZO...
UUURH?
AW, VAMOS, CHIQUITA. RIDE ON OR MOVE ASIDE.
GNUUU...
YOU'LL NEVER GET OUT OF THIS PLACE WITH THAT CAR...
...WITHOUT HELP.

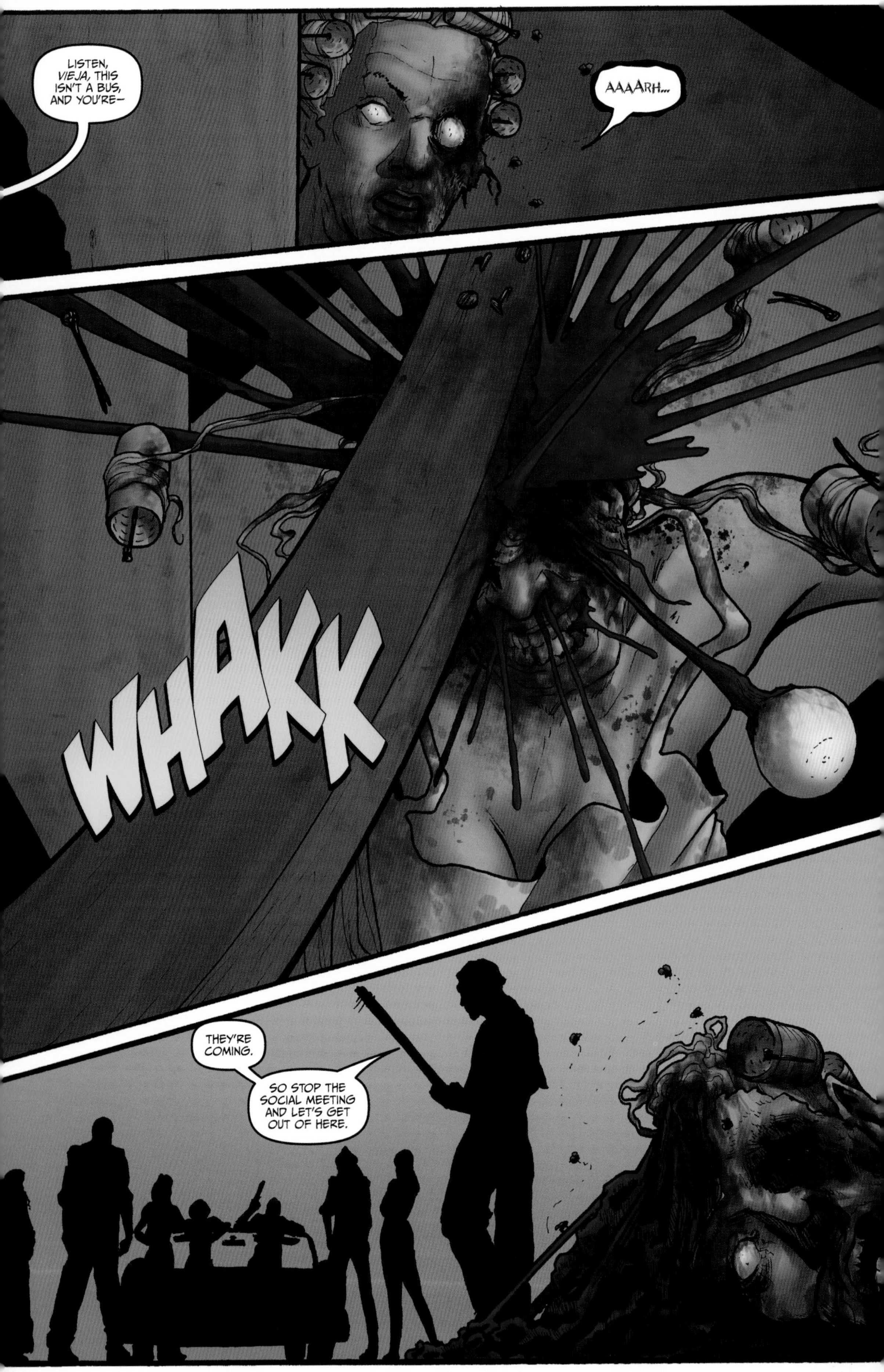
LISTEN, VIEJA, THIS ISN'T A BUS, AND YOU'RE—
AAAARH...
WHAKK
THEY'RE COMING.
SO STOP THE SOCIAL MEETING AND LET'S GET OUT OF HERE.

WHY SHOULD I GET ALL OF YOU OUT OF HERE?!

PAQUITA, YOU'RE ONE OF US. GET YOUR LITTLE ASS IN HERE *NOW*.

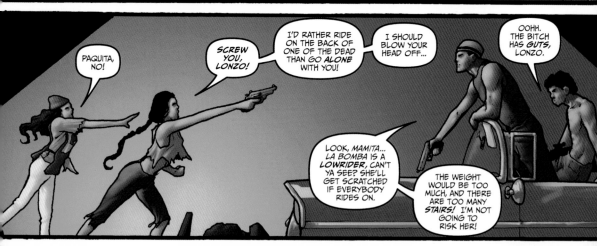

PAQUITA, NO!

SCREW YOU, LONZO!

I'D RATHER RIDE ON THE BACK OF ONE OF THE DEAD THAN GO *ALONE* WITH YOU!

I SHOULD BLOW YOUR HEAD OFF...

OOHH. THE BITCH HAS *GUTS*, LONZO.

LOOK, MAMITA... LA BOMBA IS A *LOWRIDER*, CAN'T YA SEE? SHE'LL GET SCRATCHED IF EVERYBODY RIDES ON.

THE WEIGHT WOULD BE TOO MUCH, AND THERE ARE TOO MANY *STAIRS!* I'M NOT GOING TO RISK HER!

BUT I DON'T WANT YOU TO THINK I'M A HEARTLESS LOCO.

THE GIRLS CAN COME WITH US. THE GUYS ARE ON THEIR OWN.

HEH! A TODA MADRE, CARNAL.

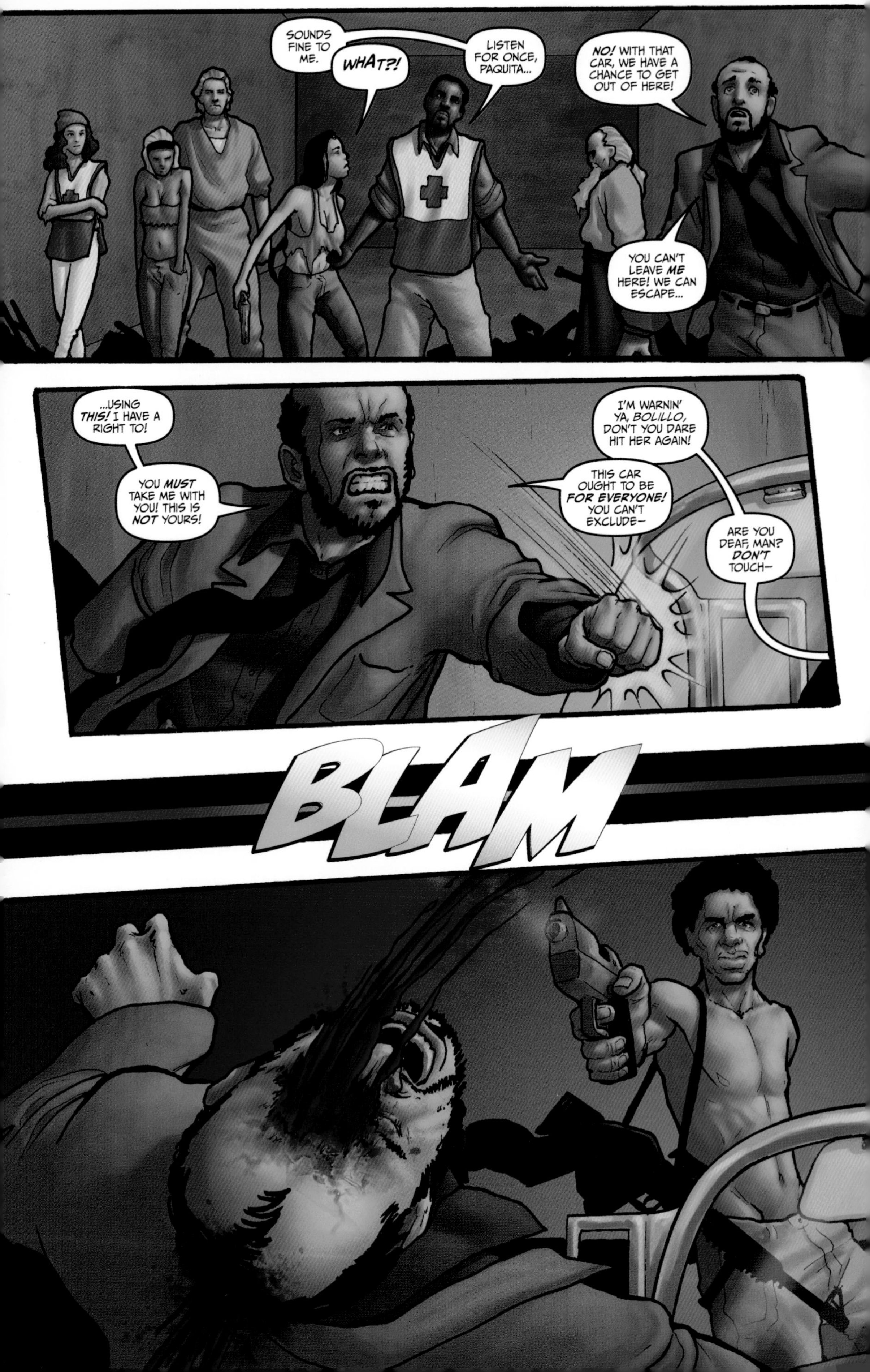
SOUNDS FINE TO ME.
WHAT?!
LISTEN FOR ONCE, PAQUITA...
NO! WITH THAT CAR, WE HAVE A CHANCE TO GET OUT OF HERE!
YOU CAN'T LEAVE ME HERE! WE CAN ESCAPE...
...USING THIS! I HAVE A RIGHT TO!
YOU MUST TAKE ME WITH YOU! THIS IS NOT YOURS!
THIS CAR OUGHT TO BE FOR EVERYONE! YOU CAN'T EXCLUDE—
I'M WARNIN' YA, BOLILLO, DON'T YOU DARE HIT HER AGAIN!
ARE YOU DEAF, MAN? DON'T TOUCH—
BLAM

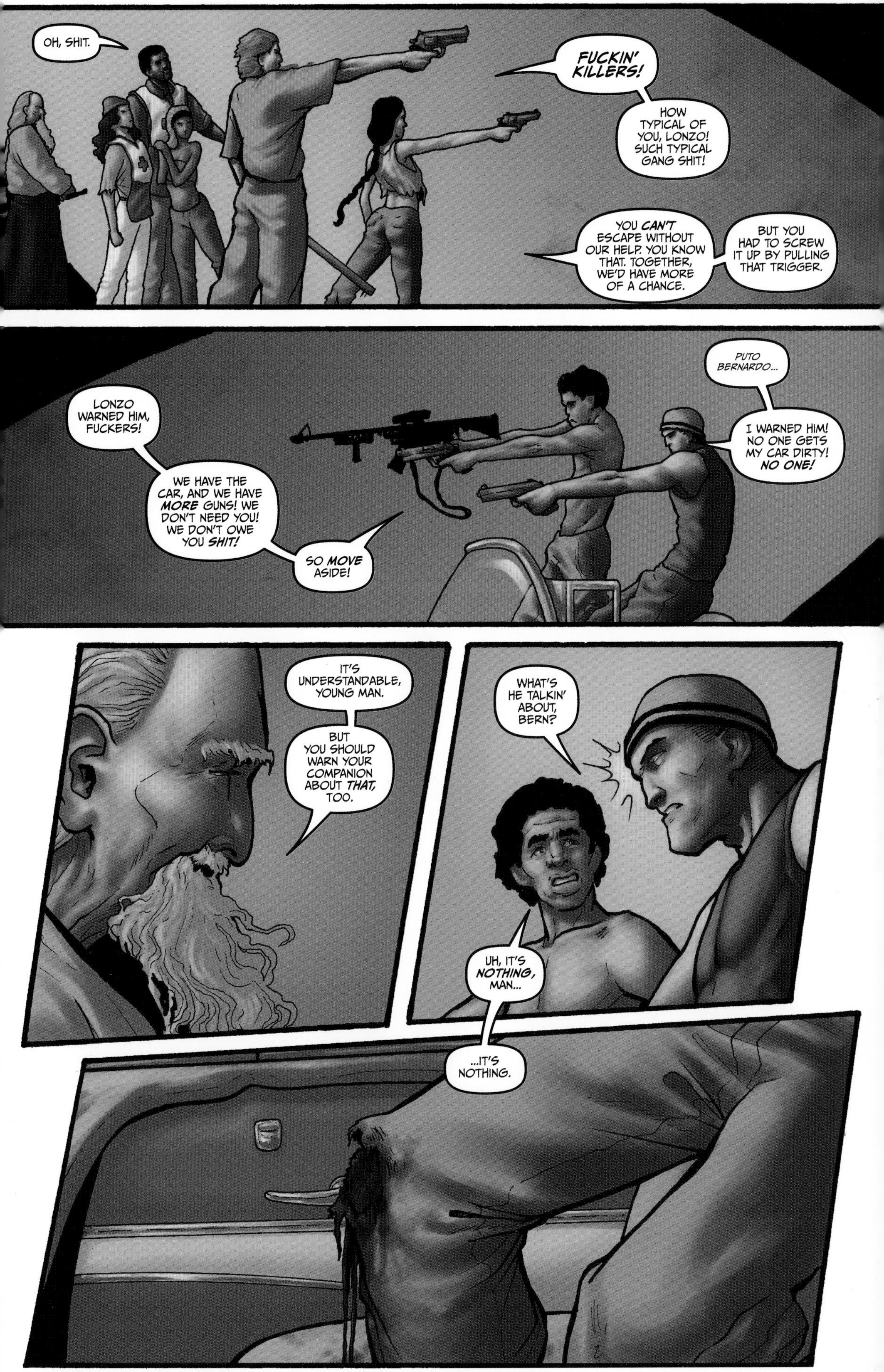
OH, SHIT.
FUCKIN' KILLERS!
HOW TYPICAL OF YOU, LONZO! SUCH TYPICAL GANG SHIT!
YOU CAN'T ESCAPE WITHOUT OUR HELP. YOU KNOW THAT. TOGETHER, WE'D HAVE MORE OF A CHANCE.
BUT YOU HAD TO SCREW IT UP BY PULLING THAT TRIGGER.
PUTO BERNARDO...
I WARNED HIM! NO ONE GETS MY CAR DIRTY! NO ONE!
LONZO WARNED HIM, FUCKERS!
WE HAVE THE CAR, AND WE HAVE MORE GUNS! WE DON'T NEED YOU! WE DON'T OWE YOU SHIT!
SO MOVE ASIDE!
IT'S UNDERSTANDABLE, YOUNG MAN.
BUT YOU SHOULD WARN YOUR COMPANION ABOUT THAT, TOO.
WHAT'S HE TALKIN' ABOUT, BERN?
UH, IT'S NOTHING, MAN...
...IT'S NOTHING.

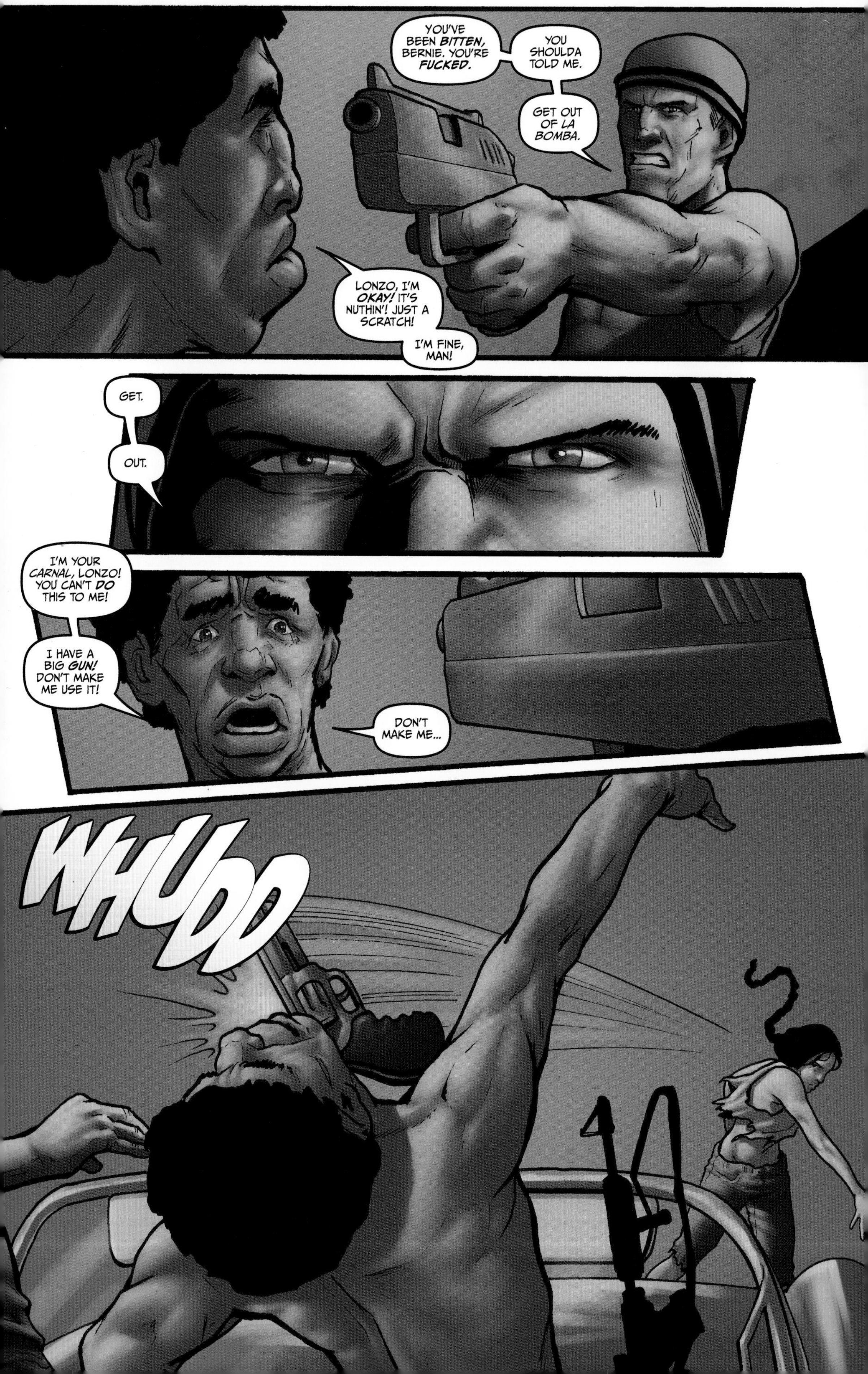
YOU'VE BEEN BITTEN, BERNIE. YOU'RE FUCKED.
YOU SHOULDA TOLD ME.
GET OUT OF LA BOMBA.
LONZO, I'M OKAY! IT'S NUTHIN'! JUST A SCRATCH!
I'M FINE, MAN!
GET.
OUT.
I'M YOUR CARNAL, LONZO! YOU CAN'T DO THIS TO ME!
I HAVE A BIG GUN! DON'T MAKE ME USE IT!
DON'T MAKE ME...
WHUDD

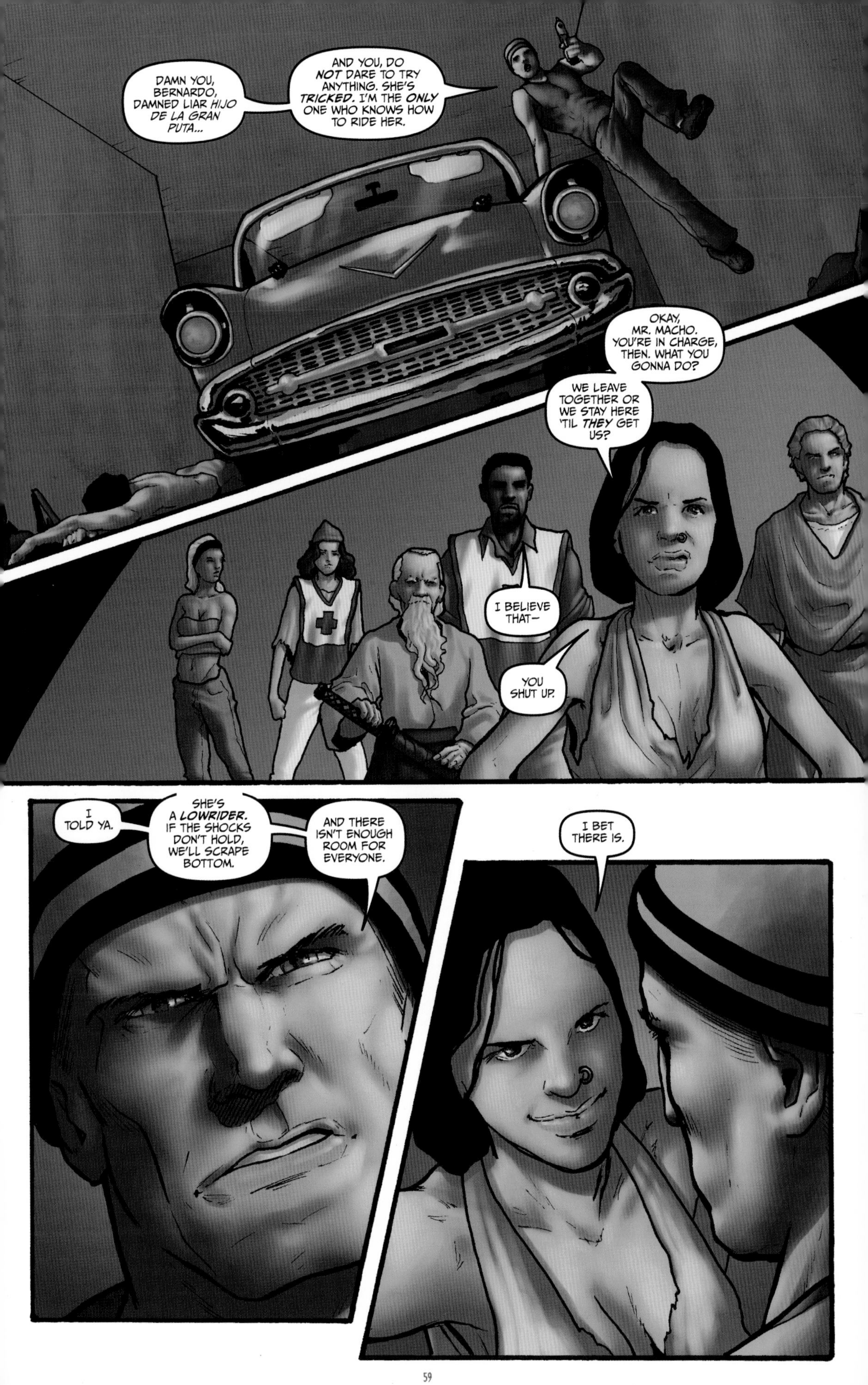
DAMN YOU, BERNARDO, DAMNED LIAR *HIJO DE LA GRAN PUTA...*
AND YOU, DO **NOT** DARE TO TRY ANYTHING. SHE'S **TRICKED.** I'M THE **ONLY** ONE WHO KNOWS HOW TO RIDE HER.
OKAY, MR. MACHO. YOU'RE IN CHARGE, THEN. WHAT YOU GONNA DO?
WE LEAVE TOGETHER OR WE STAY HERE 'TIL **THEY** GET US?
I BELIEVE THAT—
YOU SHUT UP.
I TOLD YA.
SHE'S A **LOWRIDER.** IF THE SHOCKS DON'T HOLD, WE'LL SCRAPE BOTTOM.
AND THERE ISN'T ENOUGH ROOM FOR EVERYONE.
I BET THERE IS.

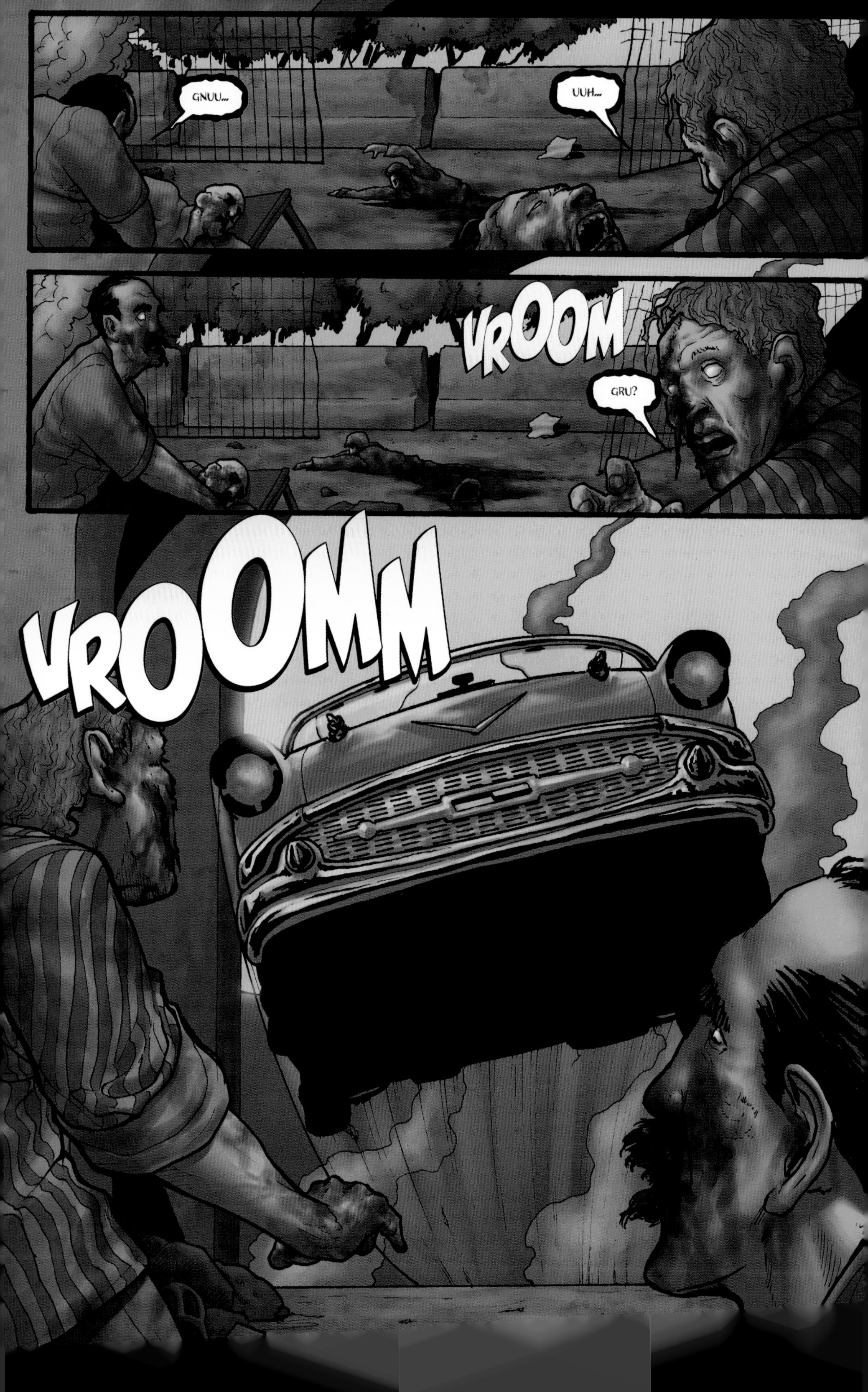
GNUU...
UUH...
VROOM
GRU?
VROOMM

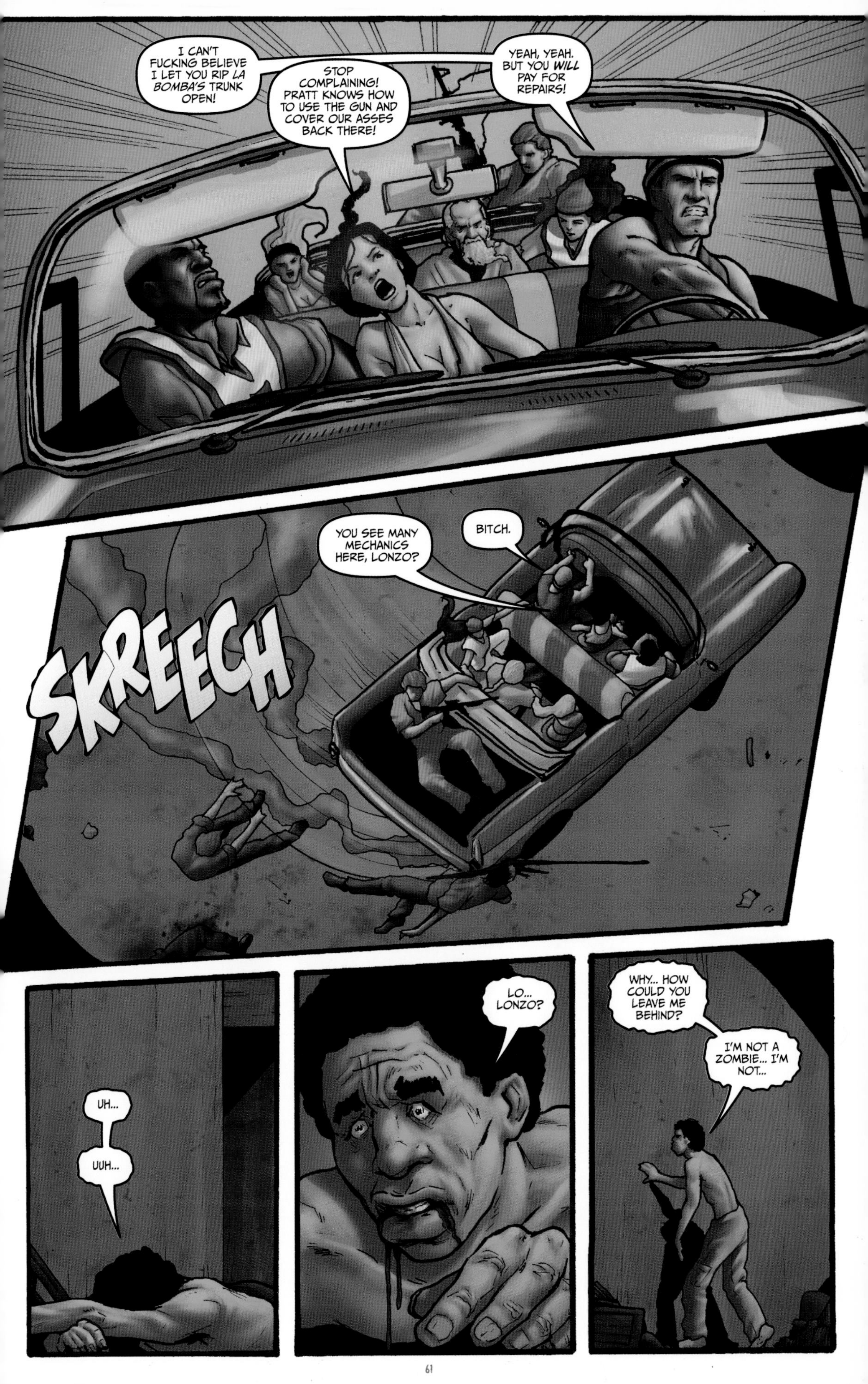
I CAN'T FUCKING BELIEVE I LET YOU RIP *LA BOMBA'S* TRUNK OPEN!
STOP COMPLAINING! PRATT KNOWS HOW TO USE THE GUN AND COVER OUR ASSES BACK THERE!
YEAH, YEAH. BUT YOU *WILL* PAY FOR REPAIRS!
YOU SEE MANY MECHANICS HERE, LONZO?
BITCH.
SKREECH
UH...
UUH...
LO... LONZO?
WHY... HOW COULD YOU LEAVE ME BEHIND?
I'M NOT A ZOMBIE... I'M NOT...

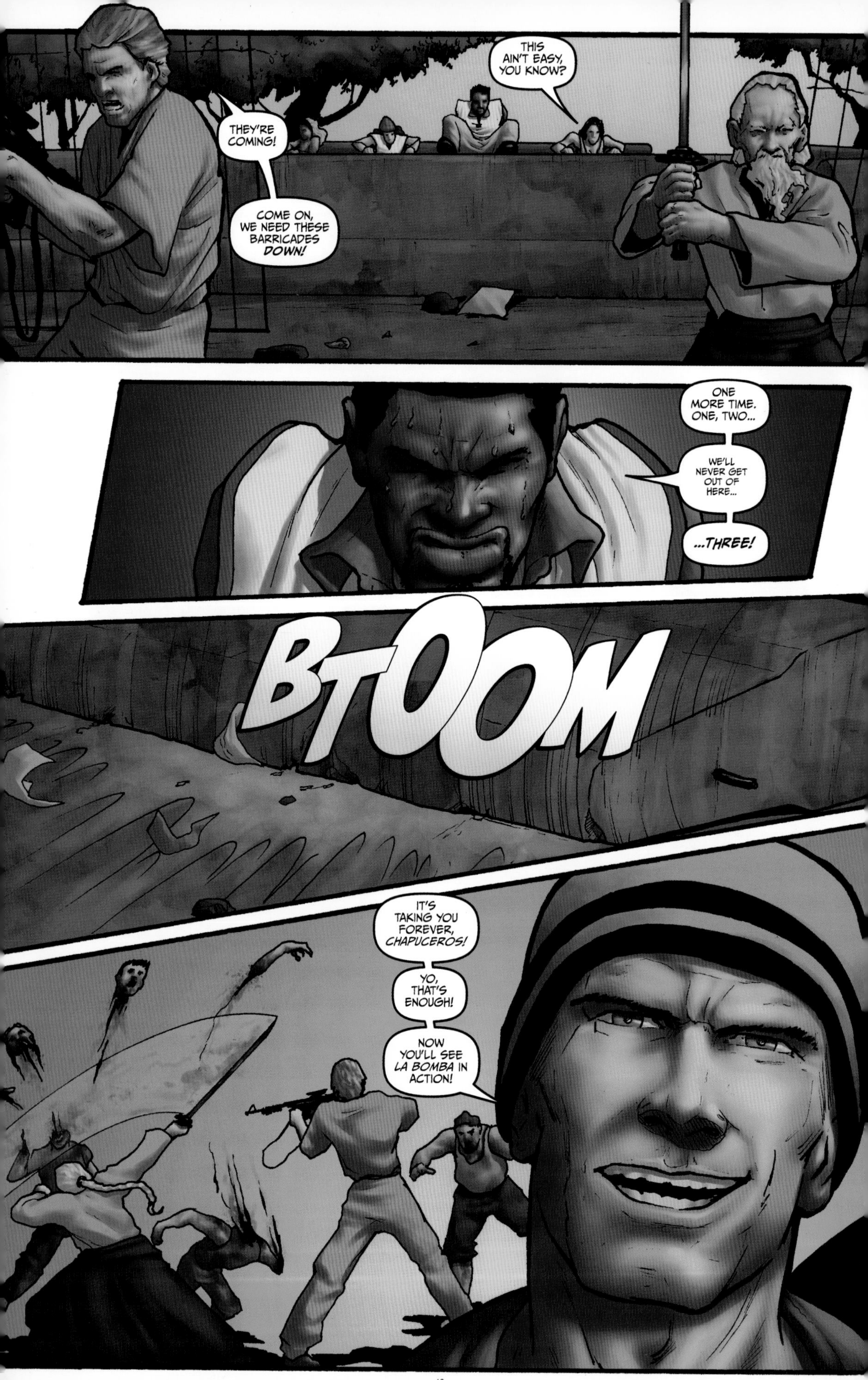
THEY'RE COMING!
COME ON, WE NEED THESE BARRICADES *DOWN!*
THIS AIN'T EASY, YOU KNOW?
ONE MORE TIME. ONE, TWO...
WE'LL NEVER GET OUT OF HERE...
...THREE!
BTOOM
IT'S TAKING YOU FOREVER, *CHAPUCEROS!*
YO, THAT'S ENOUGH!
NOW YOU'LL SEE *LA BOMBA* IN ACTION!

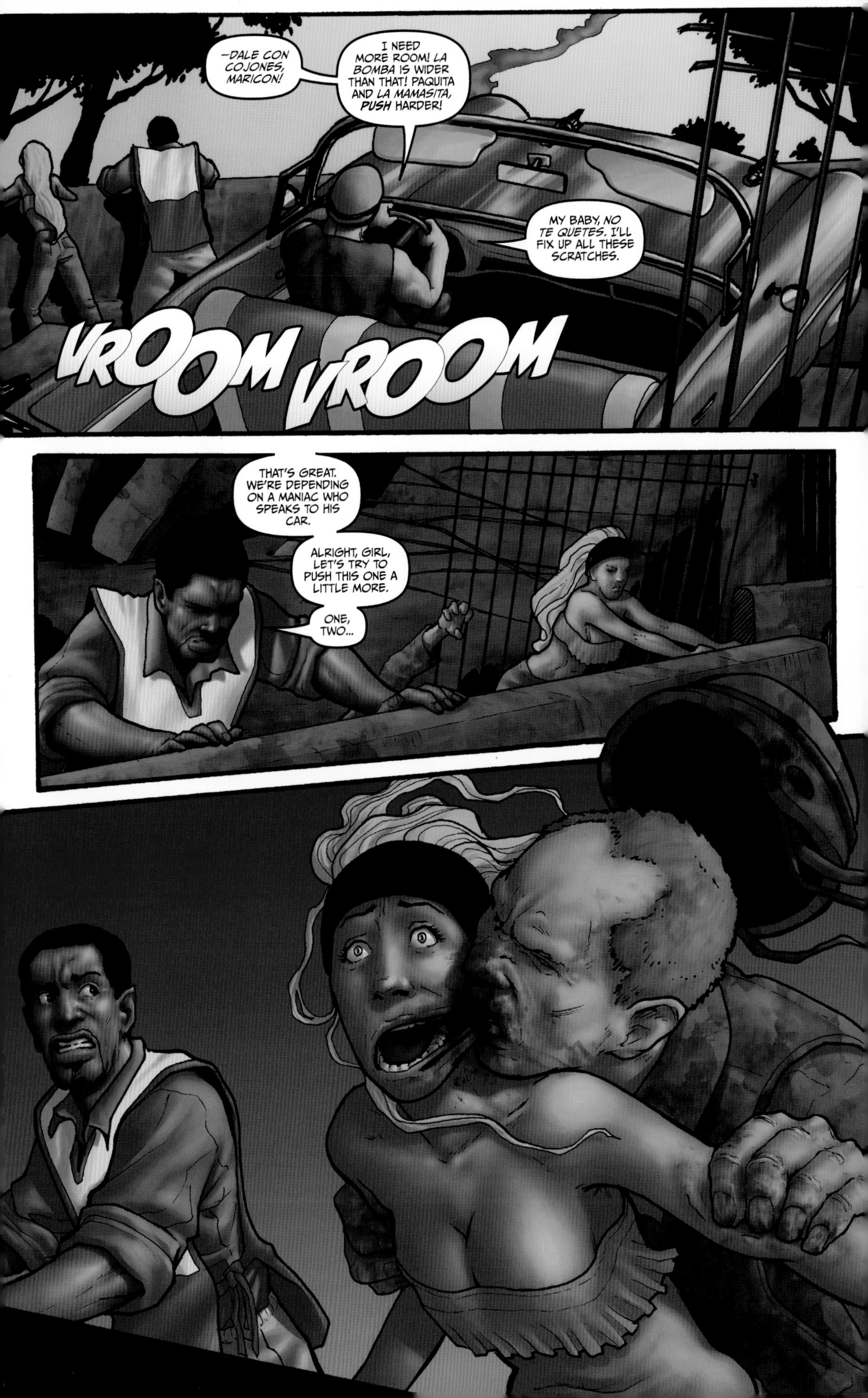

—DALE CON COJONES, MARICON!
I NEED MORE ROOM! LA BOMBA IS WIDER THAN THAT! PAQUITA AND LA MAMASITA, PUSH HARDER!
MY BABY, NO TE QUETES. I'LL FIX UP ALL THESE SCRATCHES.
VROOM VROOM
THAT'S GREAT. WE'RE DEPENDING ON A MANIAC WHO SPEAKS TO HIS CAR.
ALRIGHT, GIRL, LET'S TRY TO PUSH THIS ONE A LITTLE MORE.
ONE, TWO...

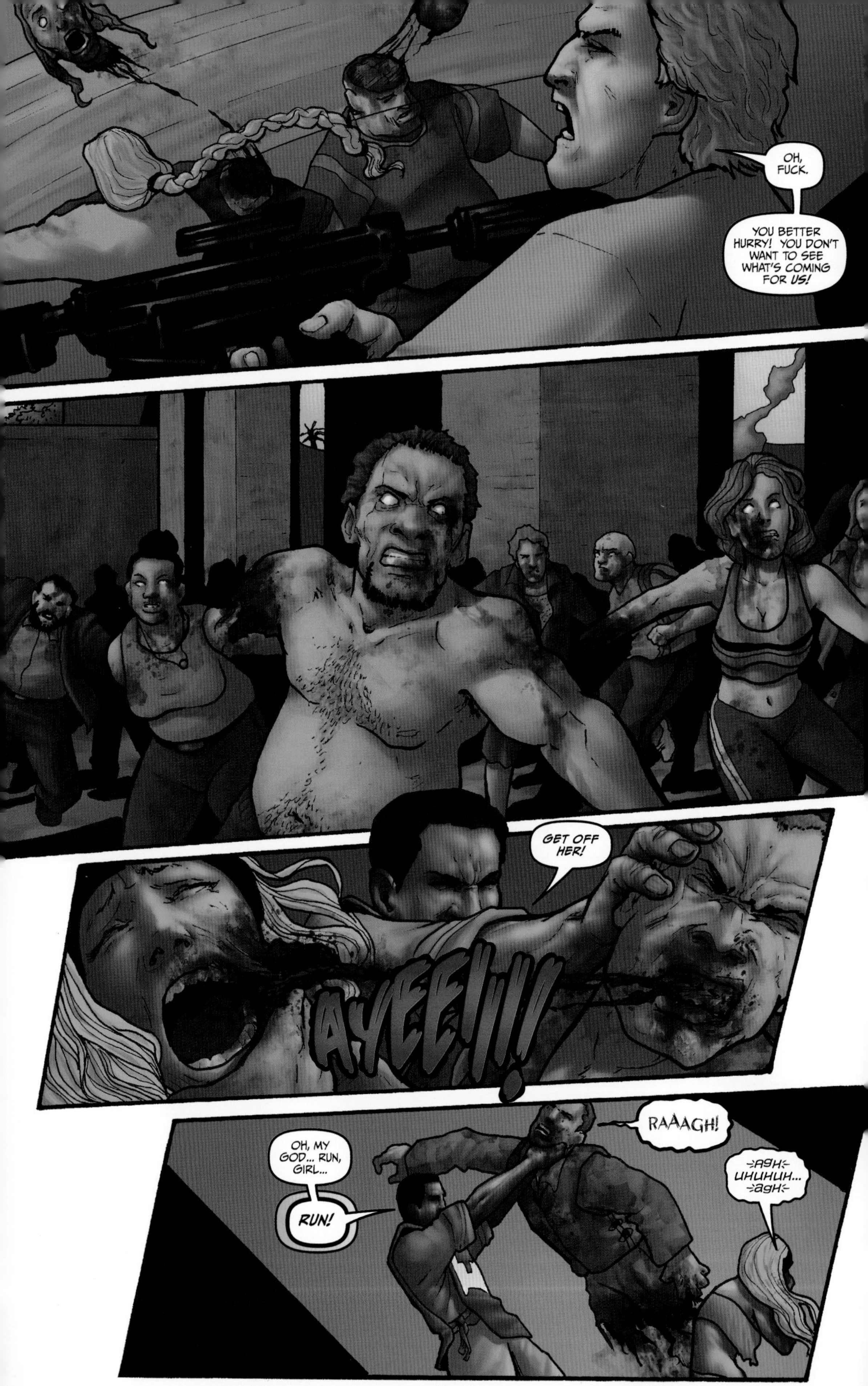
OH, FUCK.
YOU BETTER HURRY! YOU DON'T WANT TO SEE WHAT'S COMING FOR US!
GET OFF HER!
AYEE!!!!
OH, MY GOD... RUN, GIRL...
RUN!
RAAAGH!
-agh- UHUHUH... -agh-

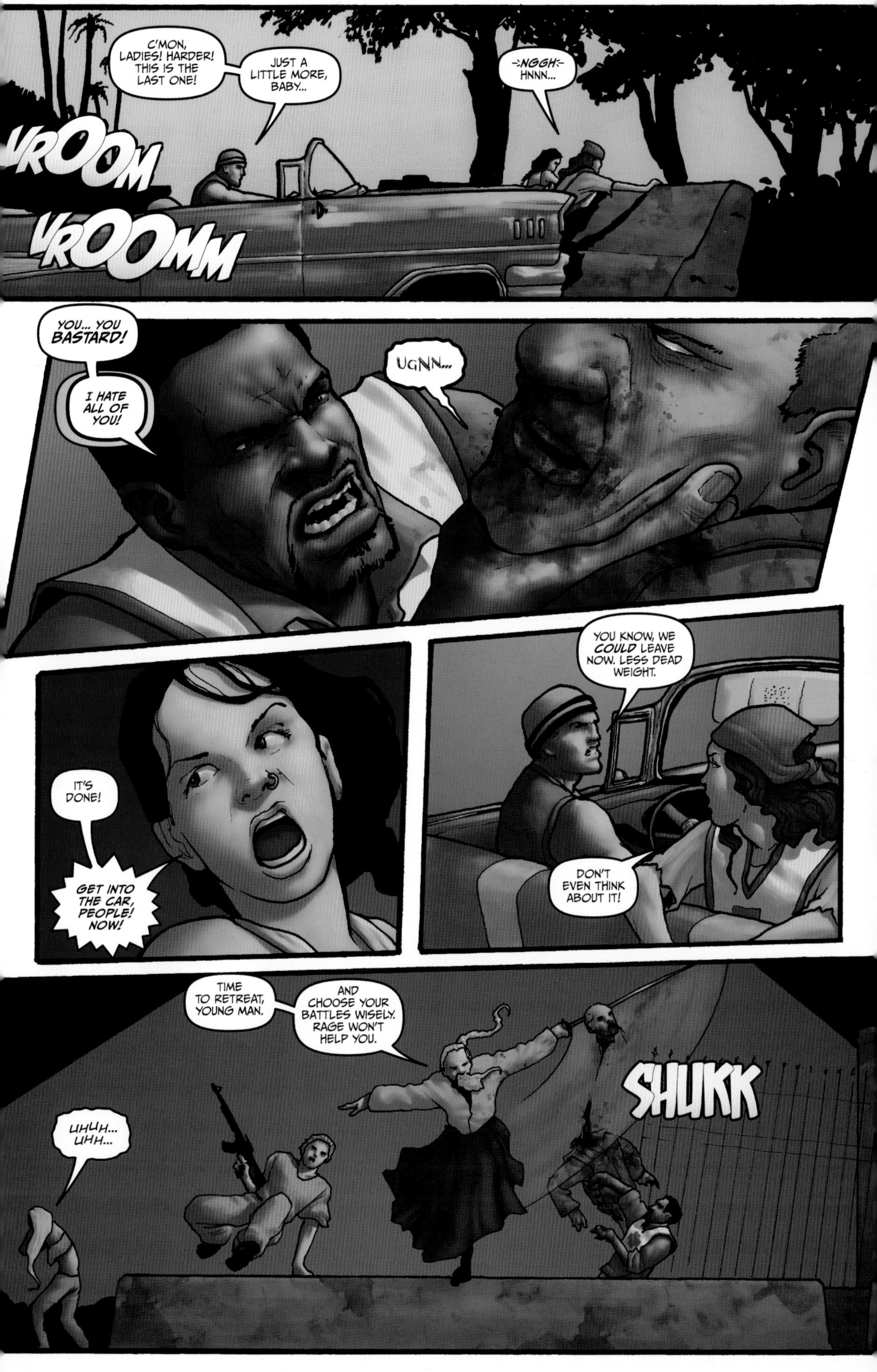
C'MON, LADIES! HARDER! THIS IS THE LAST ONE!
JUST A LITTLE MORE, BABY...
-NGGH- HNNN...
VROOM
VROOMM
YOU... YOU BASTARD!
I HATE ALL OF YOU!
UGNN...
IT'S DONE!
GET INTO THE CAR, PEOPLE! NOW!
YOU KNOW, WE COULD LEAVE NOW. LESS DEAD WEIGHT.
DON'T EVEN THINK ABOUT IT!
TIME TO RETREAT, YOUNG MAN.
AND CHOOSE YOUR BATTLES WISELY. RAGE WON'T HELP YOU.
SHUKK
UHUH... UHH...

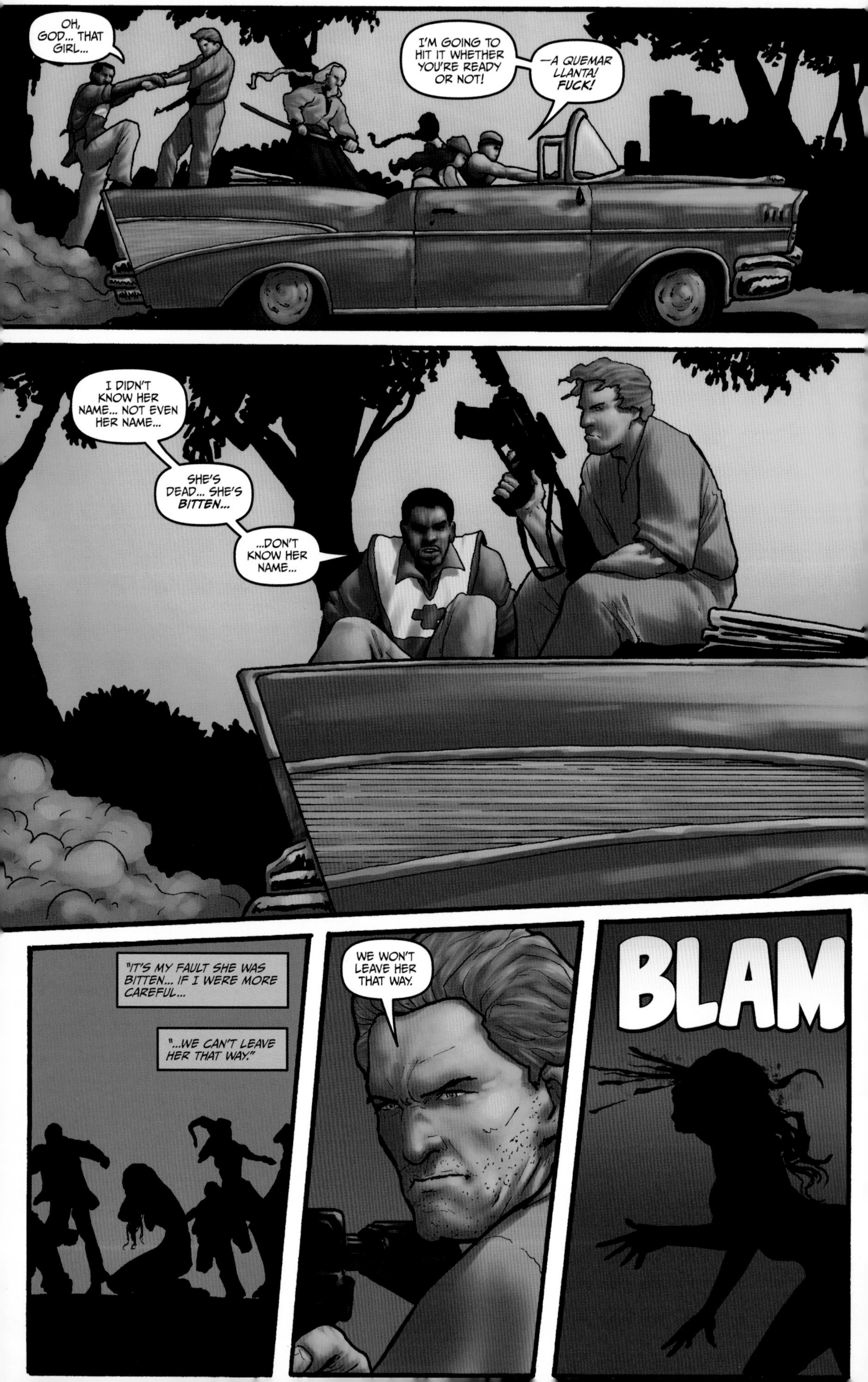
OH, GOD... THAT GIRL...
I'M GOING TO HIT IT WHETHER YOU'RE READY OR NOT!
—A QUEMAR LLANTA! FUCK!
I DIDN'T KNOW HER NAME... NOT EVEN HER NAME...
SHE'S DEAD... SHE'S BITTEN...
...DON'T KNOW HER NAME...
"IT'S MY FAULT SHE WAS BITTEN... IF I WERE MORE CAREFUL...
"...WE CAN'T LEAVE HER THAT WAY."
WE WON'T LEAVE HER THAT WAY.
BLAM

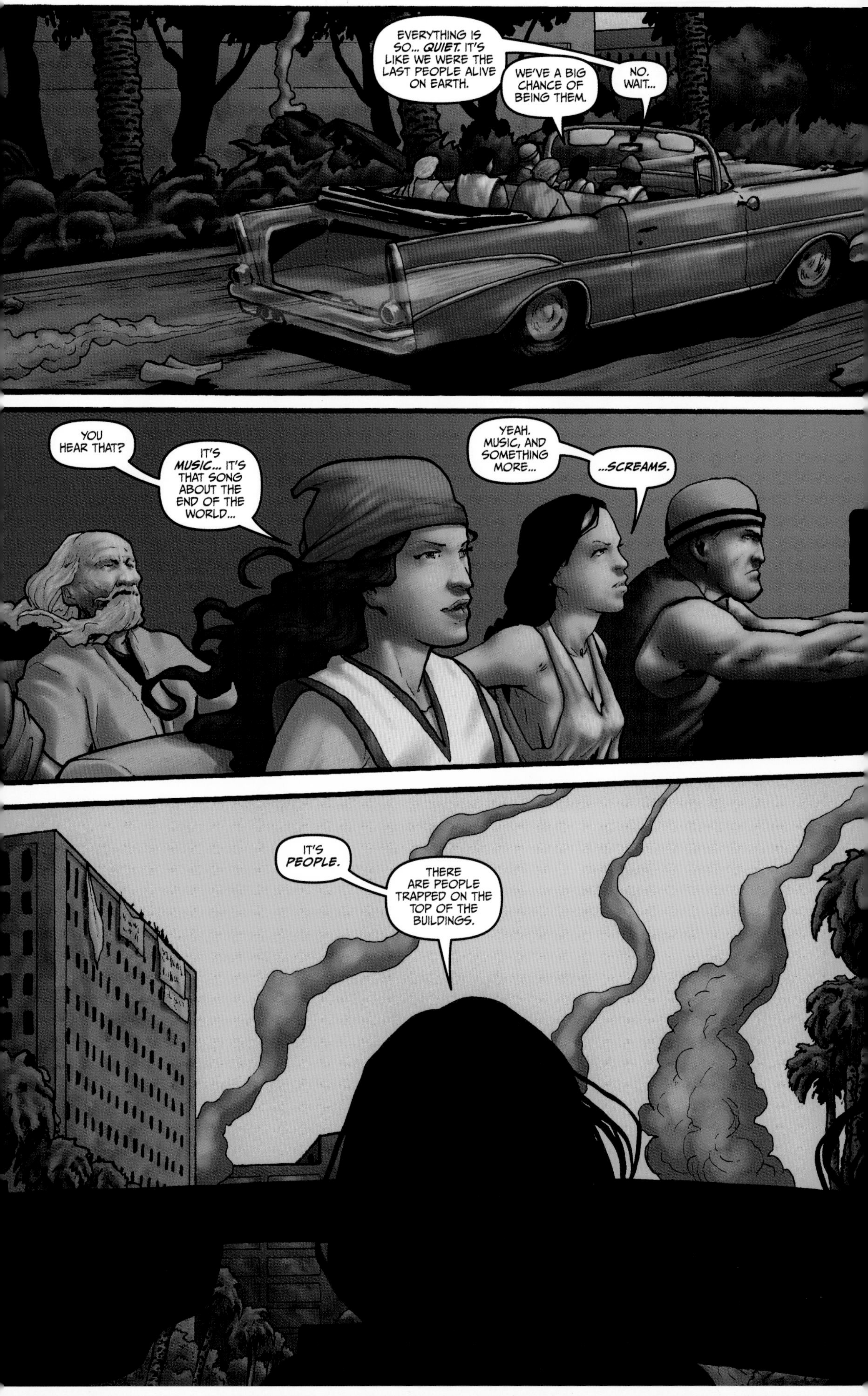
EVERYTHING IS SO... QUIET. IT'S LIKE WE WERE THE LAST PEOPLE ALIVE ON EARTH.
WE'VE A BIG CHANCE OF BEING THEM.
NO. WAIT...
YOU HEAR THAT?
IT'S MUSIC... IT'S THAT SONG ABOUT THE END OF THE WORLD...
YEAH. MUSIC, AND SOMETHING MORE...
...SCREAMS.
IT'S PEOPLE.
THERE ARE PEOPLE TRAPPED ON THE TOP OF THE BUILDINGS.

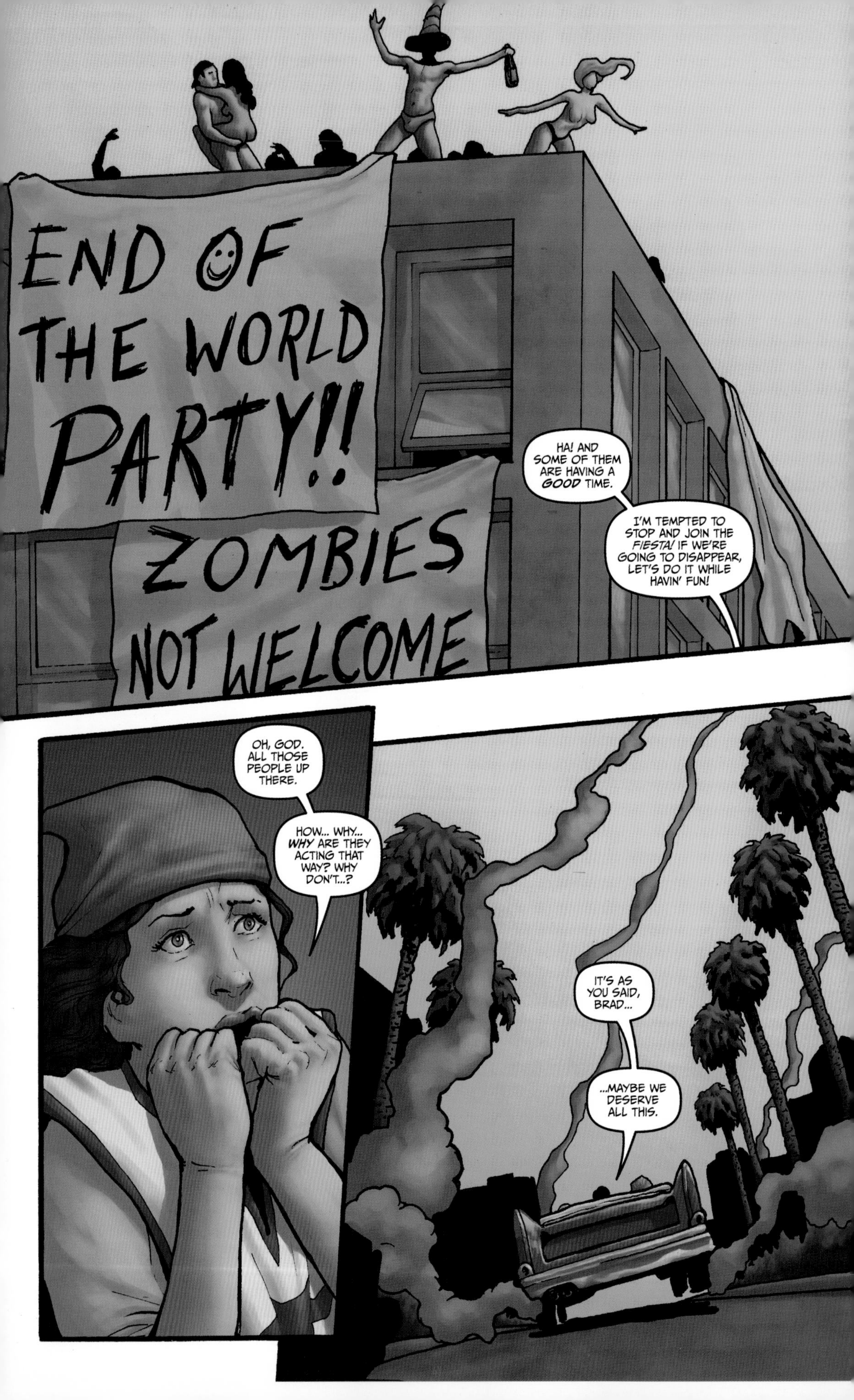
END OF THE WORLD PARTY!!
ZOMBIES NOT WELCOME
HA! AND SOME OF THEM ARE HAVING A *GOOD* TIME.
I'M TEMPTED TO STOP AND JOIN THE *FIESTA!* IF WE'RE GOING TO DISAPPEAR, LET'S DO IT WHILE HAVIN' FUN!
OH, GOD. ALL THOSE PEOPLE UP THERE.
HOW... WHY... *WHY* ARE THEY ACTING THAT WAY? WHY DON'T...?
IT'S AS YOU SAID, BRAD...
...MAYBE WE DESERVE ALL THIS.

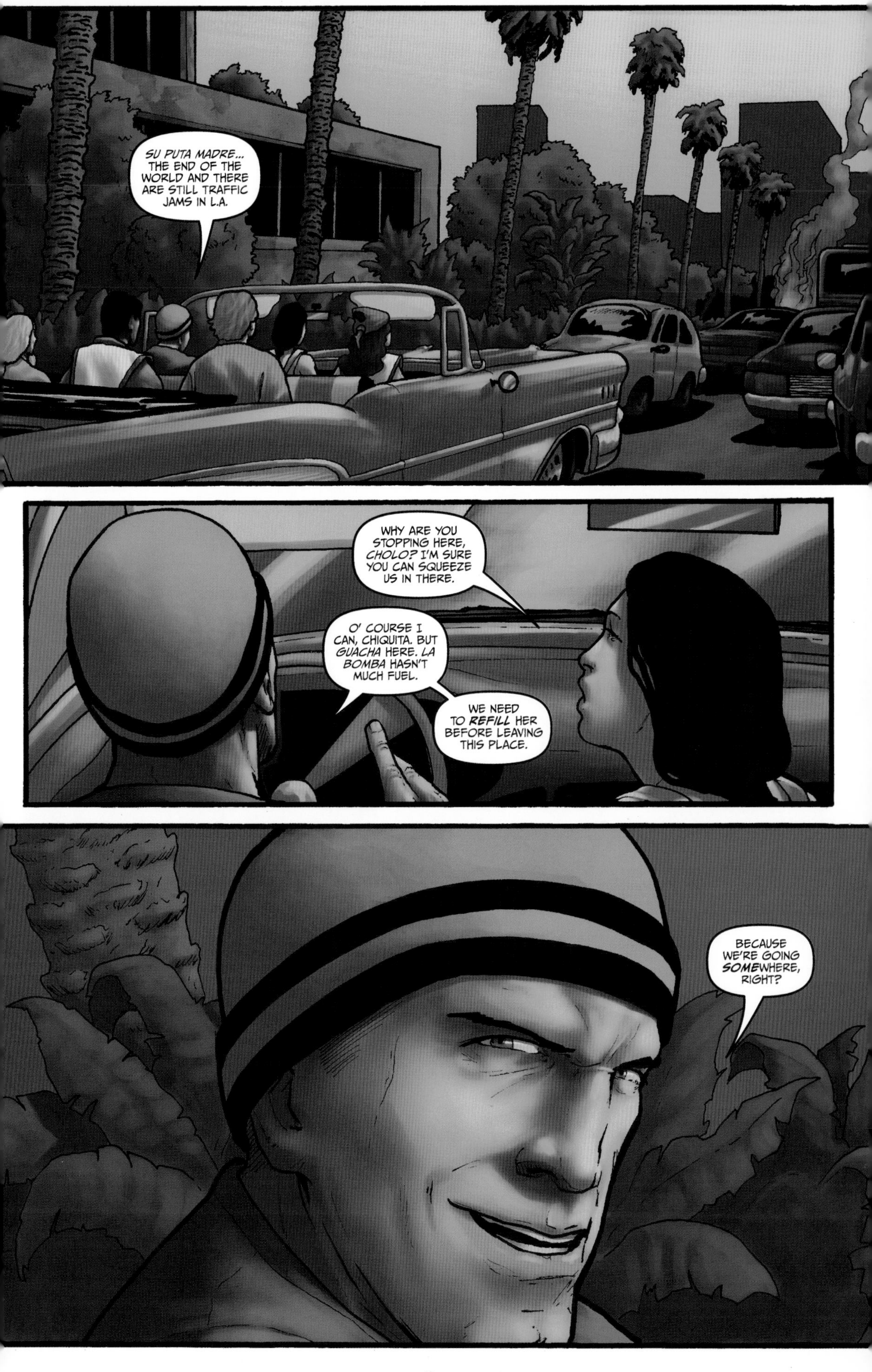
SU PUTA MADRE... THE END OF THE WORLD AND THERE ARE STILL TRAFFIC JAMS IN L.A.
WHY ARE YOU STOPPING HERE, CHOLO? I'M SURE YOU CAN SQUEEZE US IN THERE.
O' COURSE I CAN, CHIQUITA. BUT GUACHA HERE. LA BOMBA HASN'T MUCH FUEL.
WE NEED TO REFILL HER BEFORE LEAVING THIS PLACE.
BECAUSE WE'RE GOING SOMEWHERE, RIGHT?

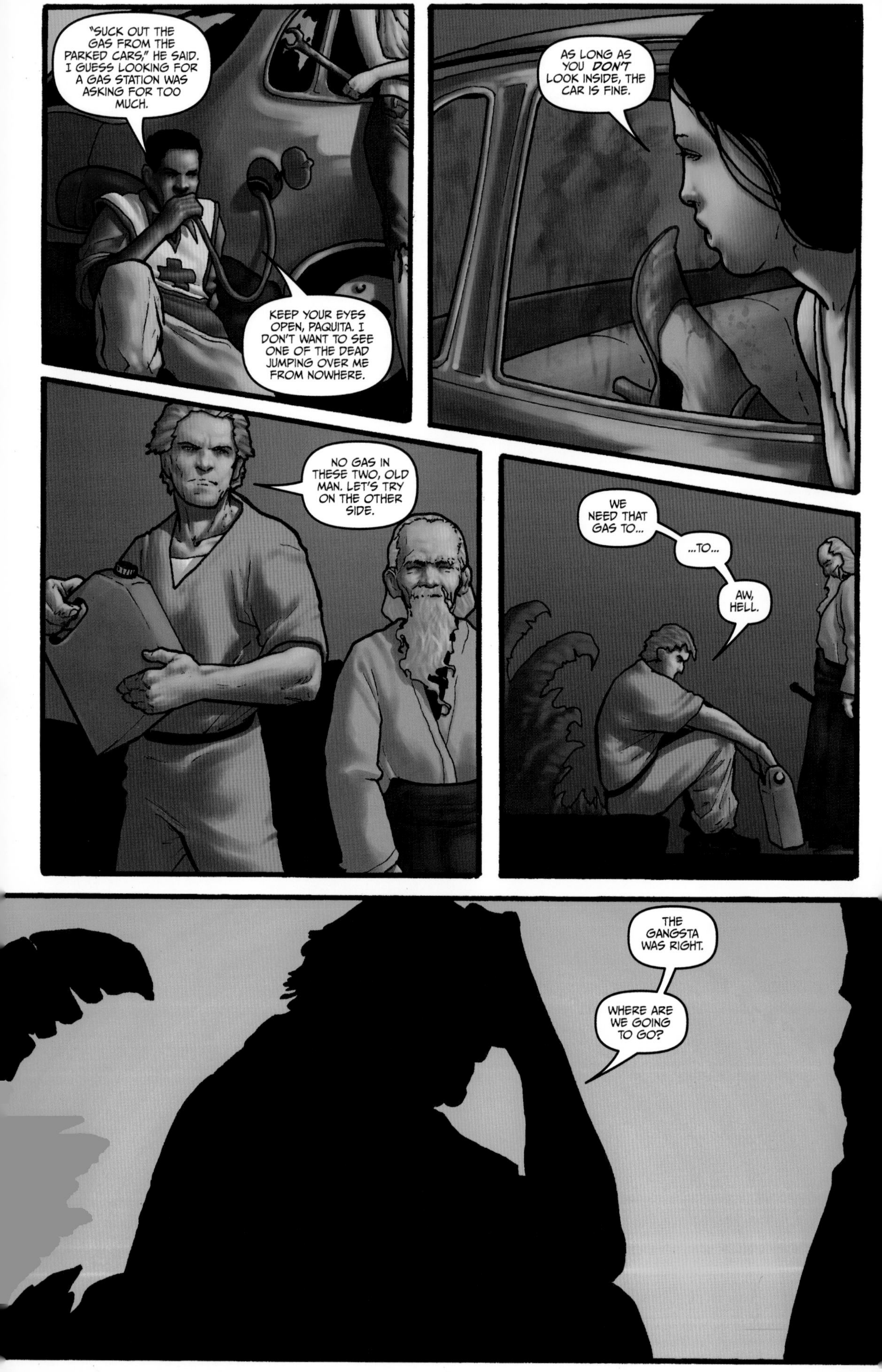
"SUCK OUT THE GAS FROM THE PARKED CARS," HE SAID. I GUESS LOOKING FOR A GAS STATION WAS ASKING FOR TOO MUCH.
KEEP YOUR EYES OPEN, PAQUITA. I DON'T WANT TO SEE ONE OF THE DEAD JUMPING OVER ME FROM NOWHERE.
AS LONG AS YOU DON'T LOOK INSIDE, THE CAR IS FINE.
NO GAS IN THESE TWO, OLD MAN. LET'S TRY ON THE OTHER SIDE.
WE NEED THAT GAS TO...
...TO...
AW, HELL.
THE GANGSTA WAS RIGHT.
WHERE ARE WE GOING TO GO?

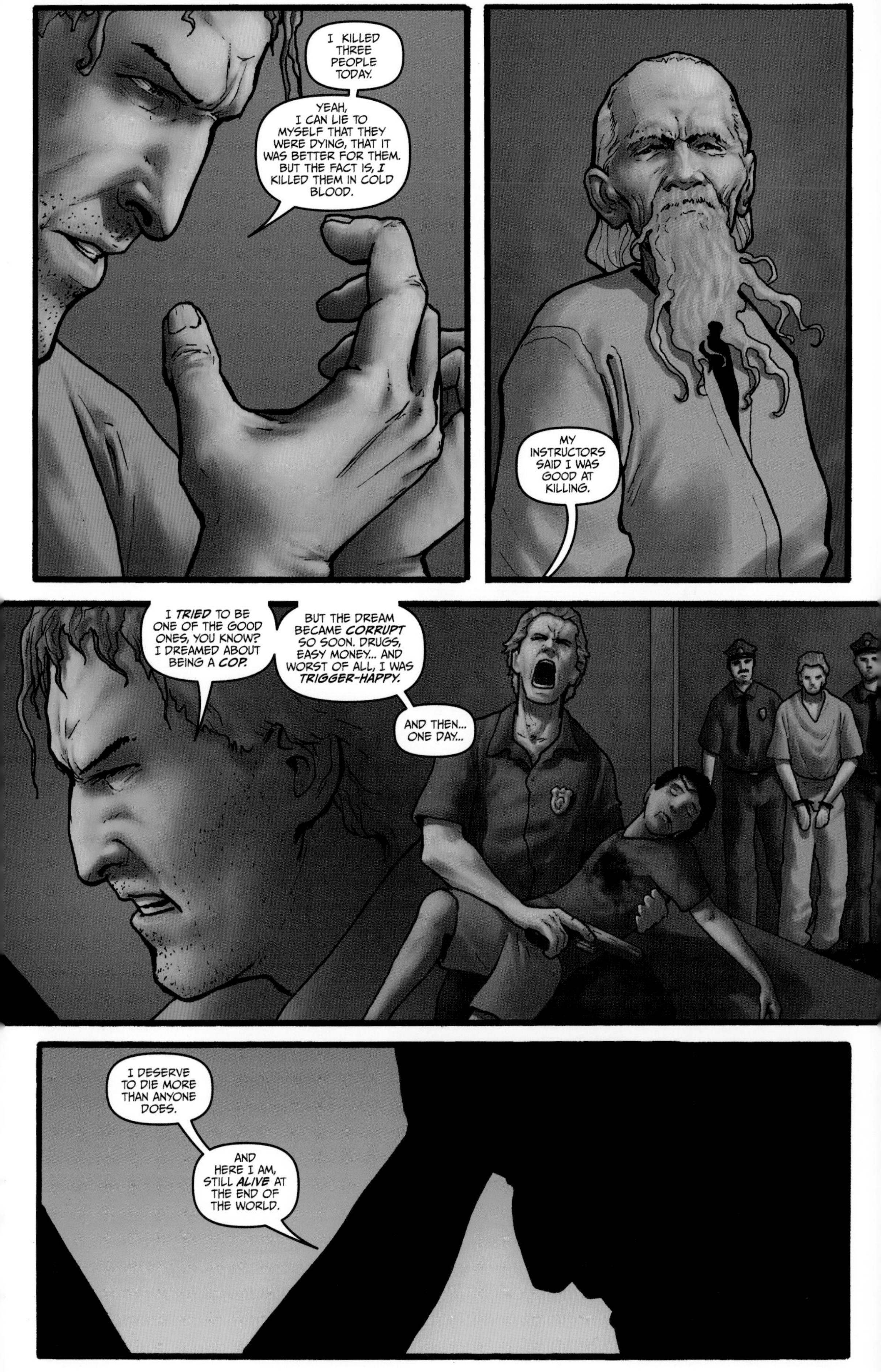
I KILLED THREE PEOPLE TODAY.
YEAH, I CAN LIE TO MYSELF THAT THEY WERE DYING, THAT IT WAS BETTER FOR THEM. BUT THE FACT IS, *I* KILLED THEM IN COLD BLOOD.
MY INSTRUCTORS SAID I WAS GOOD AT KILLING.
I *TRIED* TO BE ONE OF THE GOOD ONES, YOU KNOW? I DREAMED ABOUT BEING A *COP.*
BUT THE DREAM BECAME *CORRUPT* SO SOON. DRUGS, EASY MONEY... AND WORST OF ALL, I WAS *TRIGGER-HAPPY.*
AND THEN... ONE DAY...
I DESERVE TO DIE MORE THAN ANYONE DOES.
AND HERE I AM, STILL *ALIVE* AT THE END OF THE WORLD.

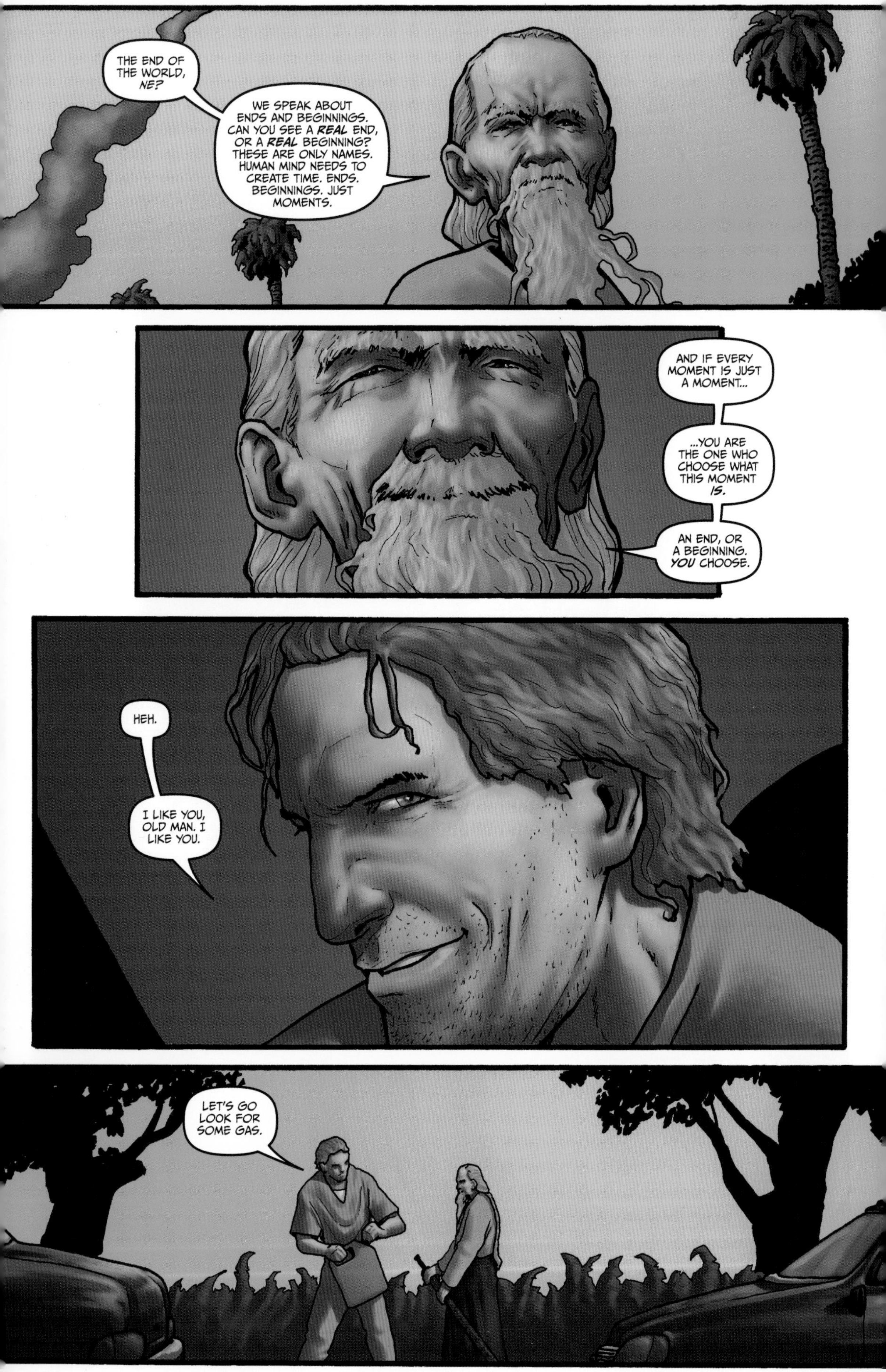

THE END OF THE WORLD, *NE?*
WE SPEAK ABOUT ENDS AND BEGINNINGS. CAN YOU SEE A ***REAL*** END, OR A ***REAL*** BEGINNING? THESE ARE ONLY NAMES. HUMAN MIND NEEDS TO CREATE TIME. ENDS. BEGINNINGS. JUST MOMENTS.
AND IF EVERY MOMENT IS JUST A MOMENT...
...YOU ARE THE ONE WHO CHOOSE WHAT THIS MOMENT *IS.*
AN END, OR A BEGINNING. ***YOU*** CHOOSE.
HEH.
I LIKE YOU, OLD MAN. I LIKE YOU.
LET'S GO LOOK FOR SOME GAS.

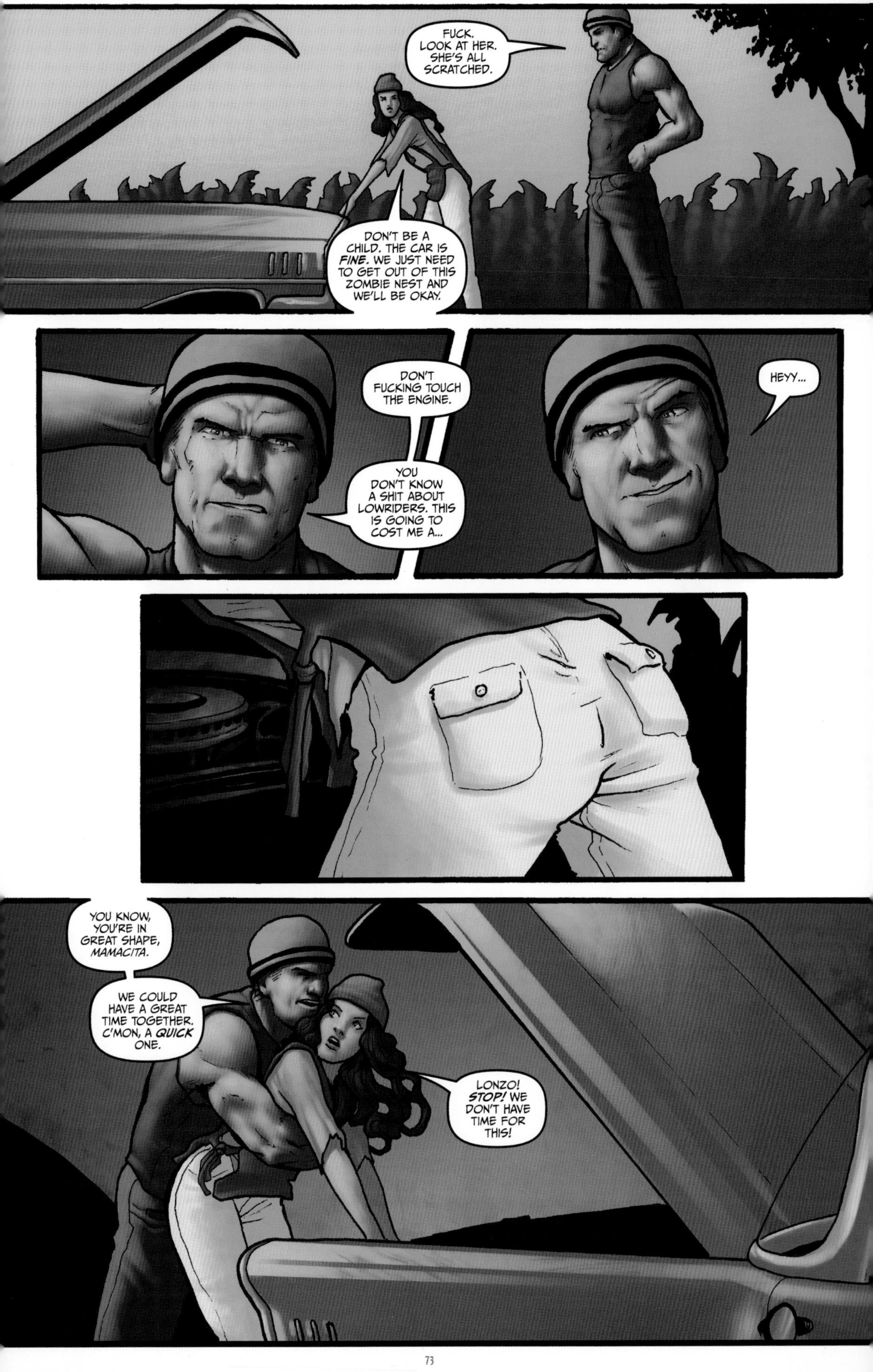
FUCK. LOOK AT HER. SHE'S ALL SCRATCHED.
DON'T BE A CHILD. THE CAR IS *FINE.* WE JUST NEED TO GET OUT OF THIS ZOMBIE NEST AND WE'LL BE OKAY.
DON'T FUCKING TOUCH THE ENGINE.
YOU DON'T KNOW A SHIT ABOUT LOWRIDERS. THIS IS GOING TO COST ME A...
HEYY...
YOU KNOW, YOU'RE IN GREAT SHAPE, *MAMACITA.*
WE COULD HAVE A GREAT TIME TOGETHER. C'MON, A *QUICK* ONE.
LONZO! *STOP!* WE DON'T HAVE TIME FOR THIS!

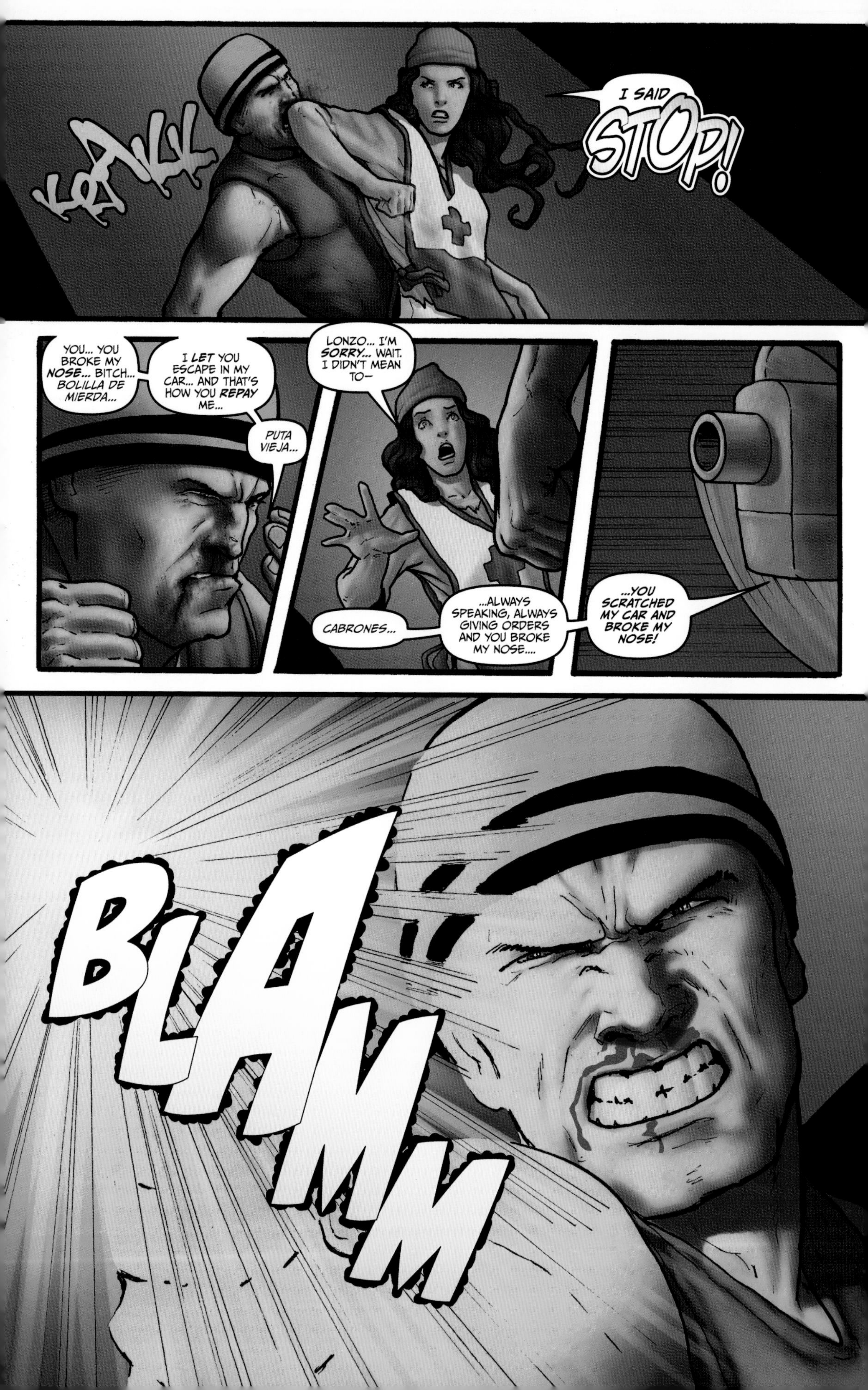
KRAKK
I SAID STOP!
YOU... YOU BROKE MY NOSE... BITCH... BOLILLA DE MIERDA...
I LET YOU ESCAPE IN MY CAR... AND THAT'S HOW YOU REPAY ME...
PUTA VIEJA...
LONZO... I'M SORRY... WAIT. I DIDN'T MEAN TO—
CABRONES...
...ALWAYS SPEAKING, ALWAYS GIVING ORDERS AND YOU BROKE MY NOSE....
...YOU SCRATCHED MY CAR AND BROKE MY NOSE!
BLAMM

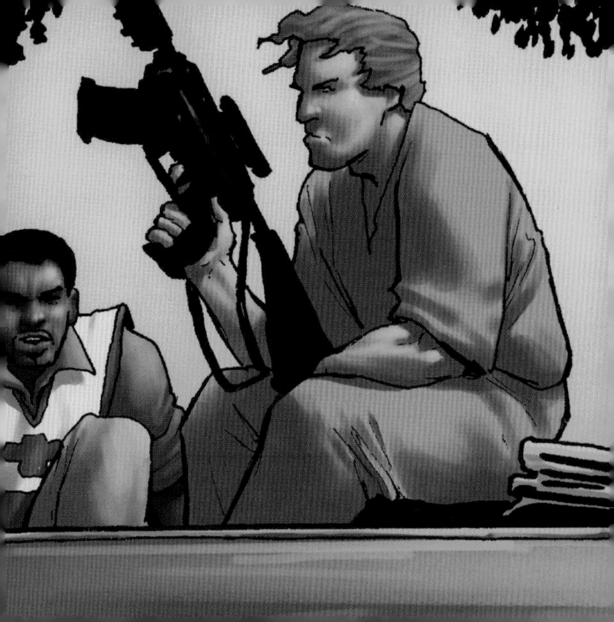

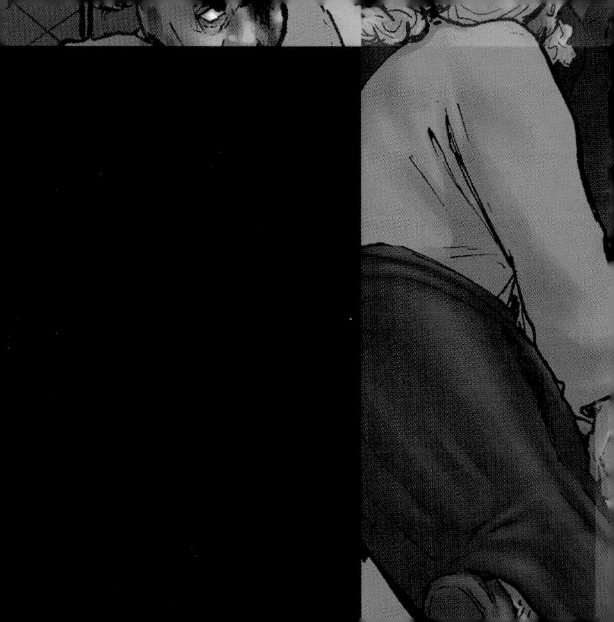

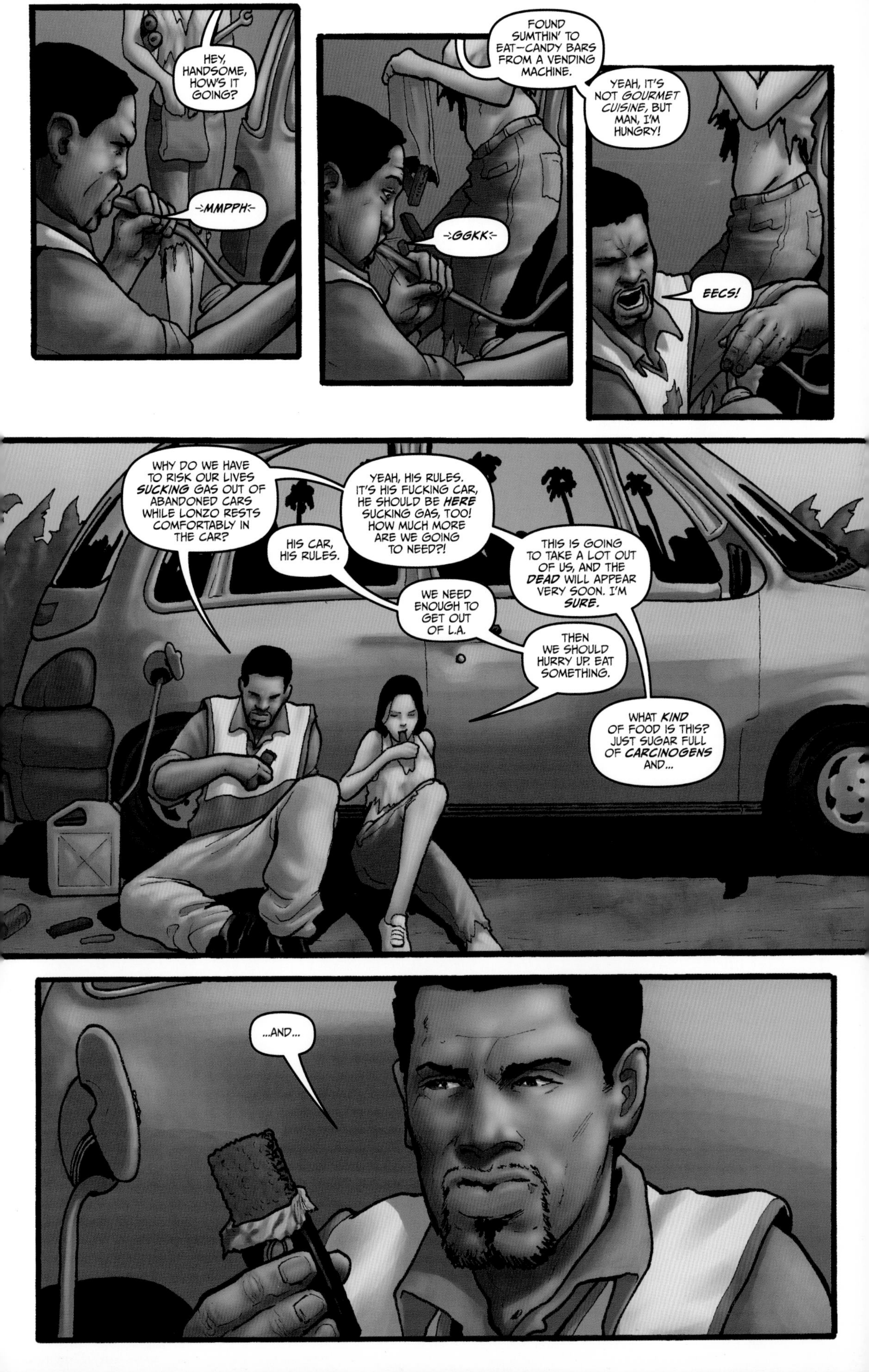
HEY, HANDSOME, HOW'S IT GOING?
MMPPH
FOUND SUMTHIN' TO EAT—CANDY BARS FROM A VENDING MACHINE.
GGKK
YEAH, IT'S NOT GOURMET CUISINE, BUT MAN, I'M HUNGRY!
EECS!
WHY DO WE HAVE TO RISK OUR LIVES SUCKING GAS OUT OF ABANDONED CARS WHILE LONZO RESTS COMFORTABLY IN THE CAR?
HIS CAR, HIS RULES.
YEAH, HIS RULES. IT'S HIS FUCKING CAR, HE SHOULD BE HERE SUCKING GAS, TOO! HOW MUCH MORE ARE WE GOING TO NEED?!
WE NEED ENOUGH TO GET OUT OF L.A.
THIS IS GOING TO TAKE A LOT OUT OF US, AND THE DEAD WILL APPEAR VERY SOON. I'M SURE.
THEN WE SHOULD HURRY UP. EAT SOMETHING.
WHAT KIND OF FOOD IS THIS? JUST SUGAR FULL OF CARCINOGENS AND...
...AND...

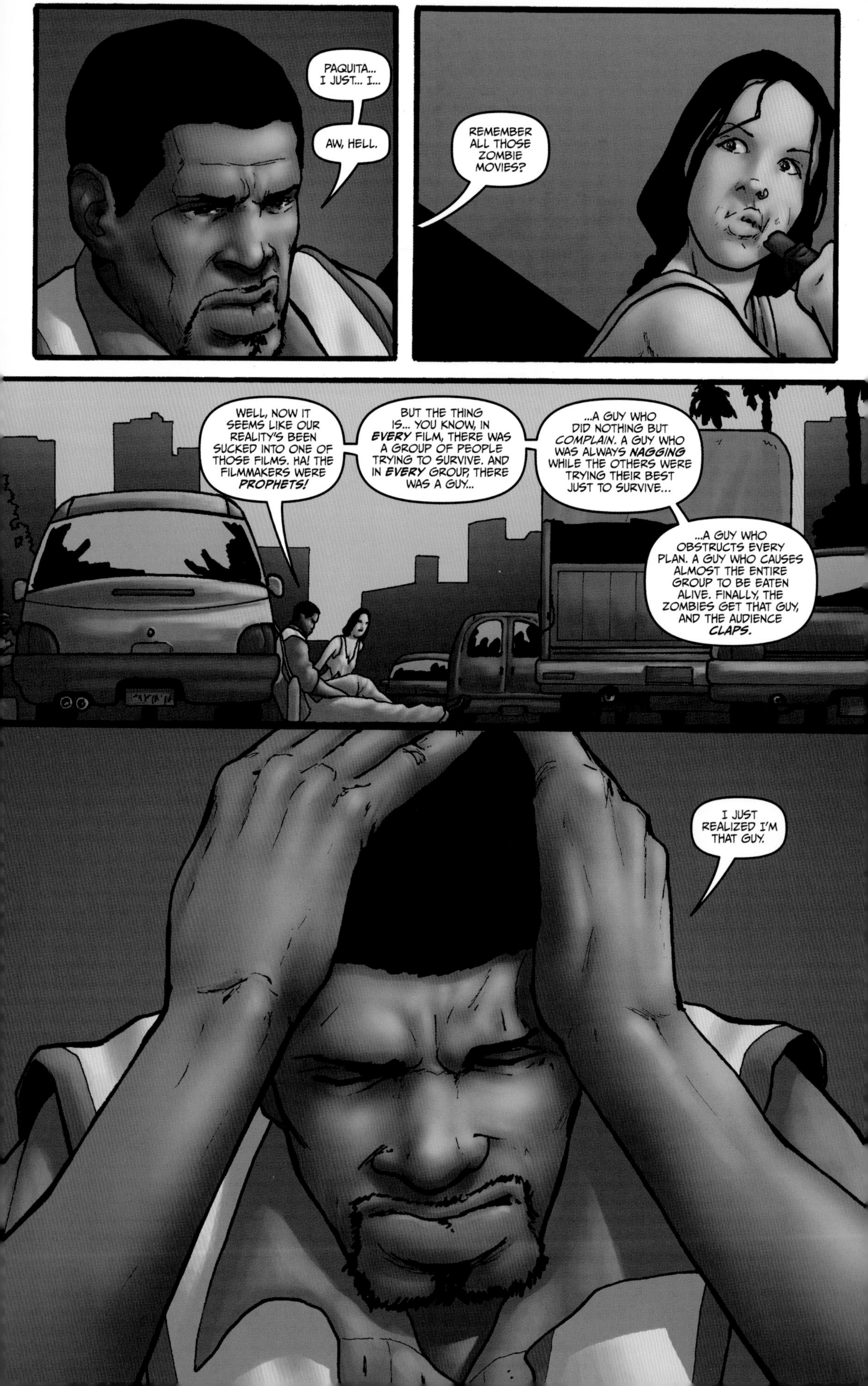
PAQUITA... I JUST... I...
AW, HELL.
REMEMBER ALL THOSE ZOMBIE MOVIES?
WELL, NOW IT SEEMS LIKE OUR REALITY'S BEEN SUCKED INTO ONE OF THOSE FILMS. HA! THE FILMMAKERS WERE PROPHETS!
BUT THE THING IS... YOU KNOW, IN EVERY FILM, THERE WAS A GROUP OF PEOPLE TRYING TO SURVIVE. AND IN EVERY GROUP, THERE WAS A GUY...
...A GUY WHO DID NOTHING BUT COMPLAIN. A GUY WHO WAS ALWAYS NAGGING WHILE THE OTHERS WERE TRYING THEIR BEST JUST TO SURVIVE...
...A GUY WHO OBSTRUCTS EVERY PLAN. A GUY WHO CAUSES ALMOST THE ENTIRE GROUP TO BE EATEN ALIVE. FINALLY, THE ZOMBIES GET THAT GUY, AND THE AUDIENCE CLAPS.
I JUST REALIZED I'M THAT GUY.

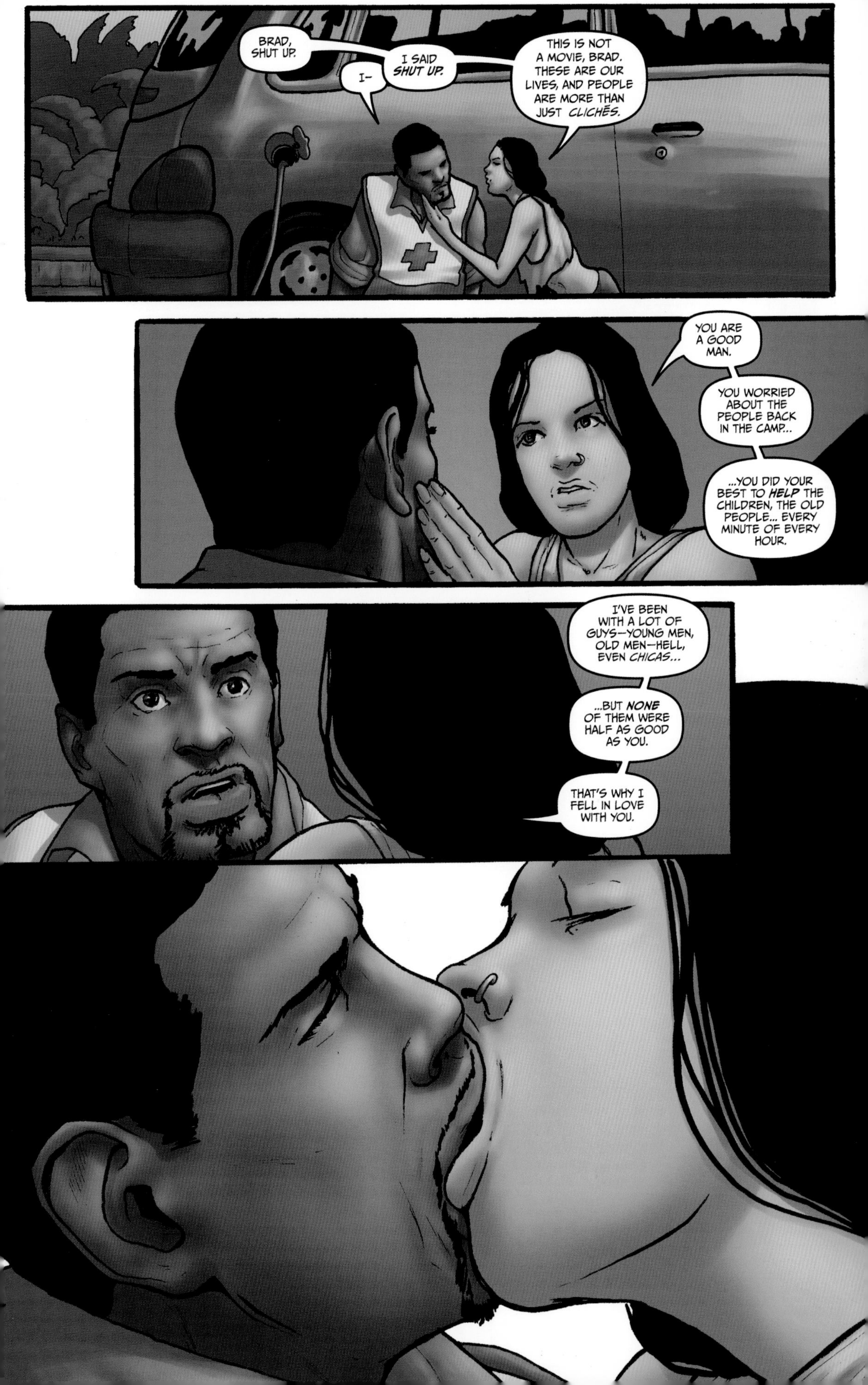
BRAD, SHUT UP.
I–
I SAID SHUT UP.
THIS IS NOT A MOVIE, BRAD. THESE ARE OUR LIVES, AND PEOPLE ARE MORE THAN JUST CLICHÉS.
YOU ARE A GOOD MAN.
YOU WORRIED ABOUT THE PEOPLE BACK IN THE CAMP...
...YOU DID YOUR BEST TO HELP THE CHILDREN, THE OLD PEOPLE... EVERY MINUTE OF EVERY HOUR.
I'VE BEEN WITH A LOT OF GUYS—YOUNG MEN, OLD MEN—HELL, EVEN CHICAS...
...BUT NONE OF THEM WERE HALF AS GOOD AS YOU.
THAT'S WHY I FELL IN LOVE WITH YOU.

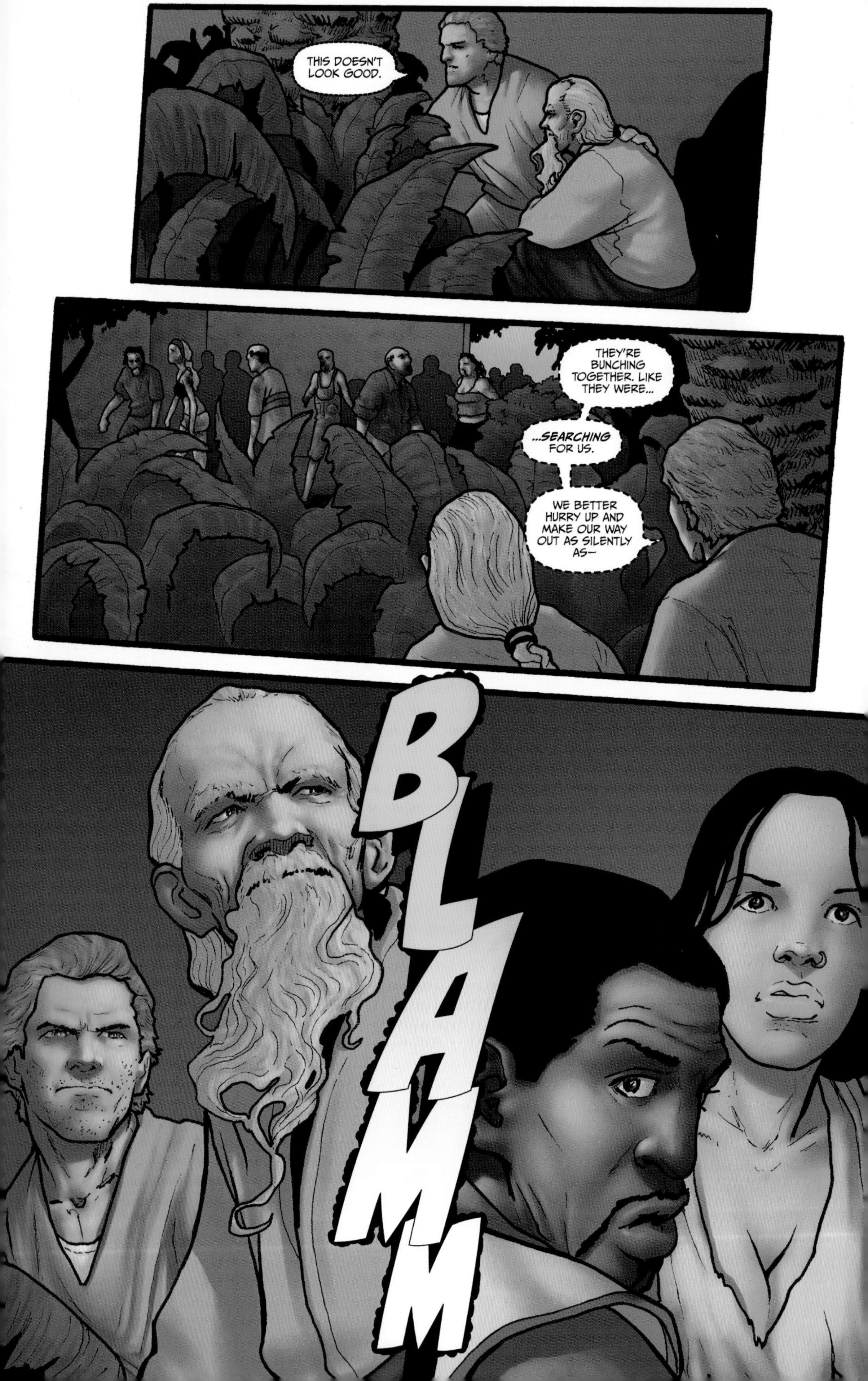
THIS DOESN'T LOOK GOOD.
THEY'RE BUNCHING TOGETHER. LIKE THEY WERE...
...SEARCHING FOR US.
WE BETTER HURRY UP AND MAKE OUR WAY OUT AS SILENTLY AS—
BLAMM

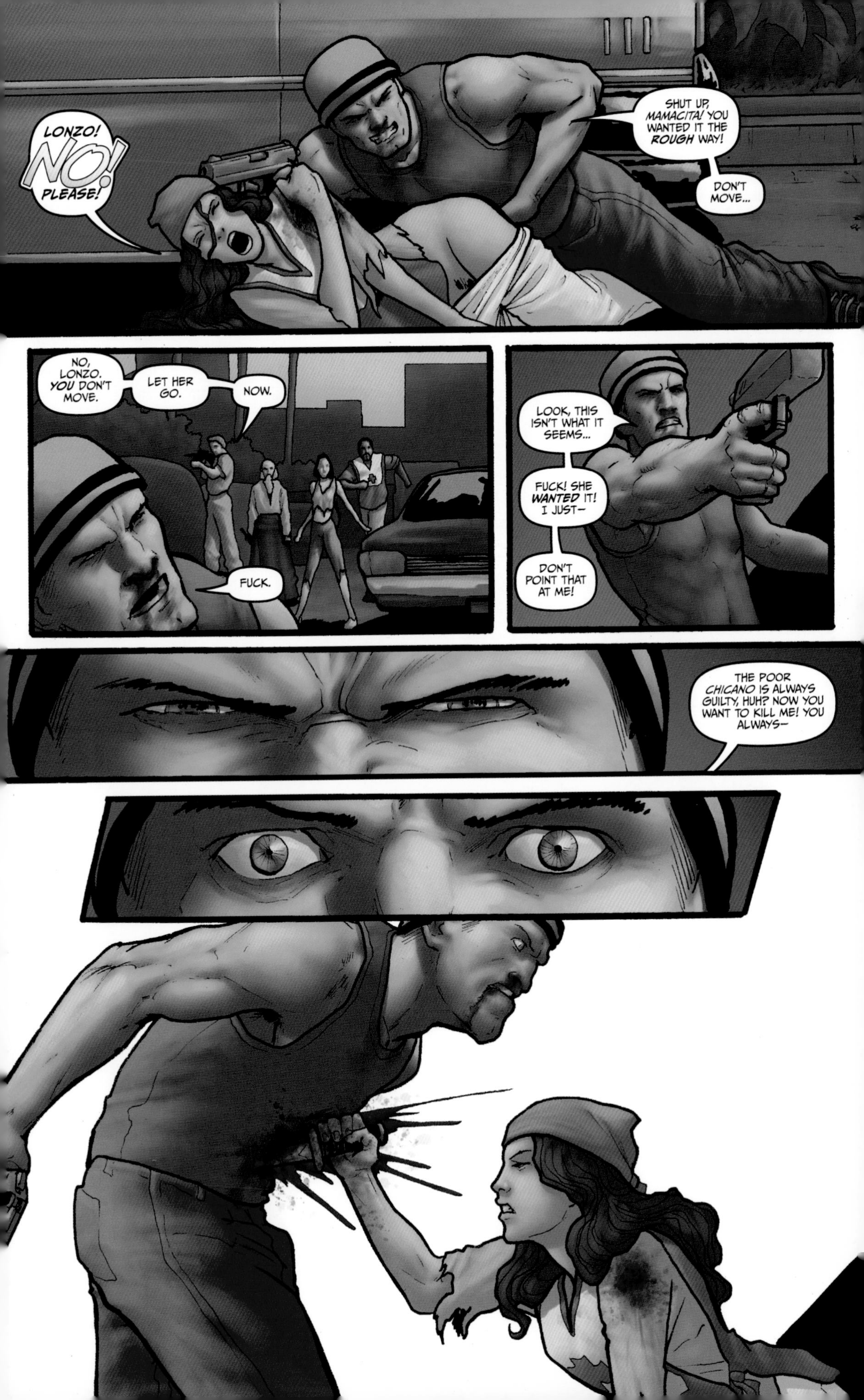
LONZO! NO! PLEASE!
SHUT UP, MAMACITA! YOU WANTED IT THE ROUGH WAY!
DON'T MOVE...
NO, LONZO. YOU DON'T MOVE.
LET HER GO.
NOW.
FUCK.
LOOK, THIS ISN'T WHAT IT SEEMS...
FUCK! SHE WANTED IT! I JUST—
DON'T POINT THAT AT ME!
THE POOR CHICANO IS ALWAYS GUILTY, HUH? NOW YOU WANT TO KILL ME! YOU ALWAYS—

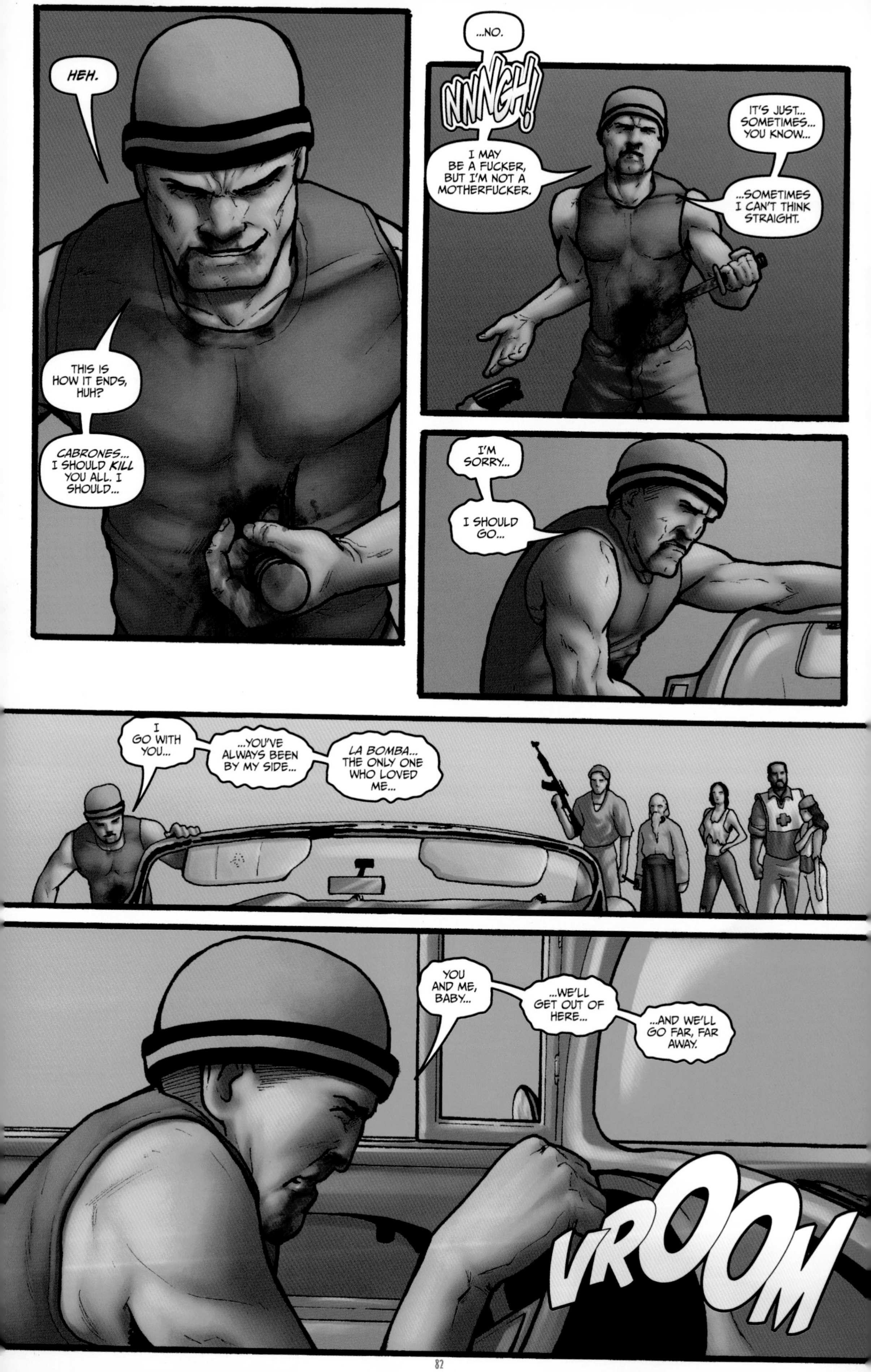
HEH.
THIS IS HOW IT ENDS, HUH?
CABRONES... I SHOULD KILL YOU ALL. I SHOULD...
...NO.
NNNGH!
I MAY BE A FUCKER, BUT I'M NOT A MOTHERFUCKER.
IT'S JUST... SOMETIMES... YOU KNOW...
...SOMETIMES I CAN'T THINK STRAIGHT.
I'M SORRY...
I SHOULD GO...
I GO WITH YOU...
...YOU'VE ALWAYS BEEN BY MY SIDE...
LA BOMBA... THE ONLY ONE WHO LOVED ME...
YOU AND ME, BABY...
...WE'LL GET OUT OF HERE...
...AND WE'LL GO FAR, FAR AWAY.
VROOOM

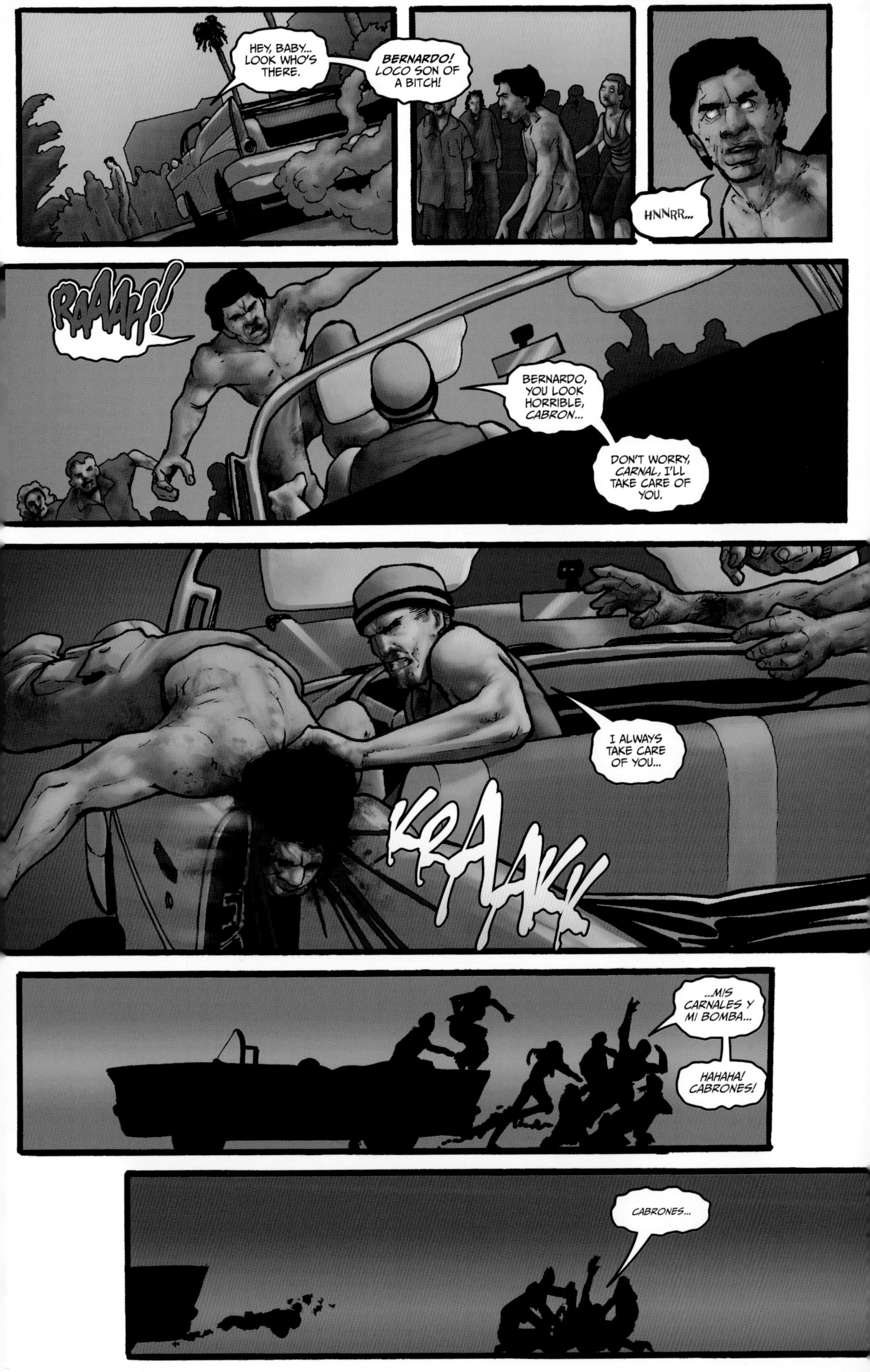
HEY, BABY... LOOK WHO'S THERE.
BERNARDO! LOCO SON OF A BITCH!
HNNRR...
RAAAH!
BERNARDO, YOU LOOK HORRIBLE, CABRON...
DON'T WORRY, CARNAL, I'LL TAKE CARE OF YOU.
I ALWAYS TAKE CARE OF YOU...
KRAAKK
...MIS CARNALES Y MI BOMBA...
HAHAHA! CABRONES!
CABRONES...

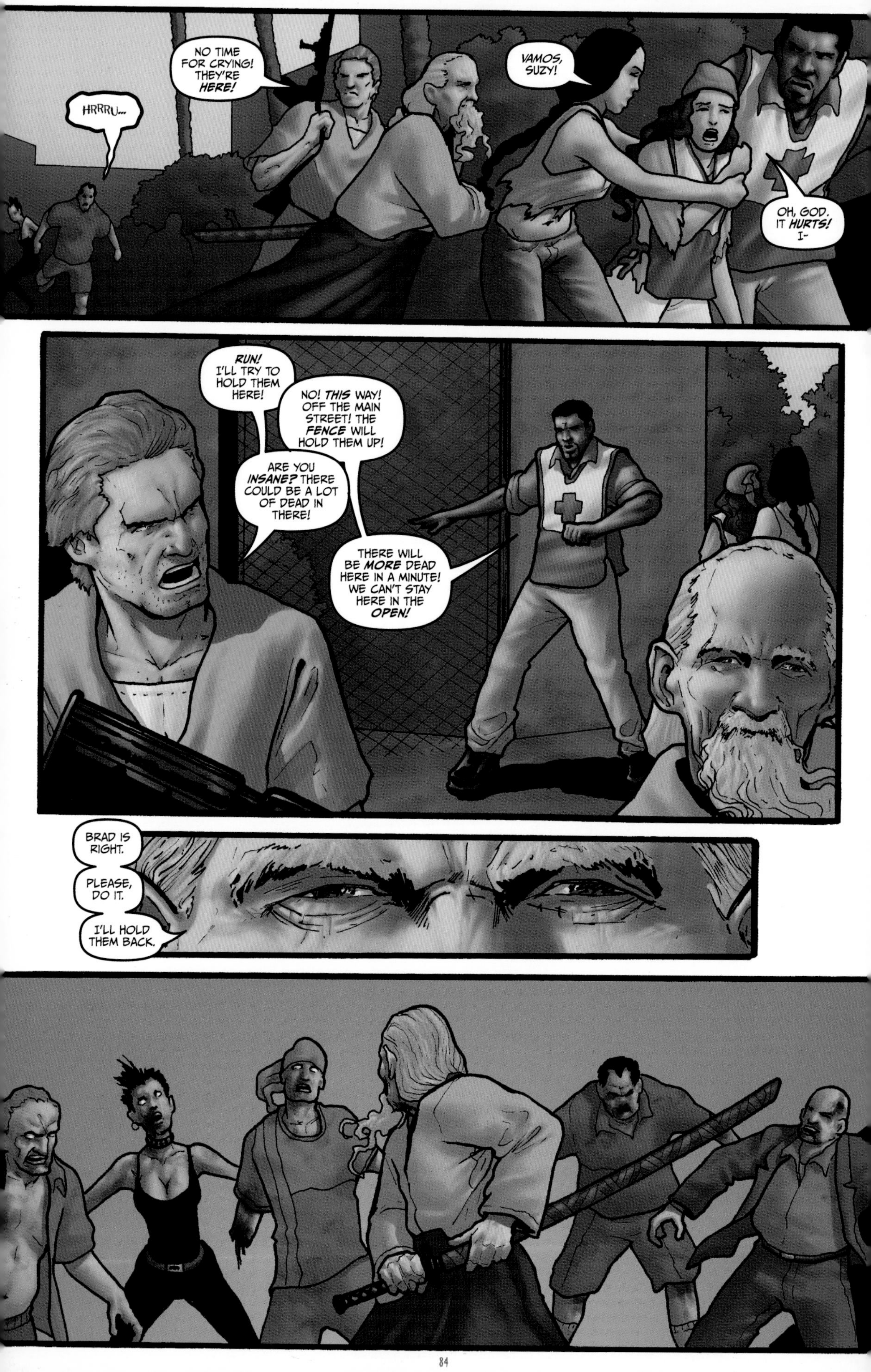
HRRRU...
NO TIME FOR CRYING! THEY'RE HERE!
VAMOS, SUZY!
OH, GOD. IT HURTS! I-
RUN! I'LL TRY TO HOLD THEM HERE!
NO! THIS WAY! OFF THE MAIN STREET! THE FENCE WILL HOLD THEM UP!
ARE YOU INSANE? THERE COULD BE A LOT OF DEAD IN THERE!
THERE WILL BE MORE DEAD HERE IN A MINUTE! WE CAN'T STAY HERE IN THE OPEN!
BRAD IS RIGHT.
PLEASE, DO IT.
I'LL HOLD THEM BACK.

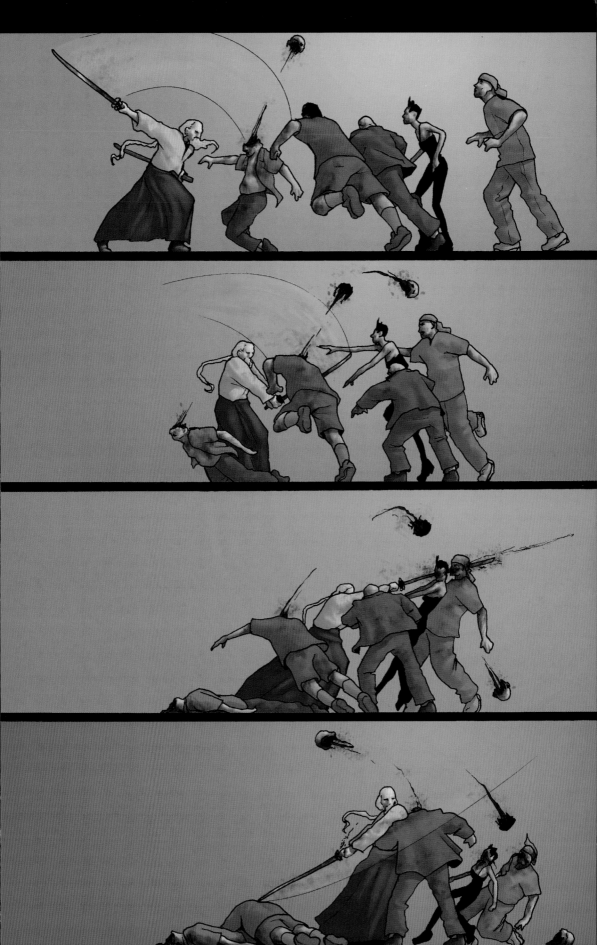

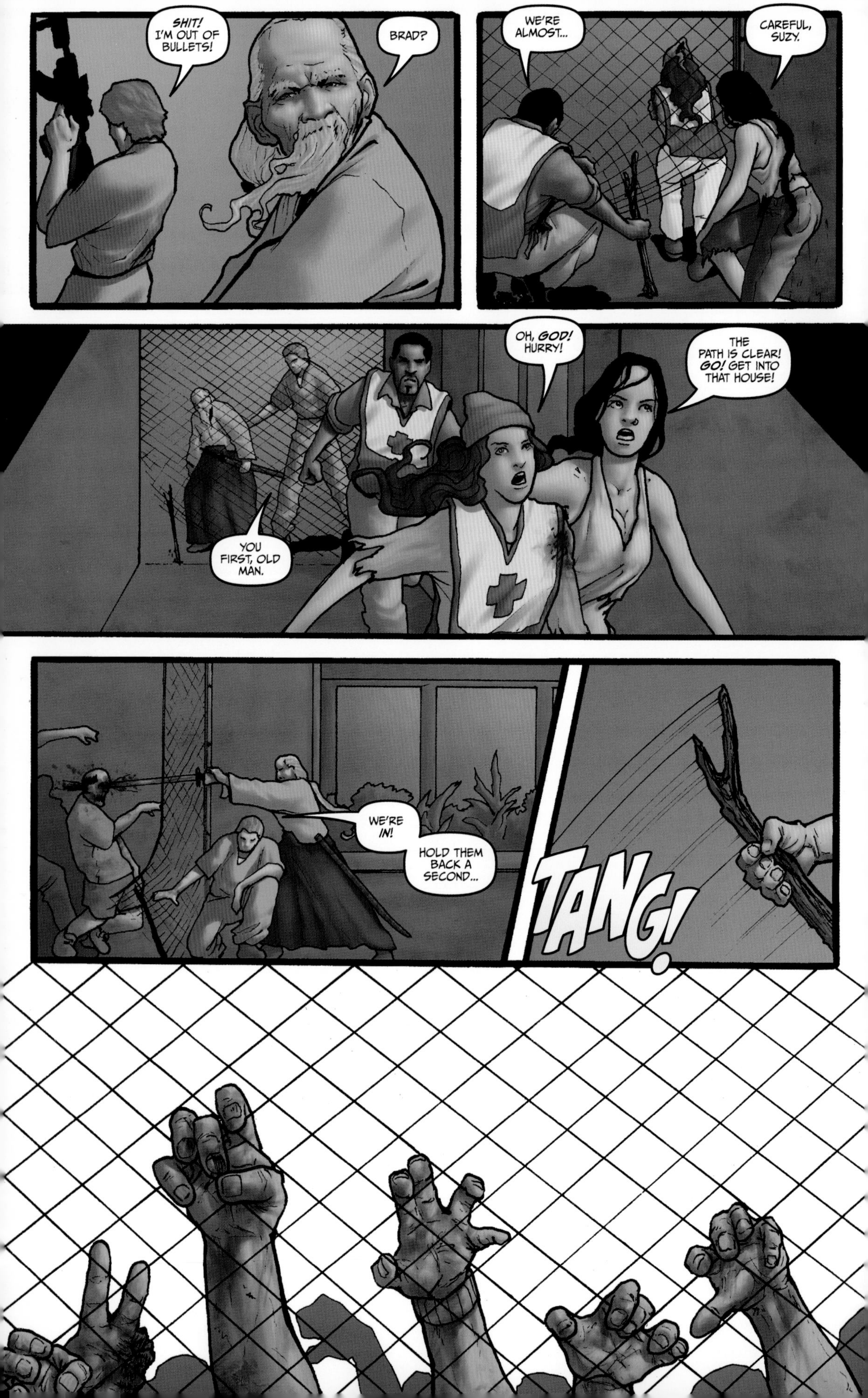
SHIT! I'M OUT OF BULLETS!
BRAD?
WE'RE ALMOST...
CAREFUL, SUZY.
OH, GOD! HURRY!
THE PATH IS CLEAR! GO! GET INTO THAT HOUSE!
YOU FIRST, OLD MAN.
WE'RE IN!
HOLD THEM BACK A SECOND...
TANG!

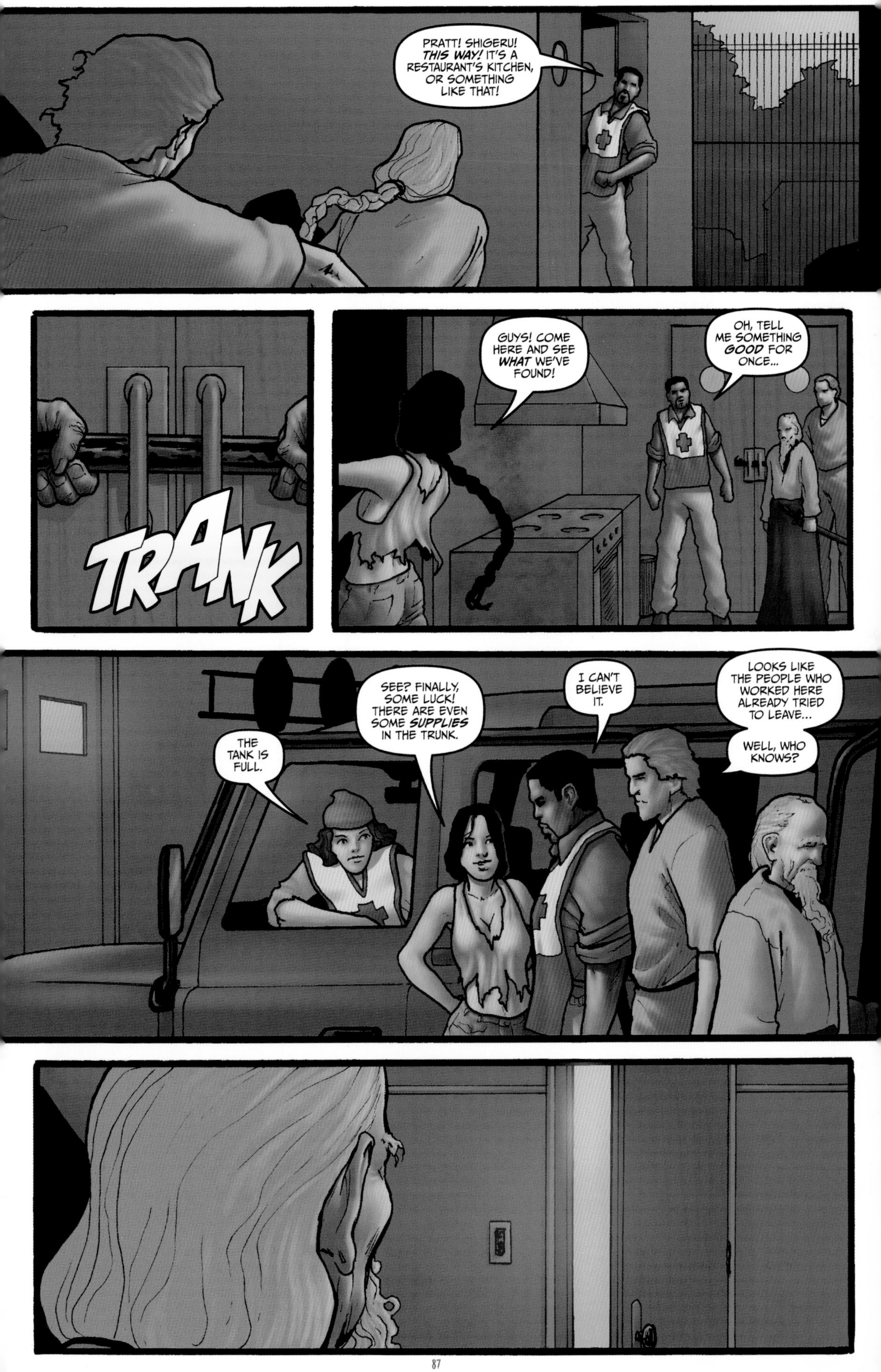
PRATT! SHIGERU! THIS WAY! IT'S A RESTAURANT'S KITCHEN, OR SOMETHING LIKE THAT!
TRANK
GUYS! COME HERE AND SEE WHAT WE'VE FOUND!
OH, TELL ME SOMETHING GOOD FOR ONCE...
THE TANK IS FULL.
SEE? FINALLY, SOME LUCK! THERE ARE EVEN SOME SUPPLIES IN THE TRUNK.
I CAN'T BELIEVE IT.
LOOKS LIKE THE PEOPLE WHO WORKED HERE ALREADY TRIED TO LEAVE...
WELL, WHO KNOWS?

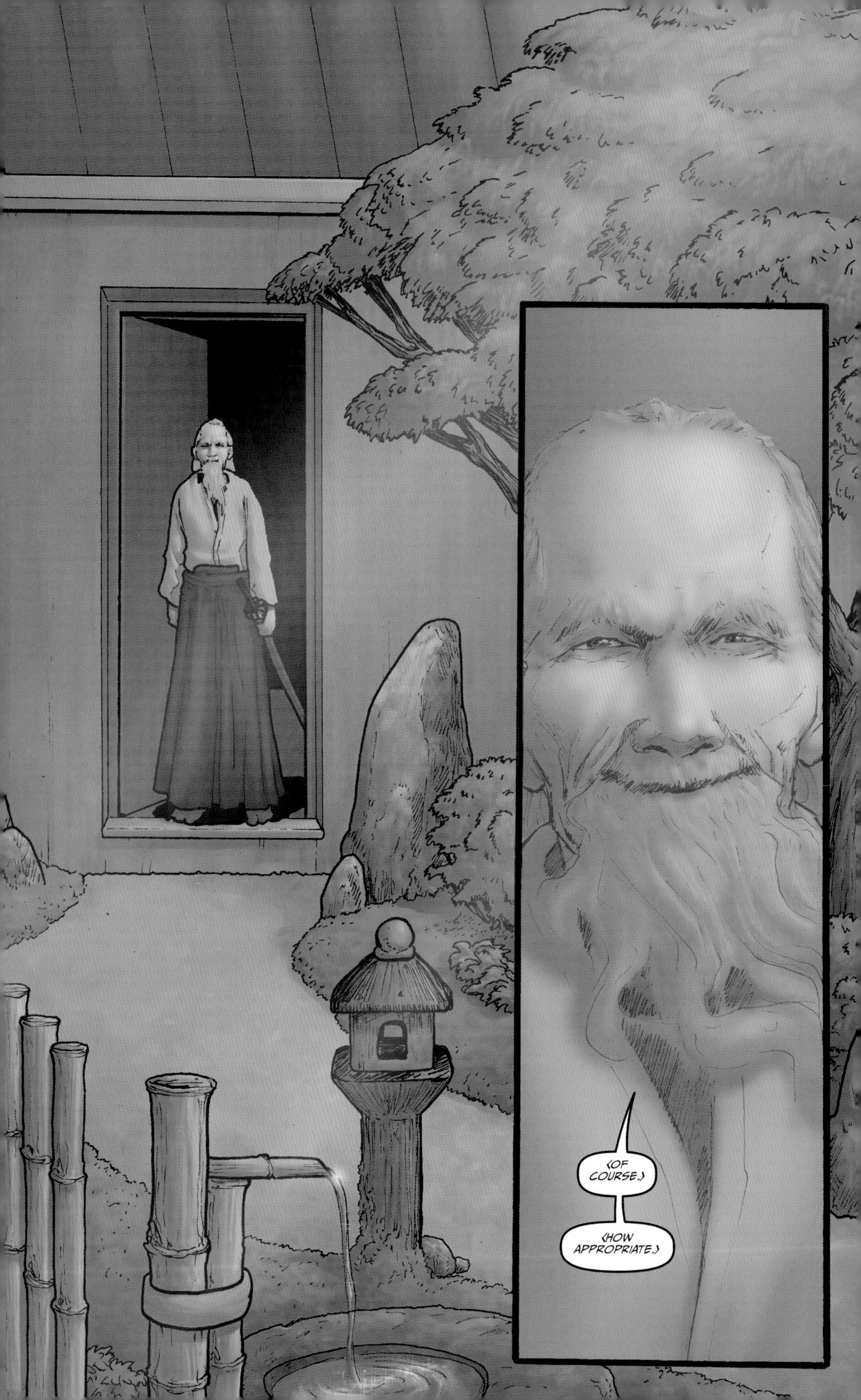
<OF COURSE.>
<HOW APPROPRIATE.>

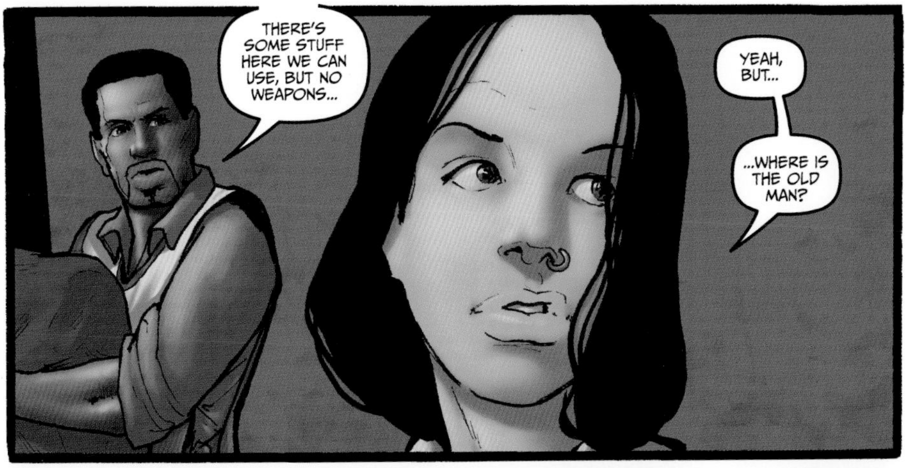
THERE'S SOME STUFF HERE WE CAN USE, BUT NO WEAPONS...
YEAH, BUT...
...WHERE IS THE OLD MAN?

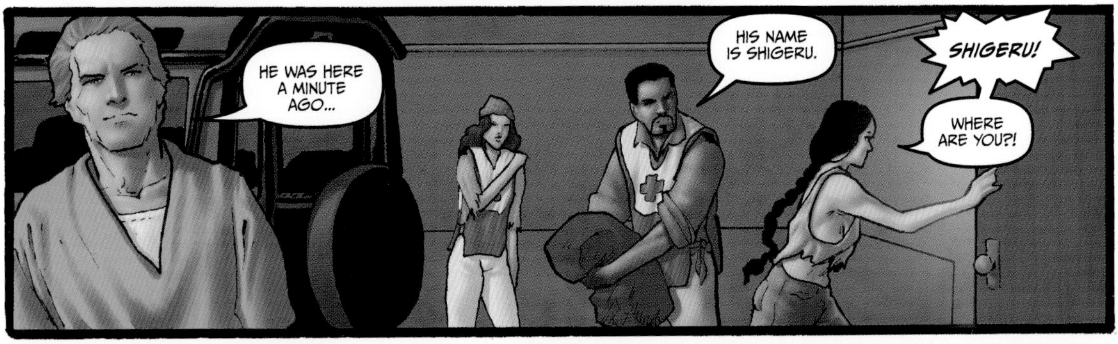
HE WAS HERE A MINUTE AGO...
HIS NAME IS SHIGERU.
SHIGERU!
WHERE ARE YOU?!

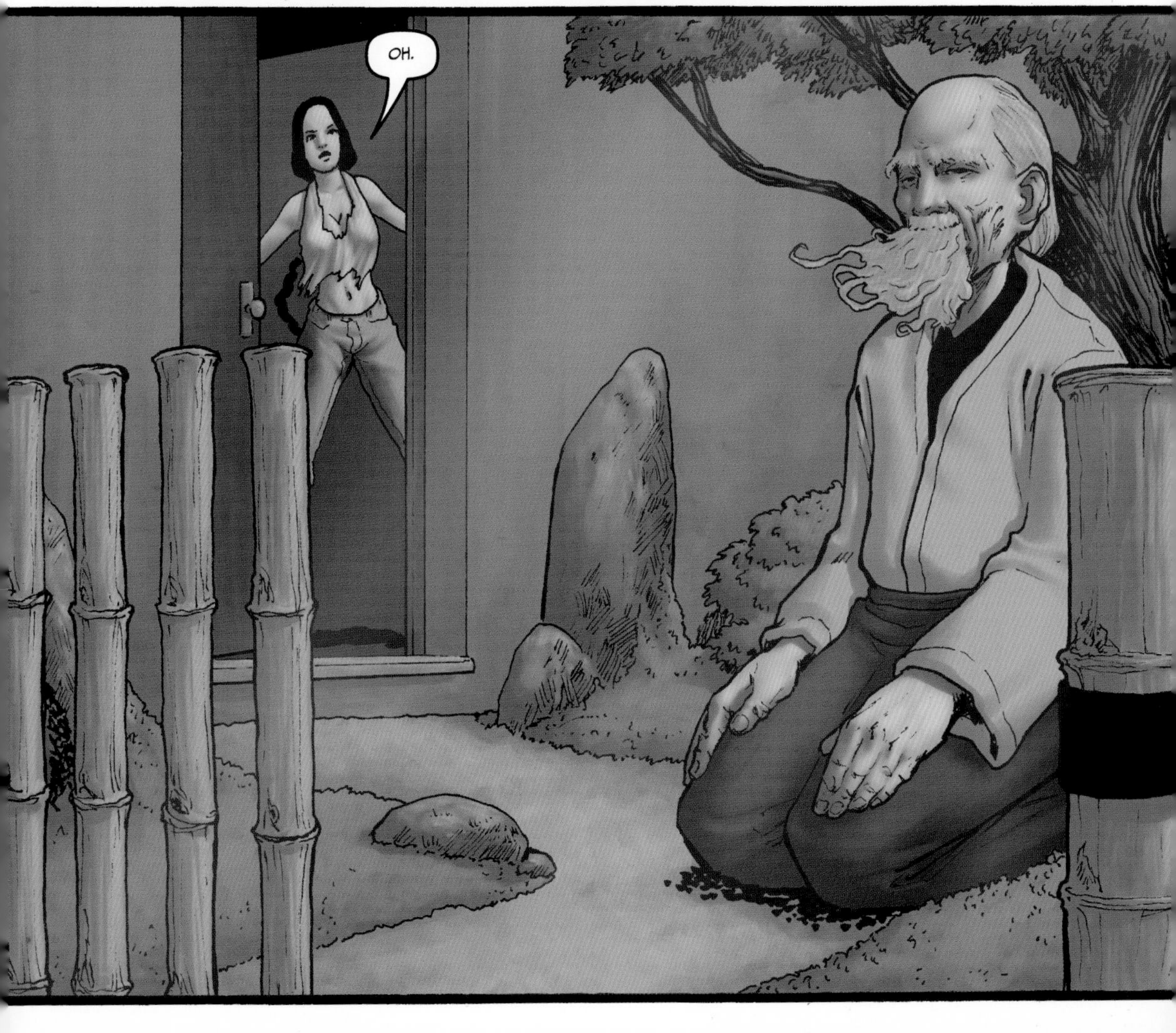
OH.

OLD MAN! WHAT ARE YOU DOING?! WE GOTTA LEAVE *NOW!*

I KNOW THIS PLACE PROBABLY REMINDS YOU OF YOUR HOMELAND, BUT...

I'M SORRY. I THINK I'LL STAY HERE.

IT'S A NICE AND QUIET PLACE.

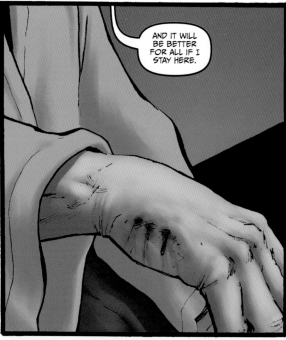

AND IT WILL BE BETTER FOR ALL IF I STAY HERE.

PLEASE, DO NOT GRIEVE FOR ME.

THIS SEEMS LIKE A GOOD PLACE AND A GOOD MOMENT TO LEAVE.

I'M AN OLD MAN, AND MY TIME PASSED LONG AGO.

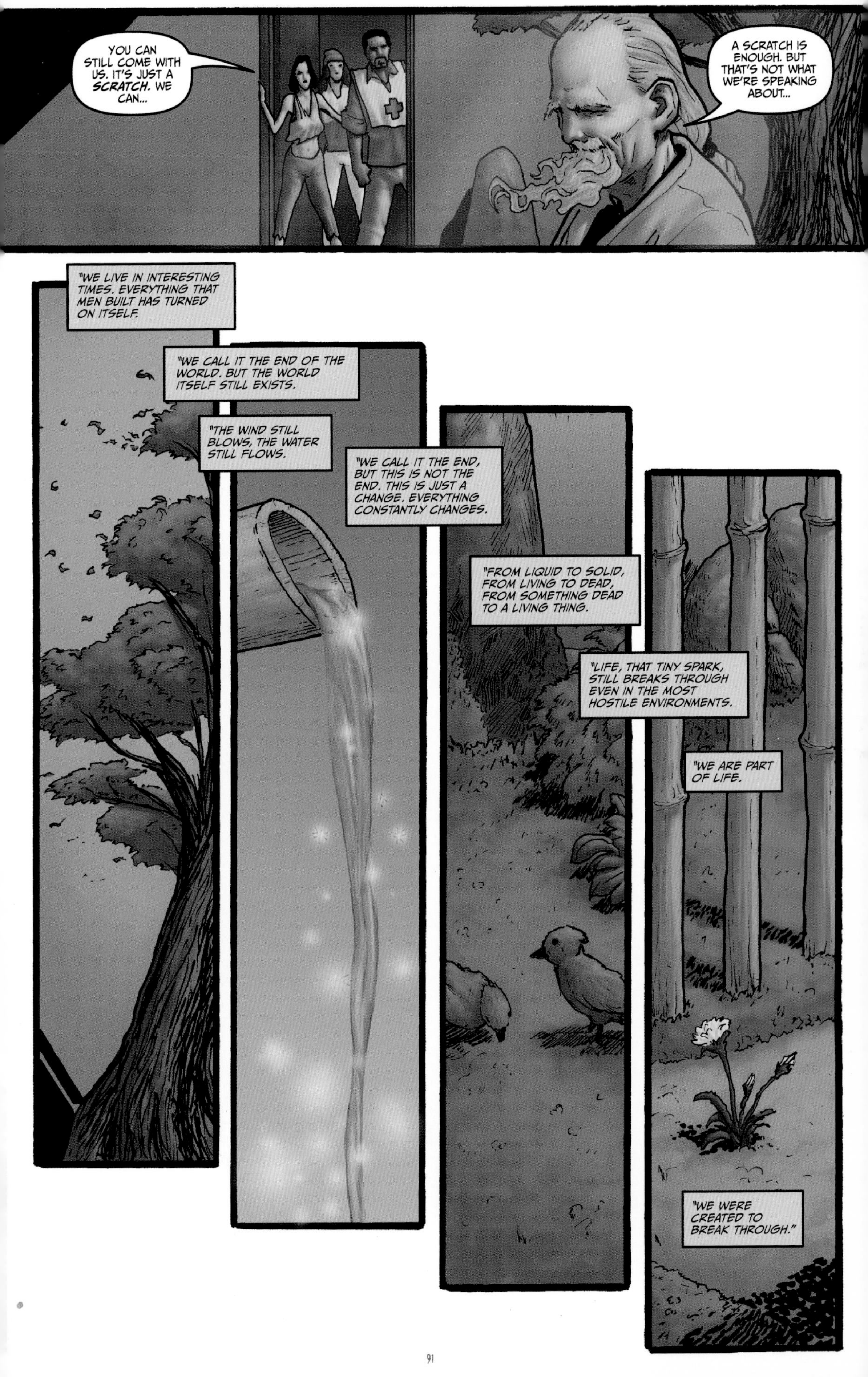
YOU CAN STILL COME WITH US. IT'S JUST A SCRATCH. WE CAN...
A SCRATCH IS ENOUGH. BUT THAT'S NOT WHAT WE'RE SPEAKING ABOUT...
"WE LIVE IN INTERESTING TIMES. EVERYTHING THAT MEN BUILT HAS TURNED ON ITSELF.
"WE CALL IT THE END OF THE WORLD. BUT THE WORLD ITSELF STILL EXISTS.
"THE WIND STILL BLOWS, THE WATER STILL FLOWS.
"WE CALL IT THE END, BUT THIS IS NOT THE END. THIS IS JUST A CHANGE. EVERYTHING CONSTANTLY CHANGES.
"FROM LIQUID TO SOLID, FROM LIVING TO DEAD, FROM SOMETHING DEAD TO A LIVING THING.
"LIFE, THAT TINY SPARK, STILL BREAKS THROUGH EVEN IN THE MOST HOSTILE ENVIRONMENTS.
"WE ARE PART OF LIFE.
"WE WERE CREATED TO BREAK THROUGH."

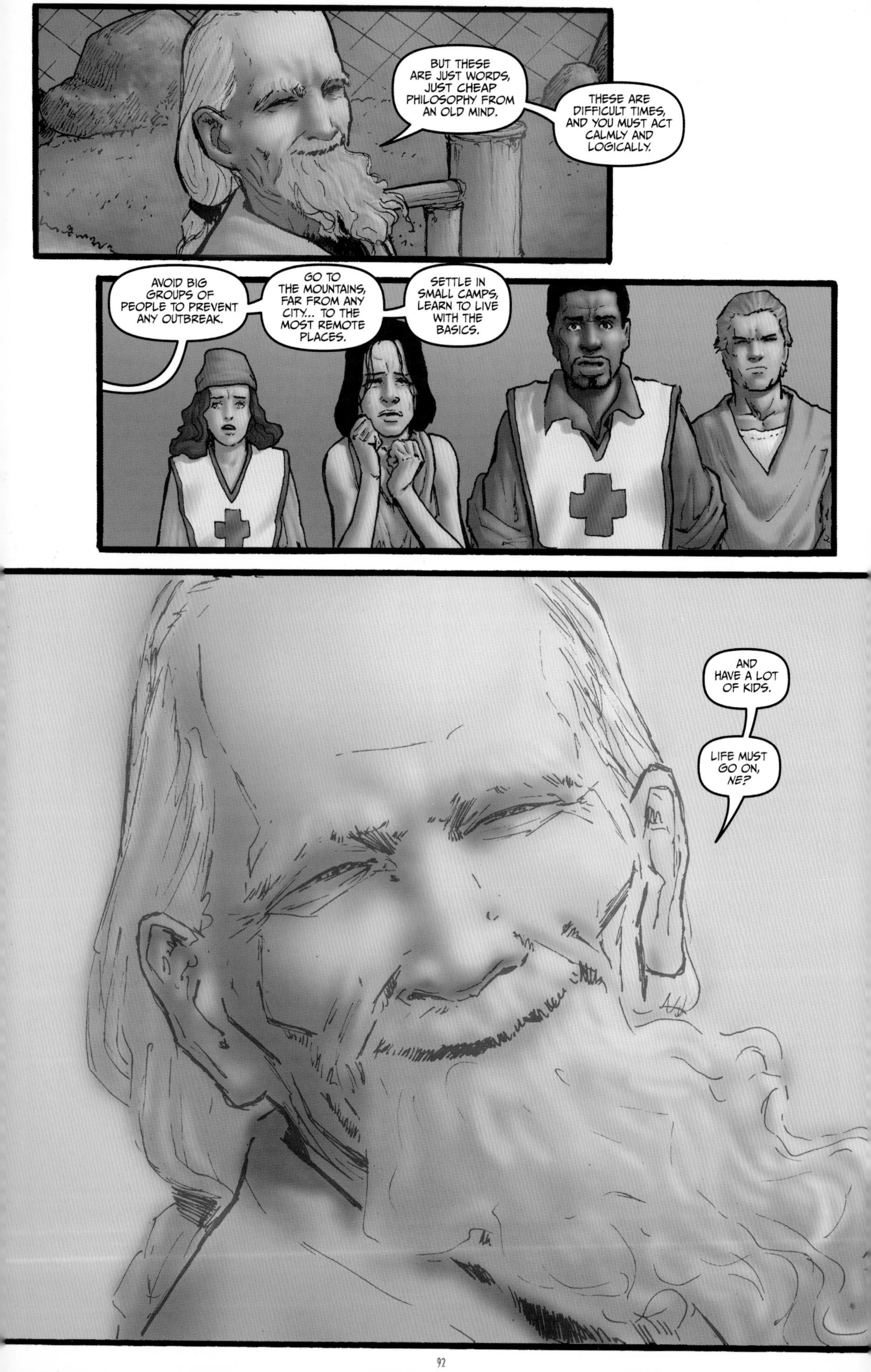
BUT THESE ARE JUST WORDS, JUST CHEAP PHILOSOPHY FROM AN OLD MIND.
THESE ARE DIFFICULT TIMES, AND YOU MUST ACT CALMLY AND LOGICALLY.
AVOID BIG GROUPS OF PEOPLE TO PREVENT ANY OUTBREAK.
GO TO THE MOUNTAINS, FAR FROM ANY CITY... TO THE MOST REMOTE PLACES.
SETTLE IN SMALL CAMPS, LEARN TO LIVE WITH THE BASICS.
AND HAVE A LOT OF KIDS.
LIFE MUST GO ON, *NE?*

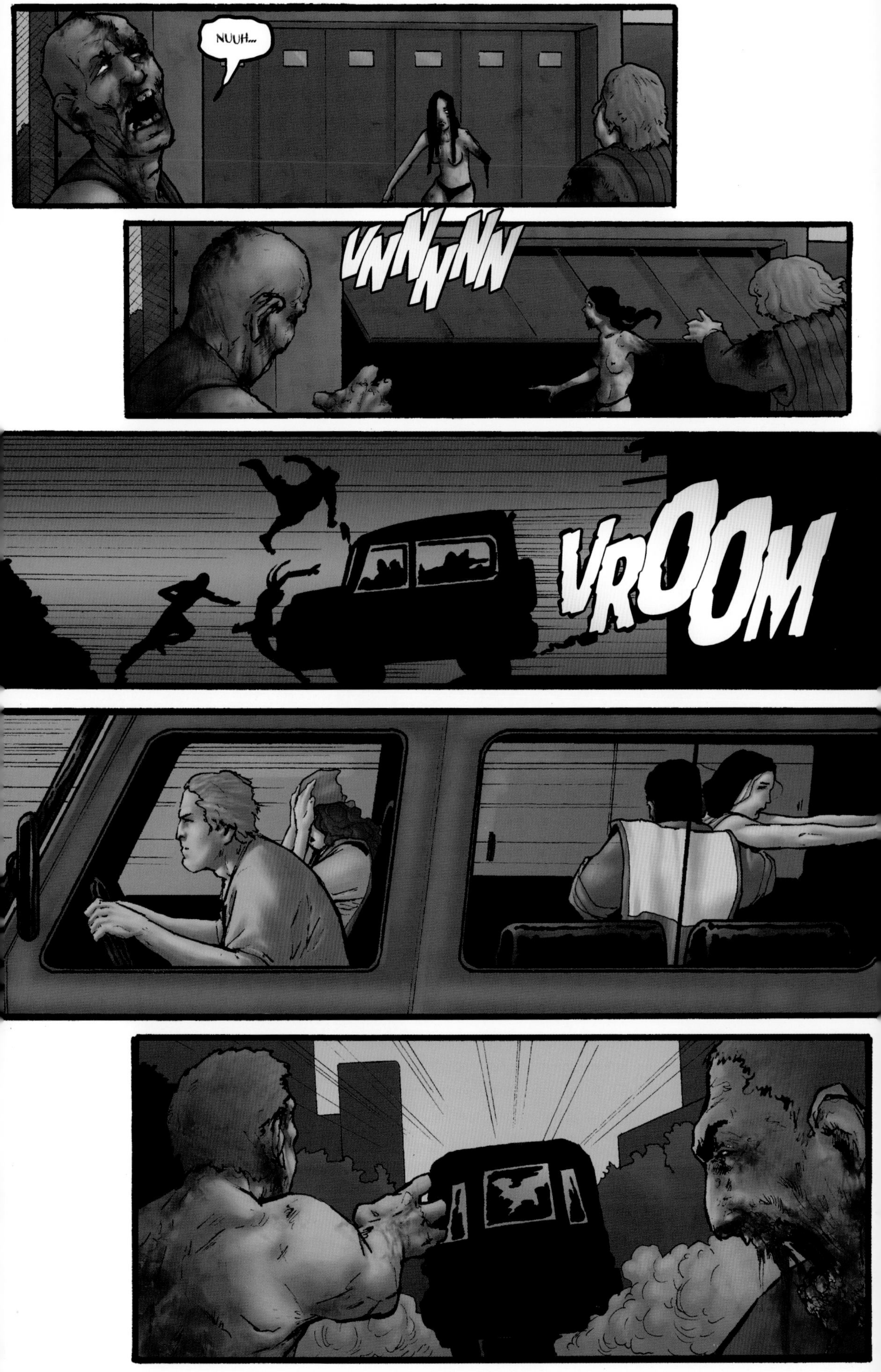
NUUH...
UNNNNNN
VROOM

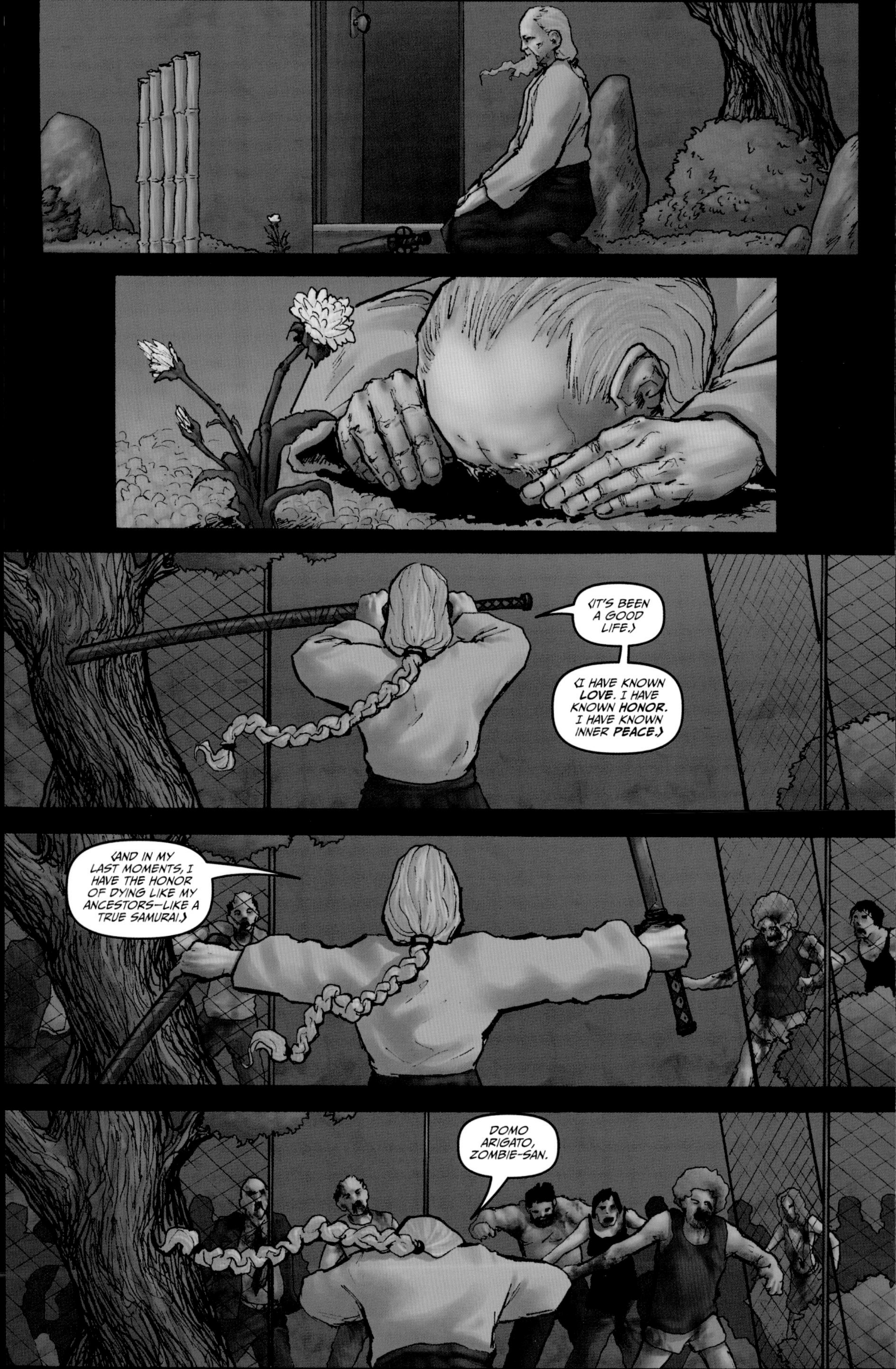
‹IT'S BEEN A GOOD LIFE.›
‹I HAVE KNOWN LOVE. I HAVE KNOWN HONOR. I HAVE KNOWN INNER PEACE.›
‹AND IN MY LAST MOMENTS, I HAVE THE HONOR OF DYING LIKE MY ANCESTORS—LIKE A TRUE SAMURAI.›
DOMO ARIGATO, ZOMBIE-SAN.

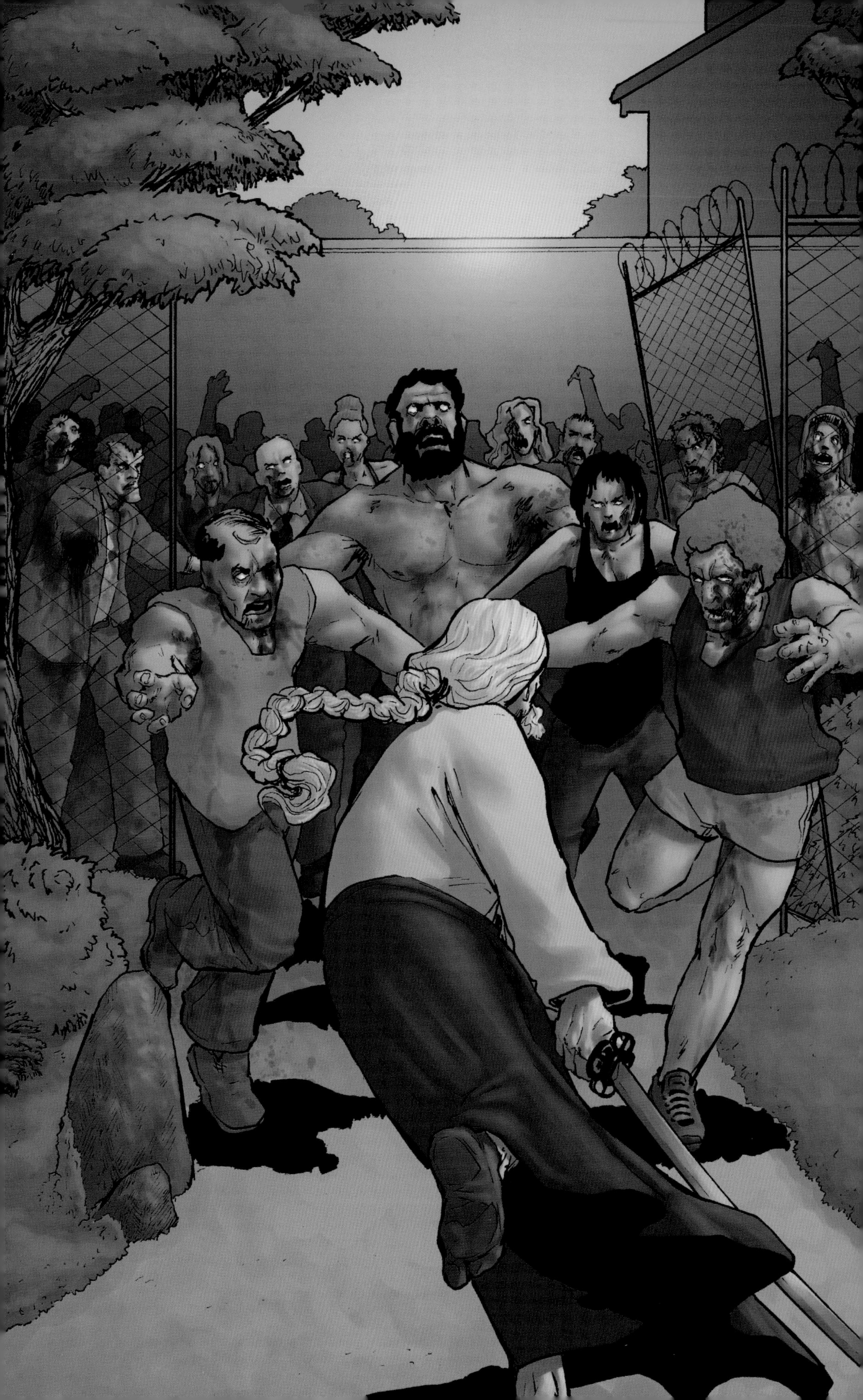

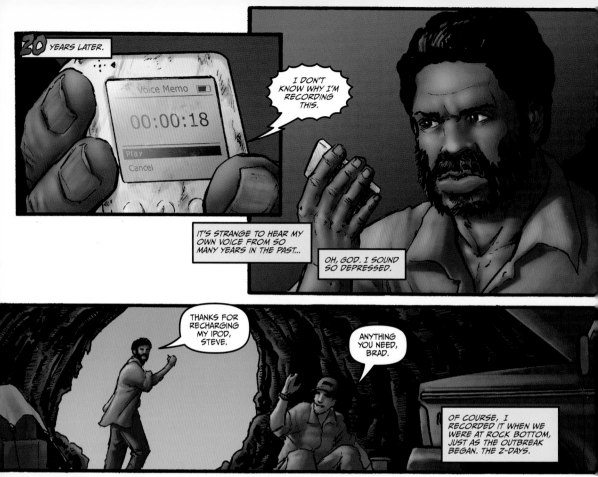

20 YEARS LATER.

Voice Memo

00:00:18

Play
Cancel

I DON'T KNOW WHY I'M RECORDING THIS.

IT'S STRANGE TO HEAR MY OWN VOICE FROM SO MANY YEARS IN THE PAST...

OH, GOD. I SOUND SO DEPRESSED.

THANKS FOR RECHARGING MY IPOD, STEVE.

ANYTHING YOU NEED, BRAD.

OF COURSE, I RECORDED IT WHEN WE WERE AT ROCK BOTTOM, JUST AS THE OUTBREAK BEGAN. THE Z-DAYS.

SHIGERU, YOU'D LIKE TO SEE THIS.

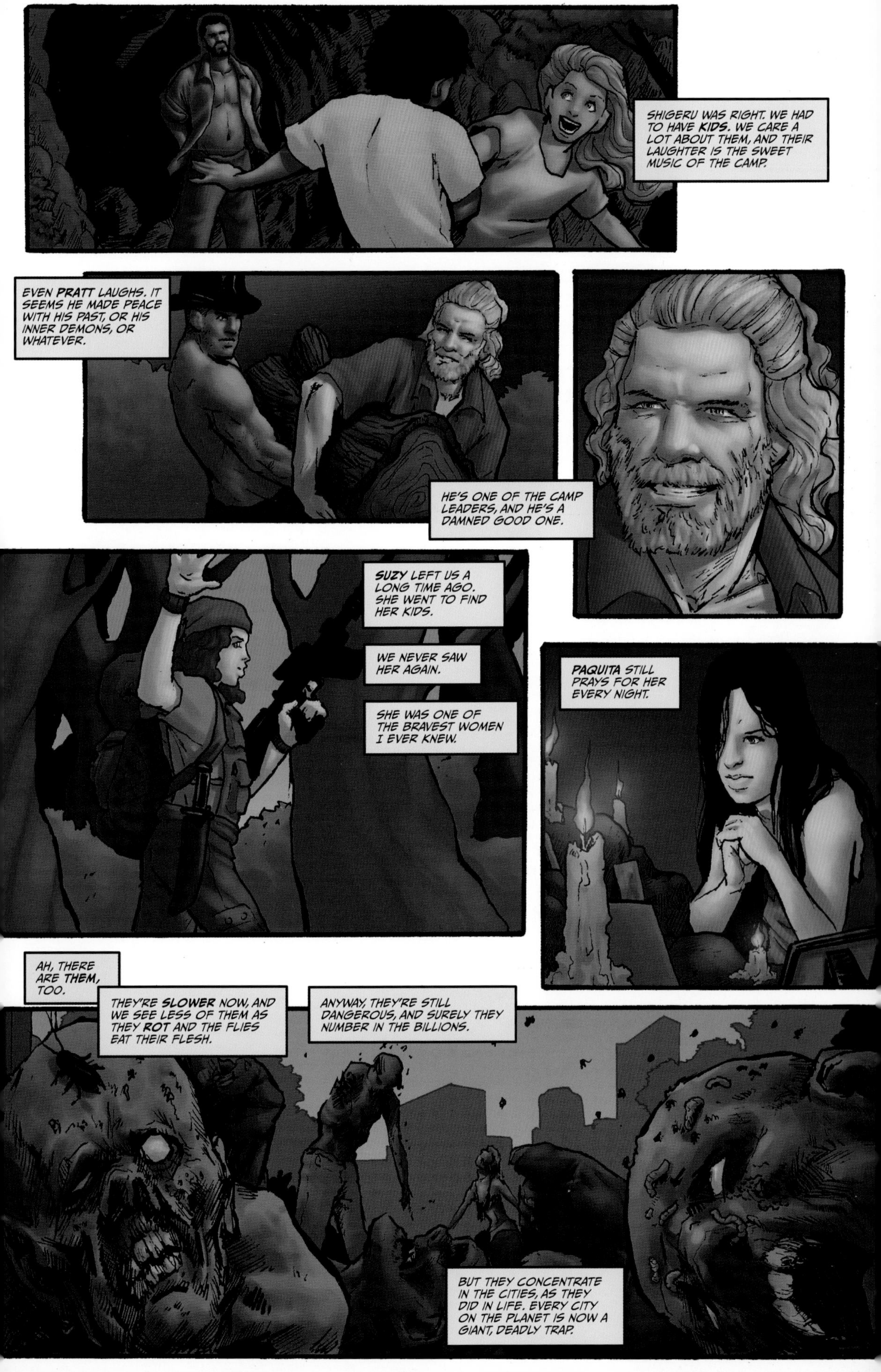

SHIGERU WAS RIGHT. WE HAD TO HAVE **KIDS**. WE CARE A LOT ABOUT THEM, AND THEIR LAUGHTER IS THE SWEET MUSIC OF THE CAMP.
EVEN **PRATT** LAUGHS. IT SEEMS HE MADE PEACE WITH HIS PAST, OR HIS INNER DEMONS, OR WHATEVER.
HE'S ONE OF THE CAMP LEADERS, AND HE'S A DAMNED GOOD ONE.
SUZY LEFT US A LONG TIME AGO. SHE WENT TO FIND HER KIDS.
WE NEVER SAW HER AGAIN.
SHE WAS ONE OF THE BRAVEST WOMEN I EVER KNEW.
PAQUITA STILL PRAYS FOR HER EVERY NIGHT.
AH, THERE ARE **THEM**, TOO.
THEY'RE **SLOWER** NOW, AND WE SEE LESS OF THEM AS THEY **ROT** AND THE FLIES EAT THEIR FLESH.
ANYWAY, THEY'RE STILL DANGEROUS, AND SURELY THEY NUMBER IN THE BILLIONS.
BUT THEY CONCENTRATE IN THE CITIES, AS THEY DID IN LIFE. EVERY CITY ON THE PLANET IS NOW A GIANT, DEADLY TRAP.

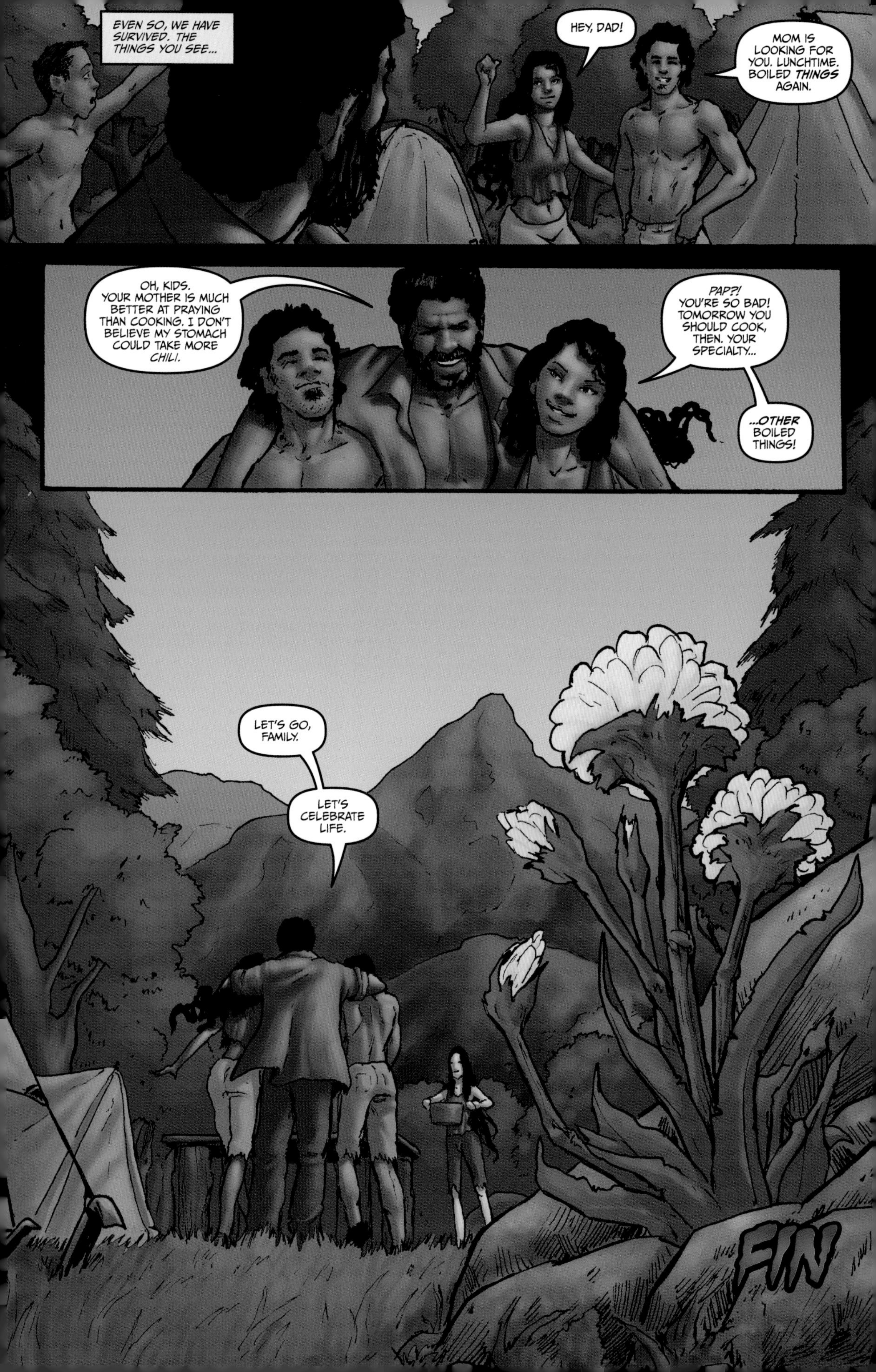
EVEN SO, WE HAVE SURVIVED. THE THINGS YOU SEE...
HEY, DAD!
MOM IS LOOKING FOR YOU. LUNCHTIME. BOILED THINGS AGAIN.
OH, KIDS. YOUR MOTHER IS MUCH BETTER AT PRAYING THAN COOKING. I DON'T BELIEVE MY STOMACH COULD TAKE MORE CHILI.
PAP?! YOU'RE SO BAD! TOMORROW YOU SHOULD COOK, THEN. YOUR SPECIALTY...
...OTHER BOILED THINGS!
LET'S GO, FAMILY.
LET'S CELEBRATE LIFE.
FIN

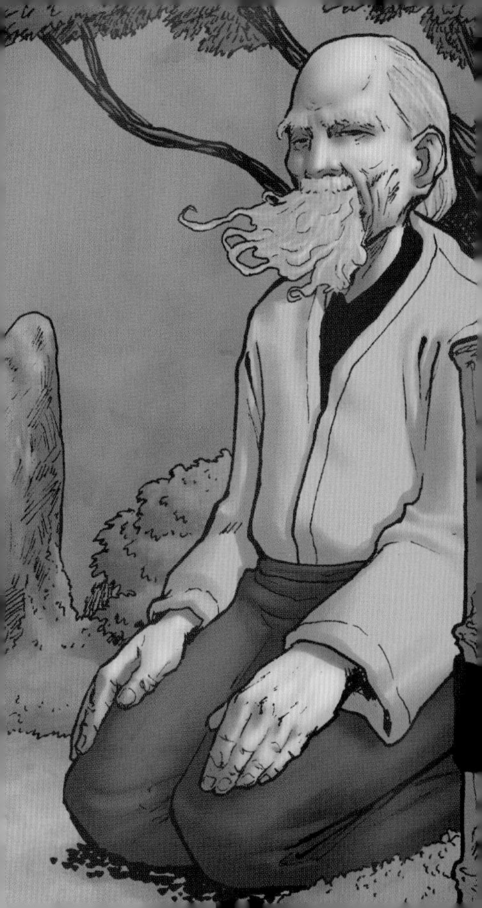

ZOMBiES! ™
eclipse of the undead

cover gallery

opposite page issue 1 cover by Yair Herrera

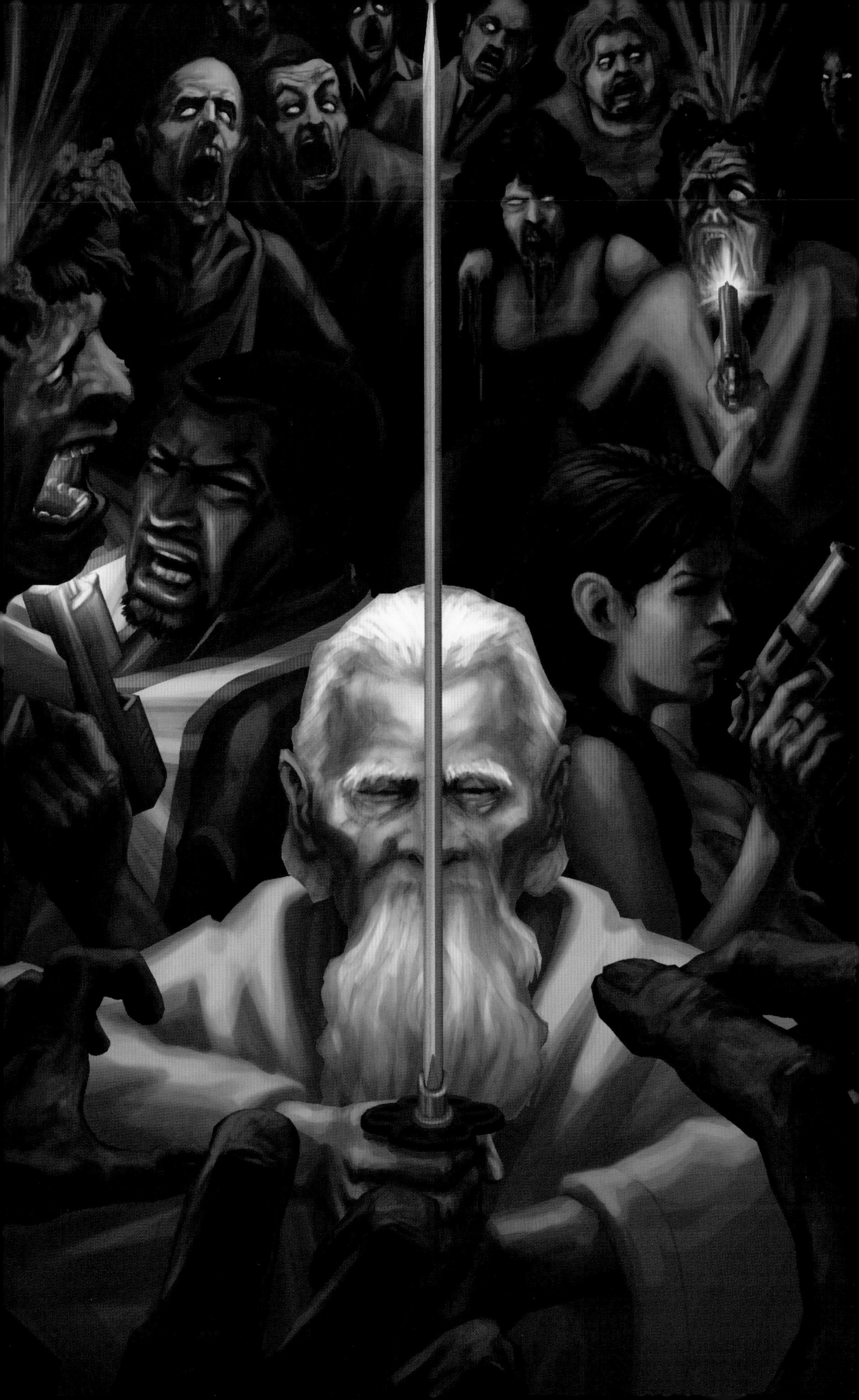

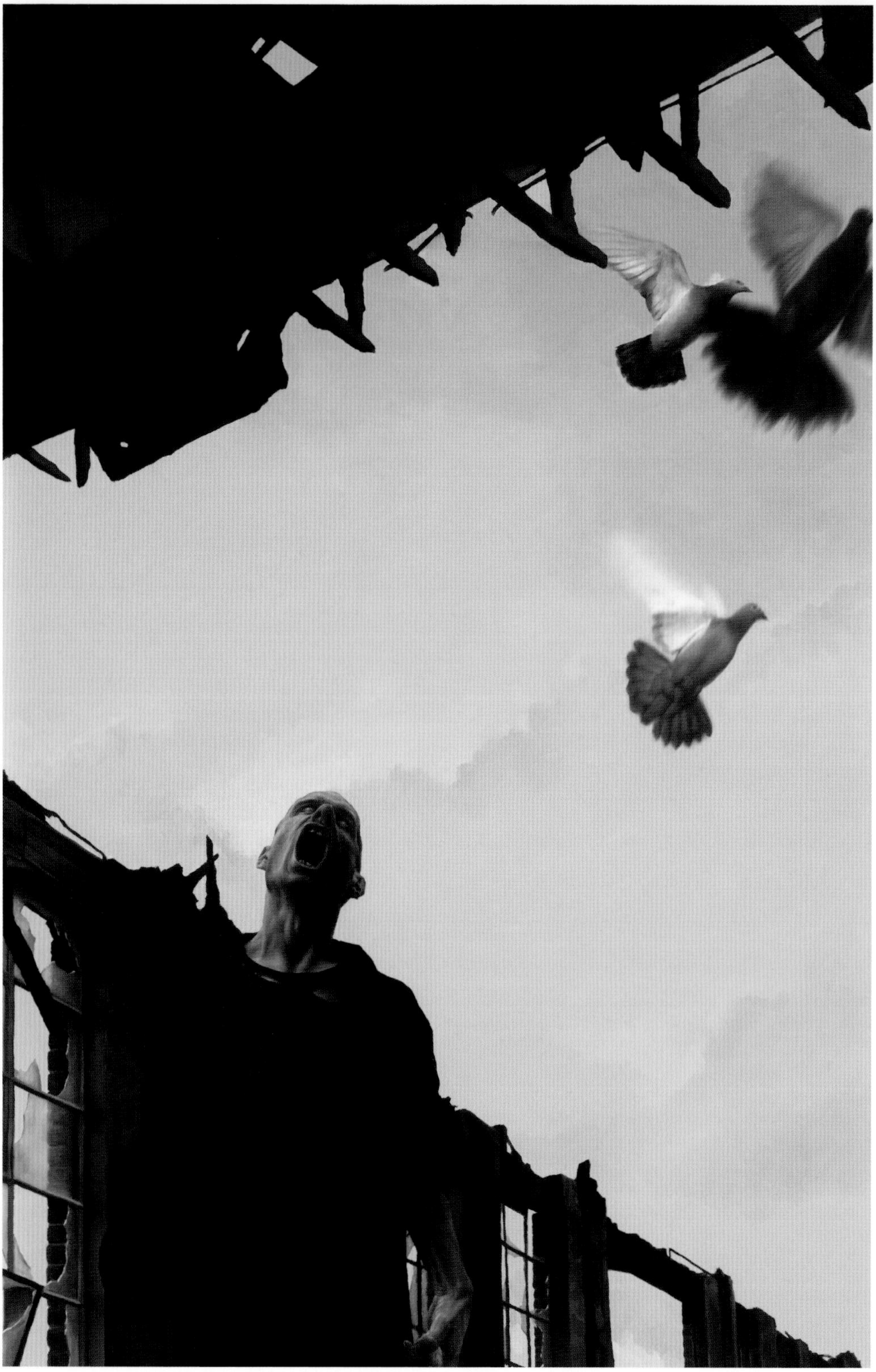

issue 1 RI cover by jeremy geddes

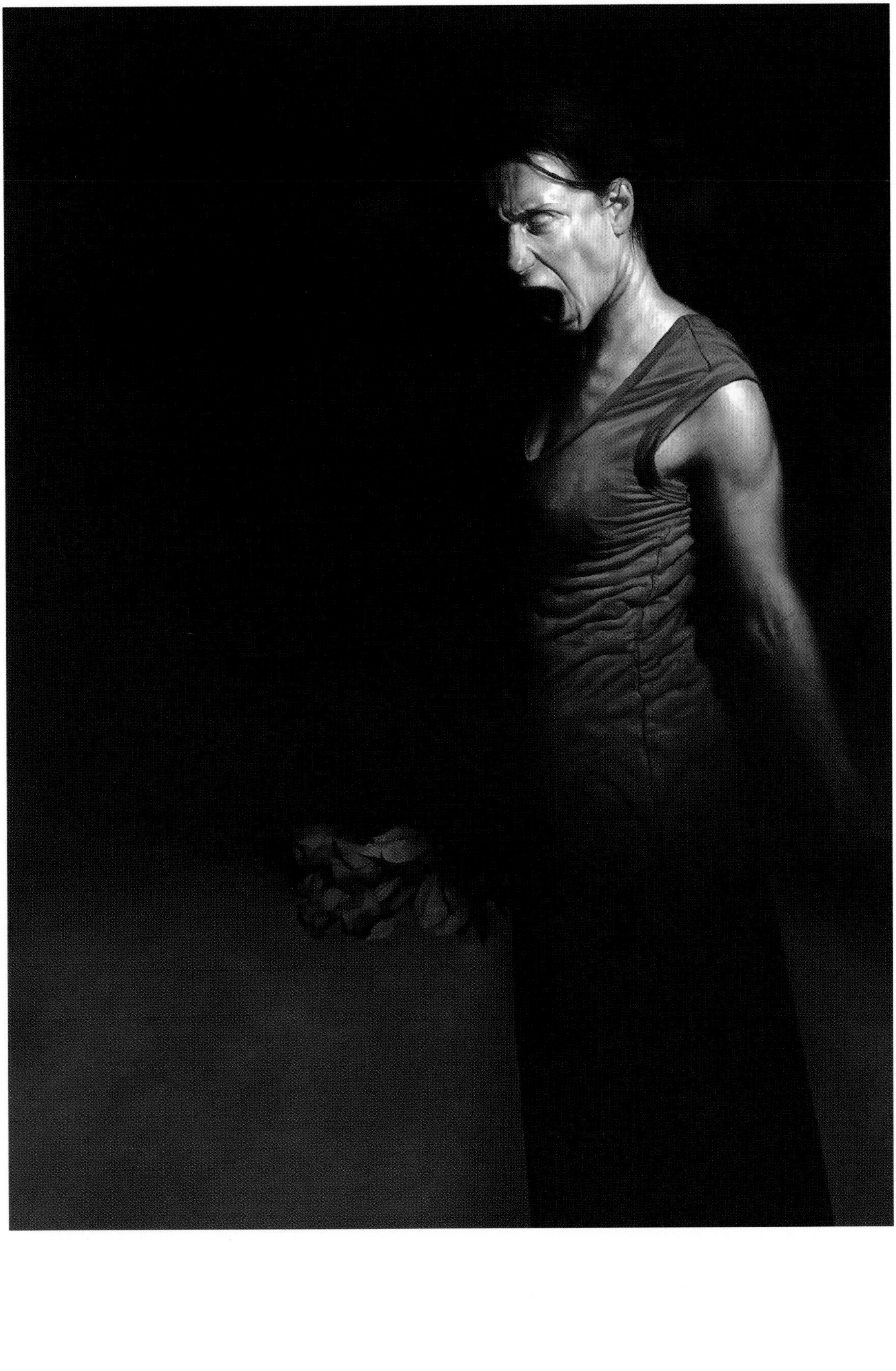

issue 2 RI cover by jeremy geddes

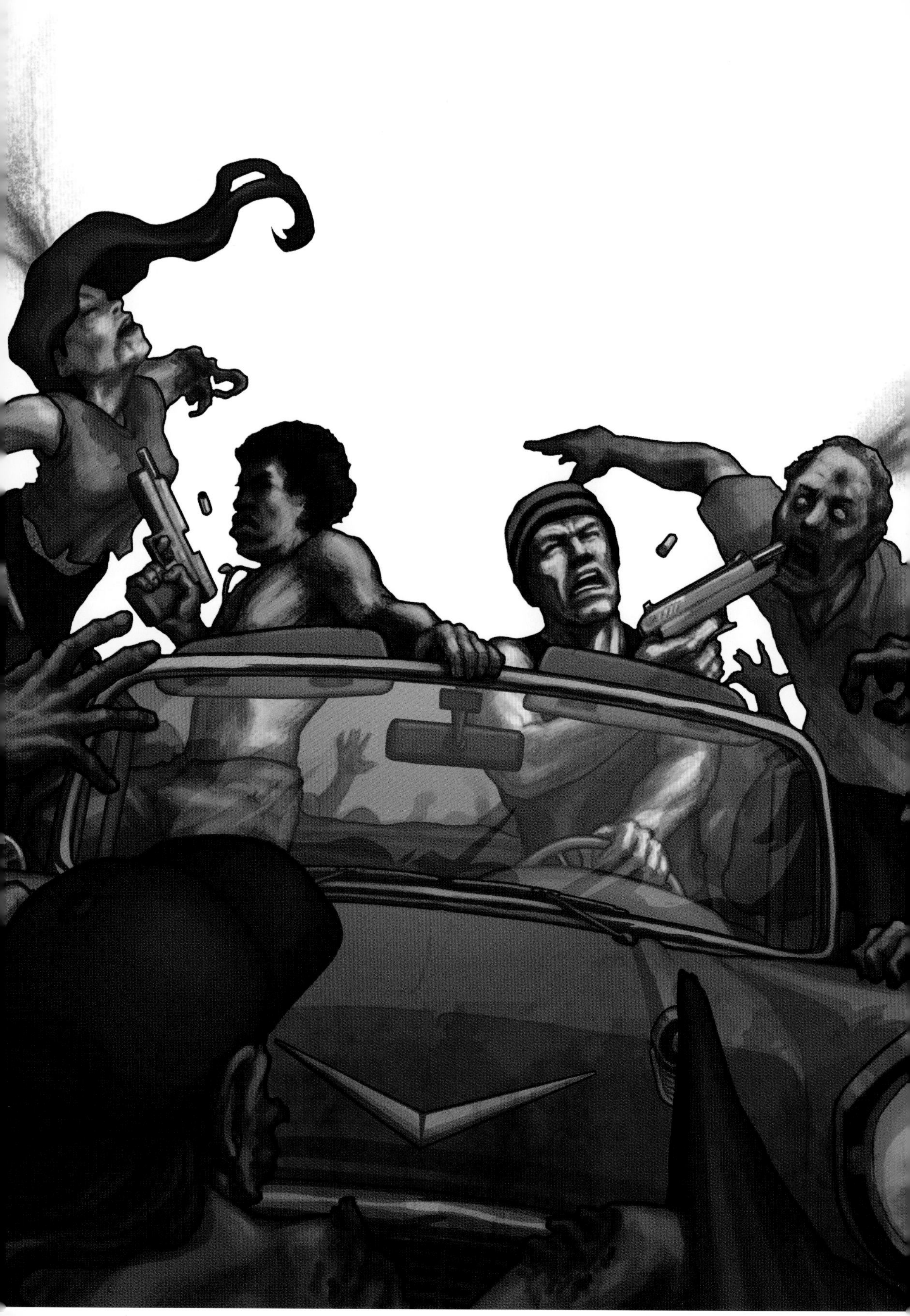

issue 2 cover by yair herrera

opposite page issue 3 cover by yair herrera

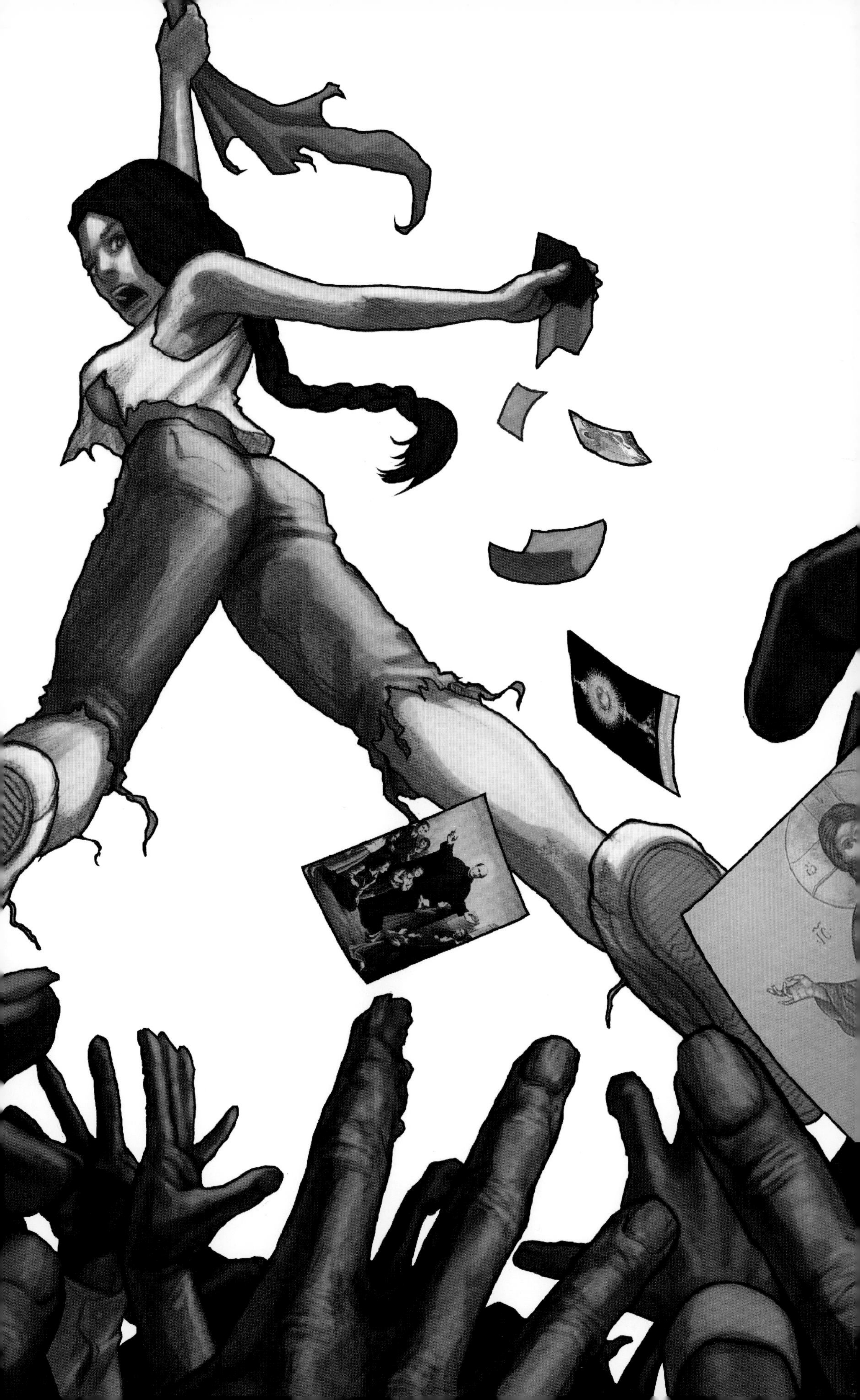

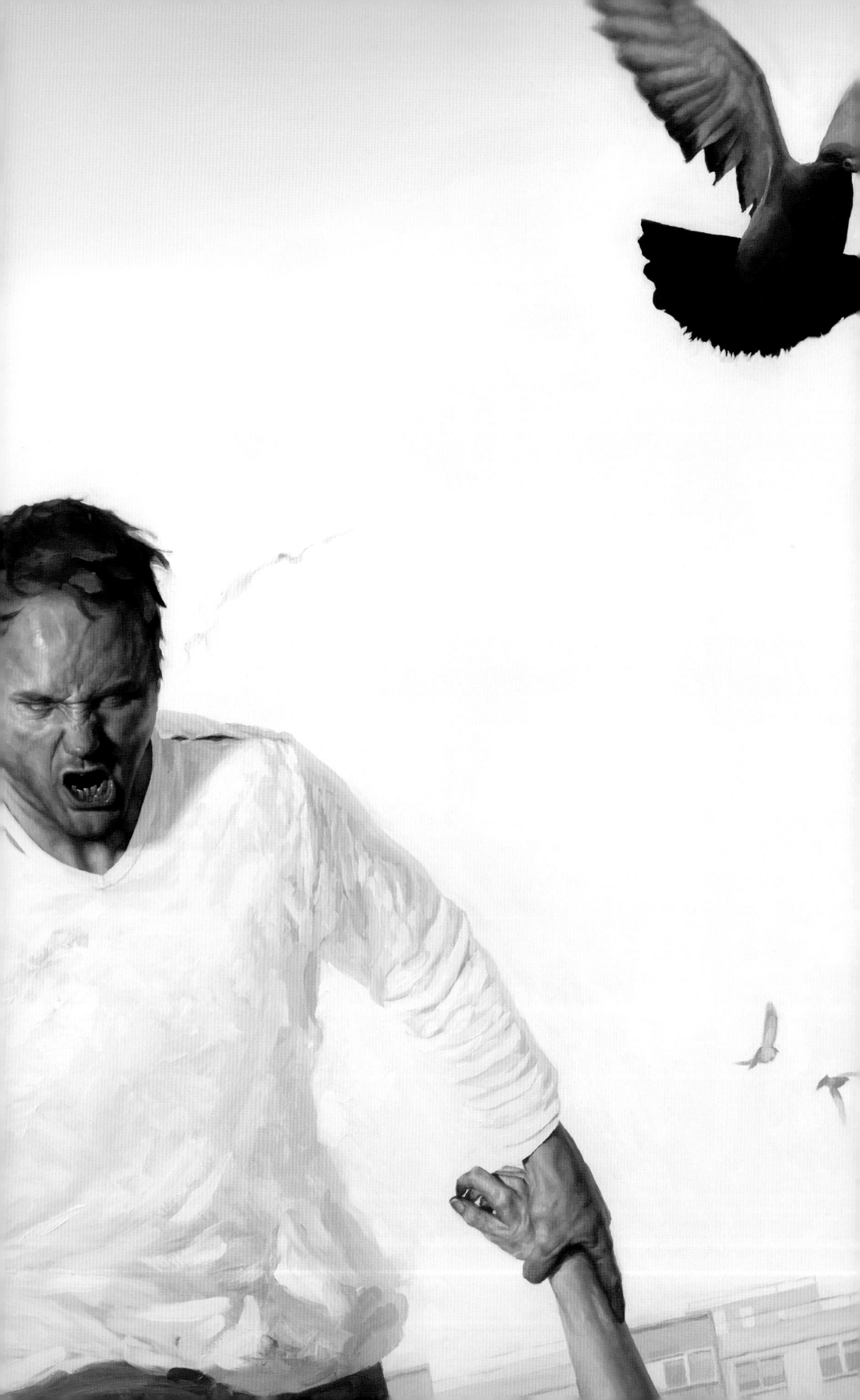

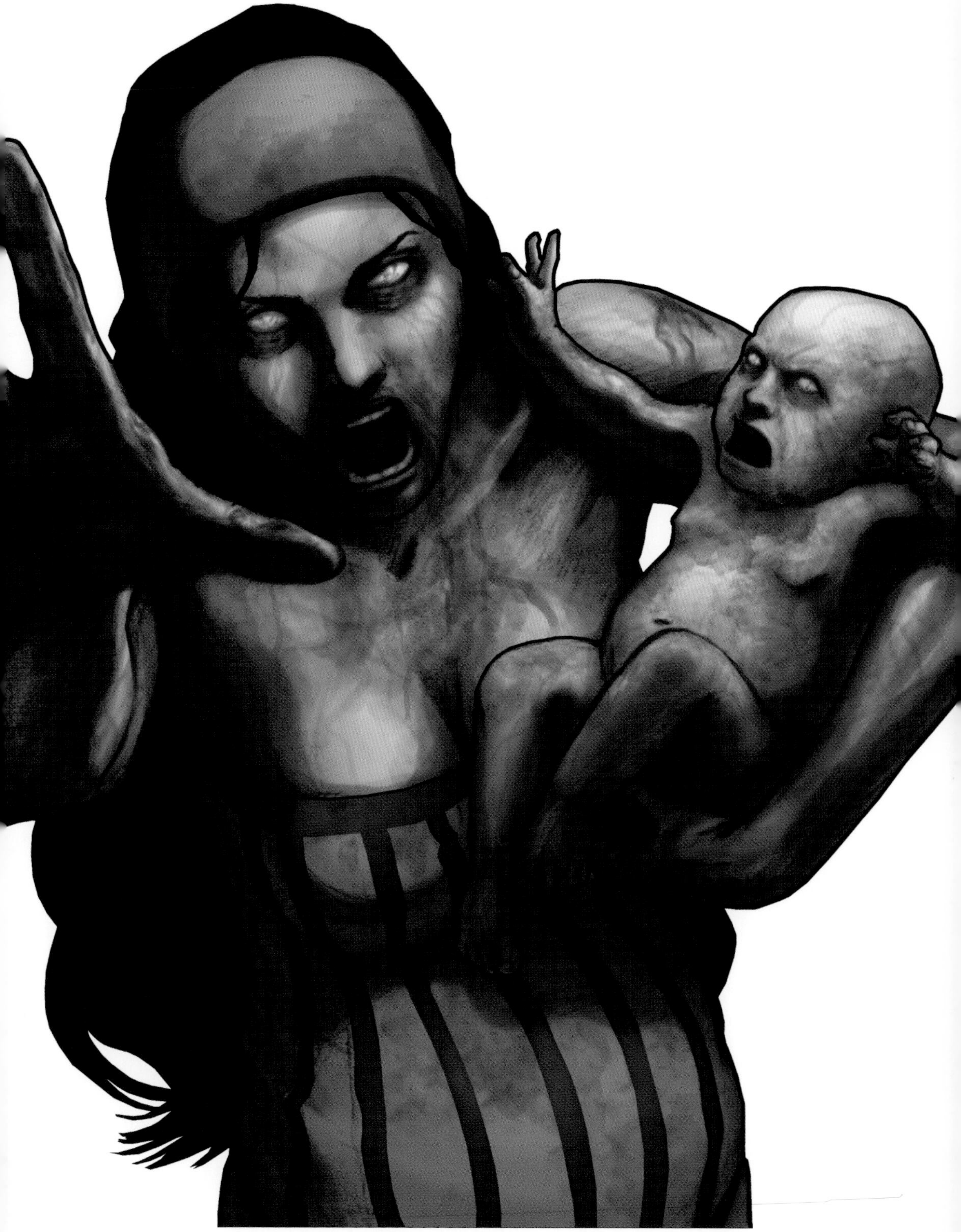

opposite page: issue 3 RI cover by Jeremy Geddes

issue 4 cover by Yair Herrera

ZOMBIES!™
feast

An event of nightmarish proportions has begun! The dead are walking the Earth and tearing the living limb from limb in an endless pursuit to quench their insatiable hunger for flesh. Yet not all killers are undead. Eight of the country's most notorious murderers are being transferred across state when their bus enters a town overrun with feasting corpses. Now, the town's remaining survivors find themselves fighting a battle on two sides. Five innocents, countless zombies, eight killers and a wide variety of blunt instruments—whether they make it out or not, it promises to be very bloody and incredibly gruesome. In the end, it's not the nightmare outside you need to worry about, but the monsters beside you.

This collection includes all five stories from ***Zombies!: Feast***, a variant cover gallery, a collection of developmental sketches from artist **Chris Bolton**, and a special foreword by series writer **Shane McCarthy**.

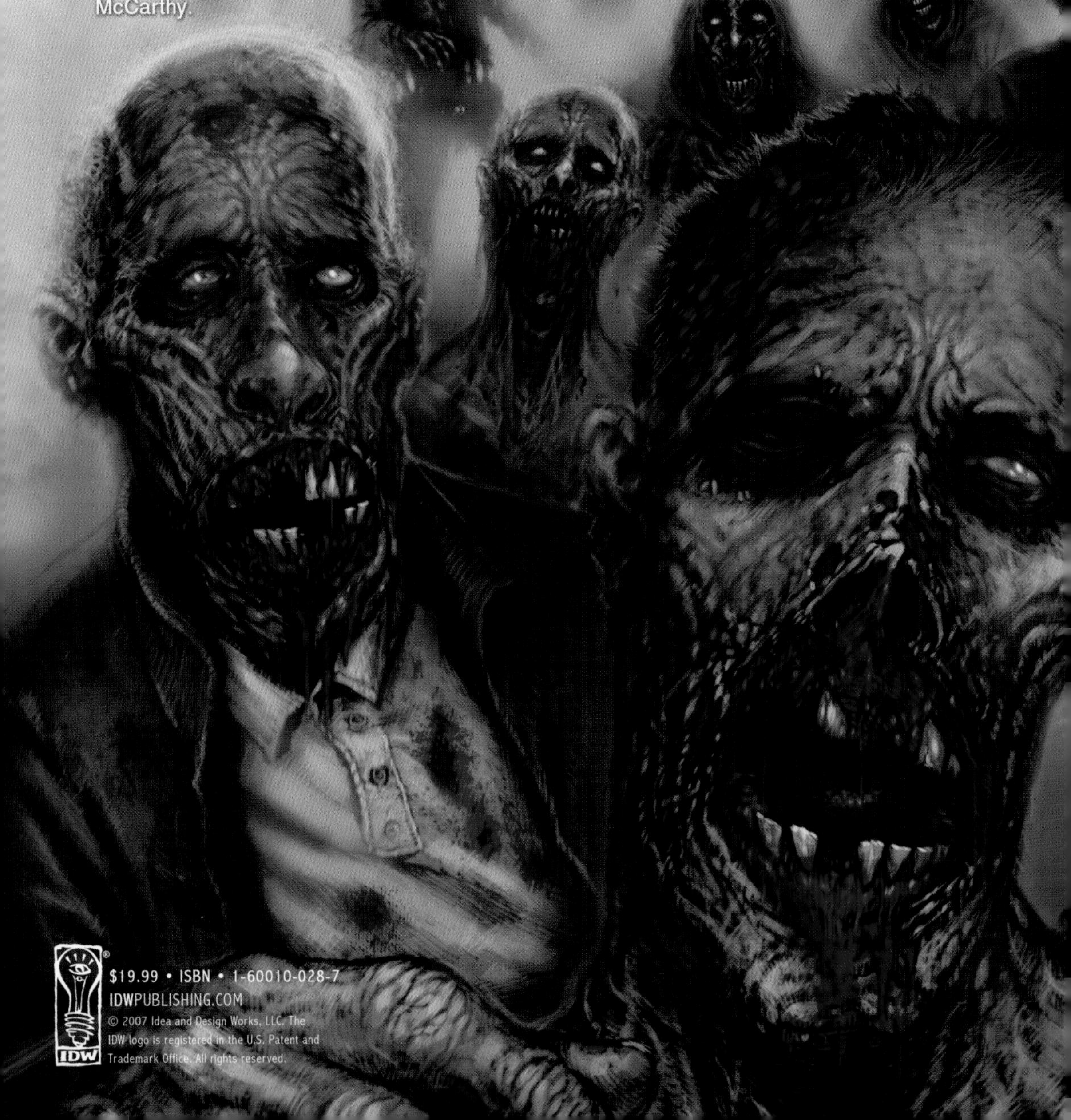

$19.99 • ISBN • 1-60010-028-7
IDWPUBLISHING.COM

CONTINUE ON FOR A CREEP PEEK AT THE
ZOMBIES: FEAST TRADE PAPERBACK

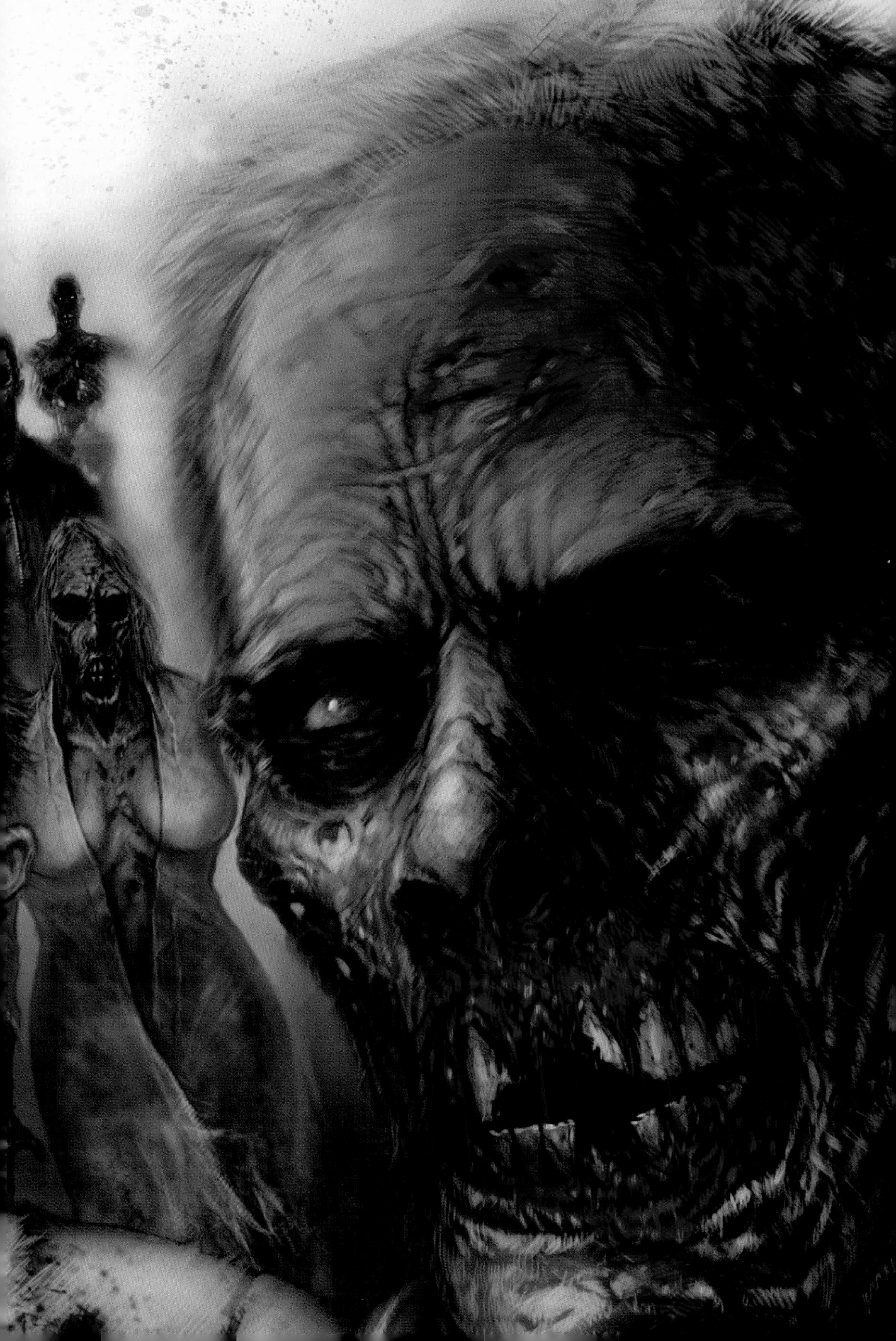

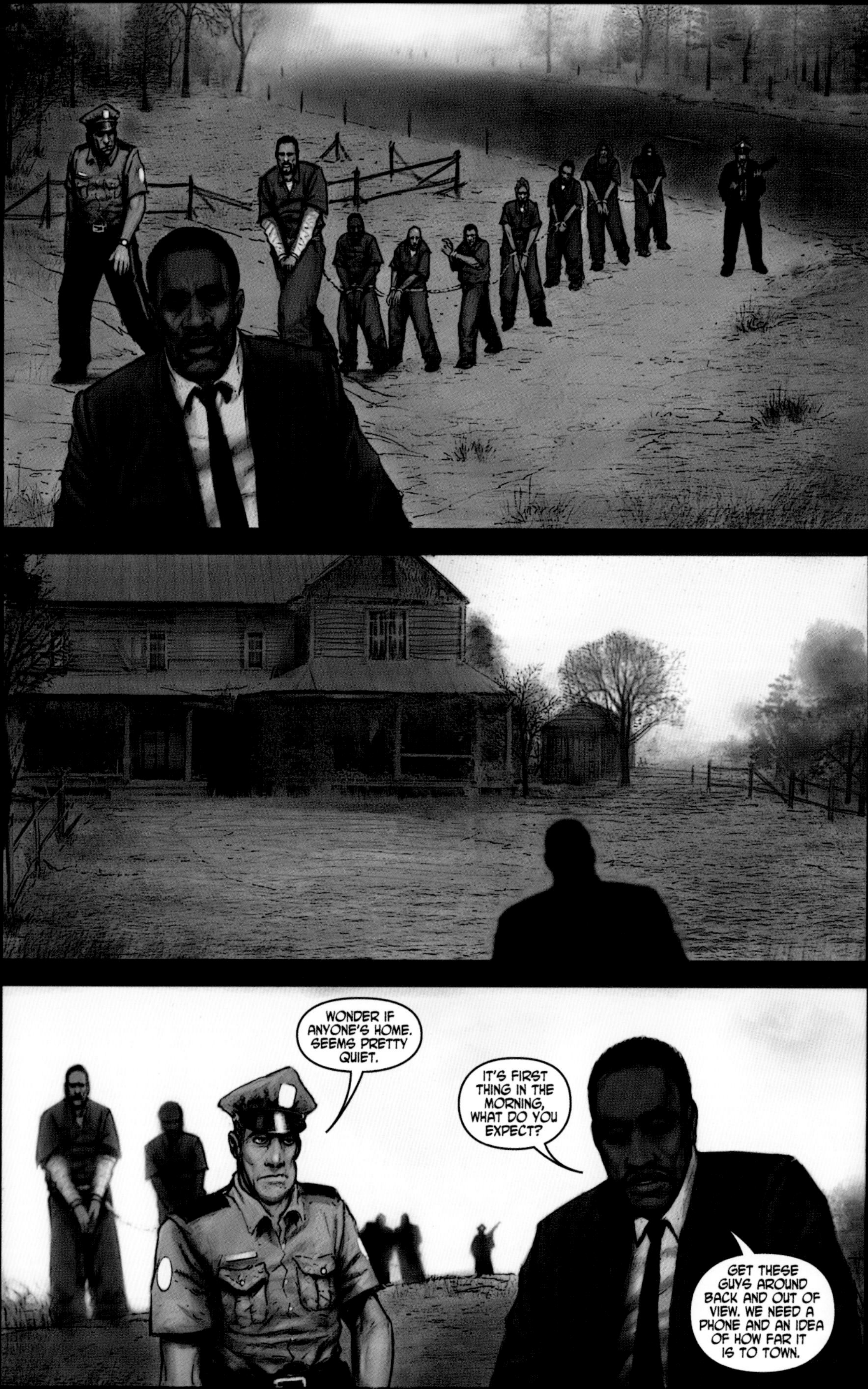
WONDER IF ANYONE'S HOME. SEEMS PRETTY QUIET.
IT'S FIRST THING IN THE MORNING, WHAT DO YOU EXPECT?
GET THESE GUYS AROUND BACK AND OUT OF VIEW. WE NEED A PHONE AND AN IDEA OF HOW FAR IT IS TO TOWN.

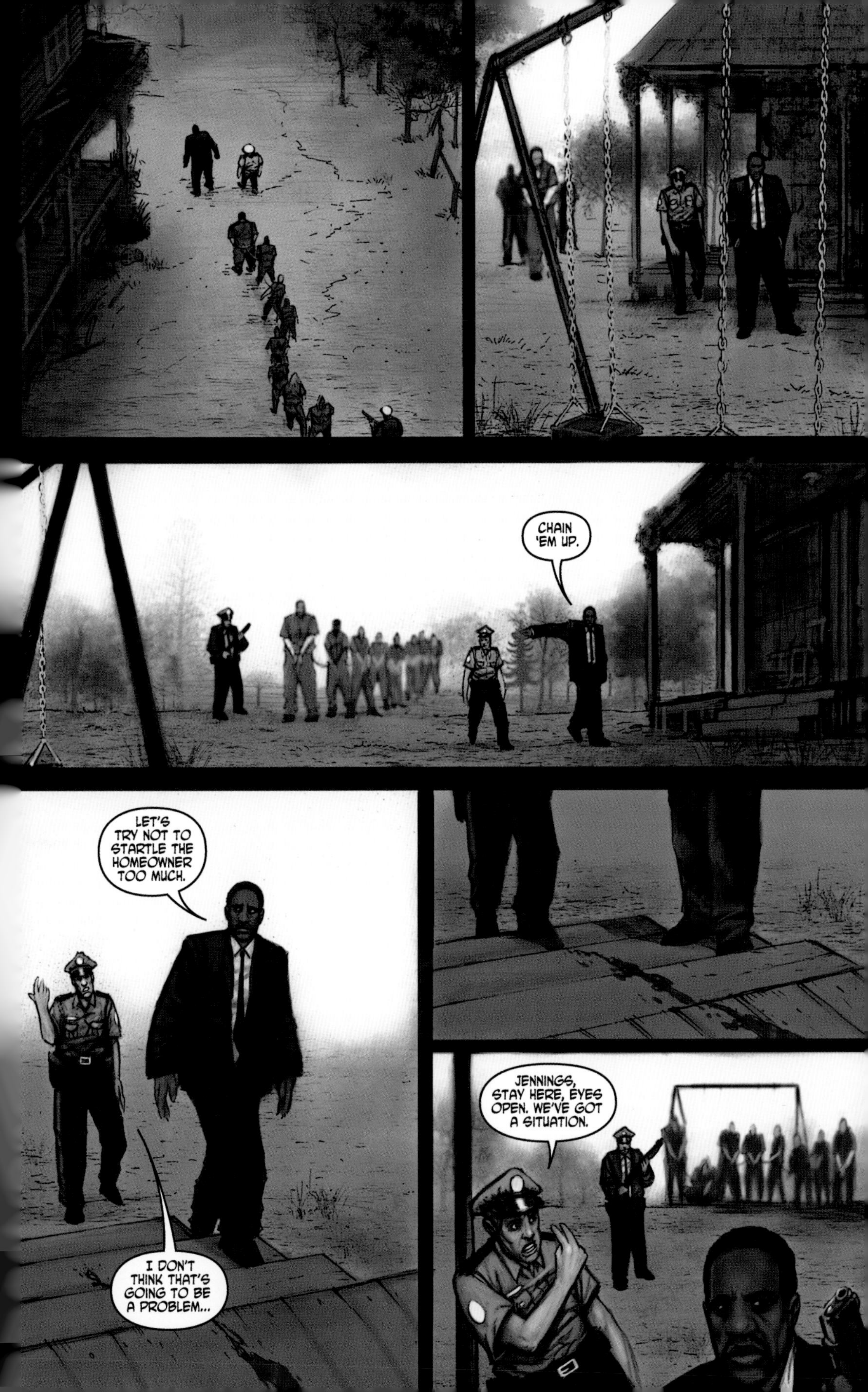
CHAIN 'EM UP.
LET'S TRY NOT TO STARTLE THE HOMEOWNER TOO MUCH.
I DON'T THINK THAT'S GOING TO BE A PROBLEM...
JENNINGS, STAY HERE, EYES OPEN. WE'VE GOT A SITUATION.

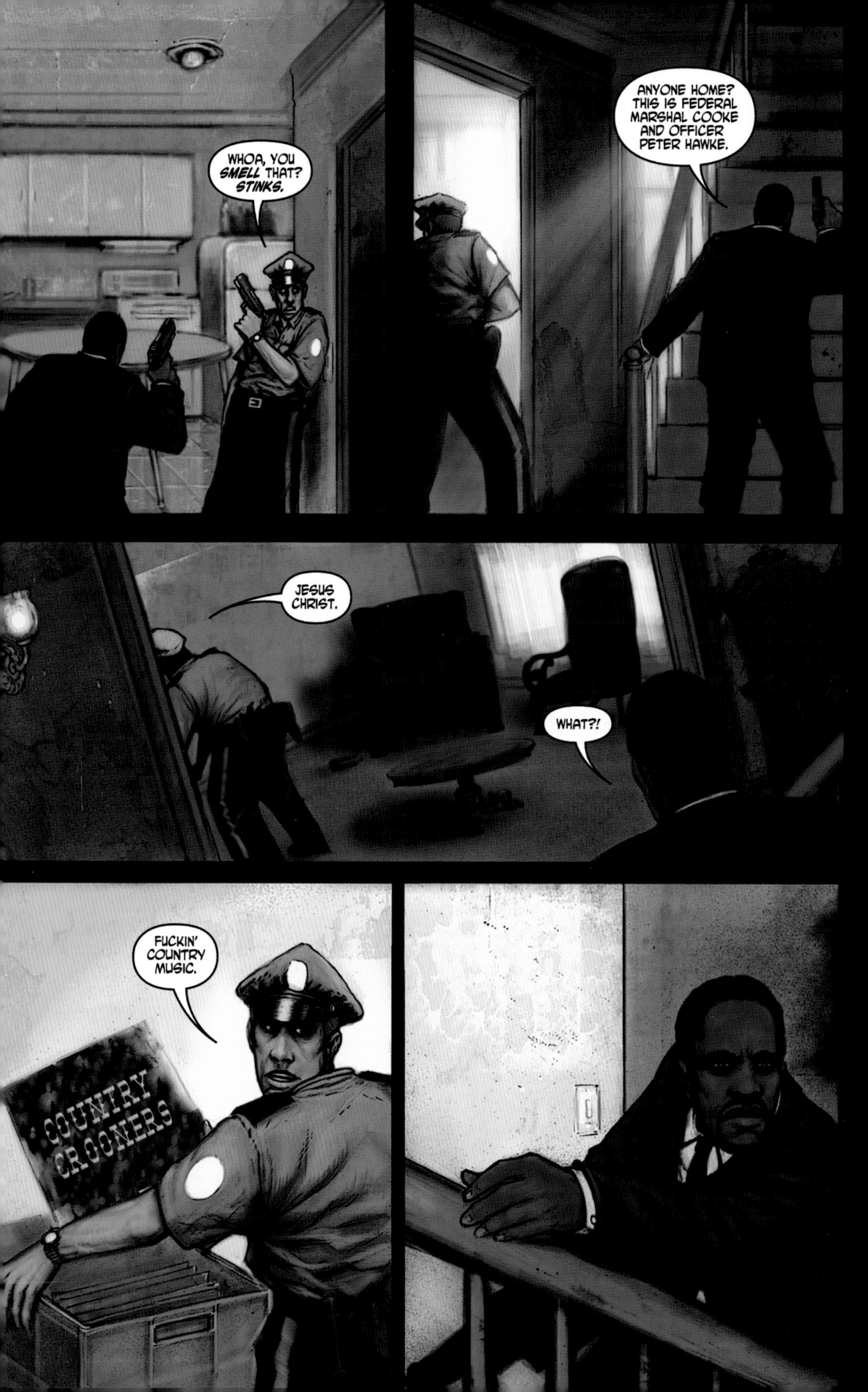
WHOA, YOU SMELL THAT? STINKS.
ANYONE HOME? THIS IS FEDERAL MARSHAL COOKE AND OFFICER PETER HAWKE.
JESUS CHRIST.
WHAT?!
FUCKIN' COUNTRY MUSIC.
COUNTRY CROONERS

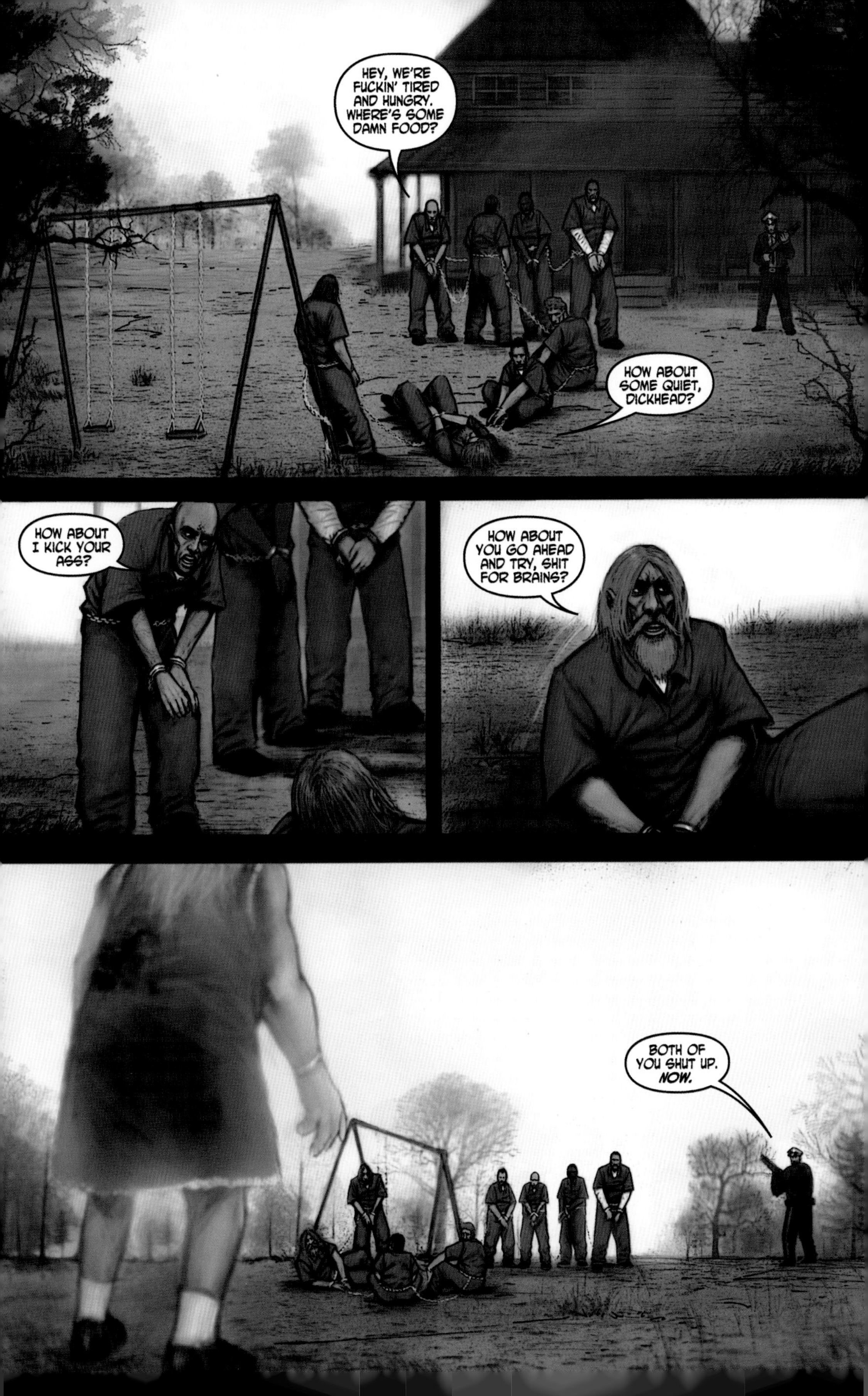
HEY, WE'RE FUCKIN' TIRED AND HUNGRY. WHERE'S SOME DAMN FOOD?
HOW ABOUT SOME QUIET, DICKHEAD?
HOW ABOUT I KICK YOUR ASS?
HOW ABOUT YOU GO AHEAD AND TRY, SHIT FOR BRAINS?
BOTH OF YOU SHUT UP. *NOW.*

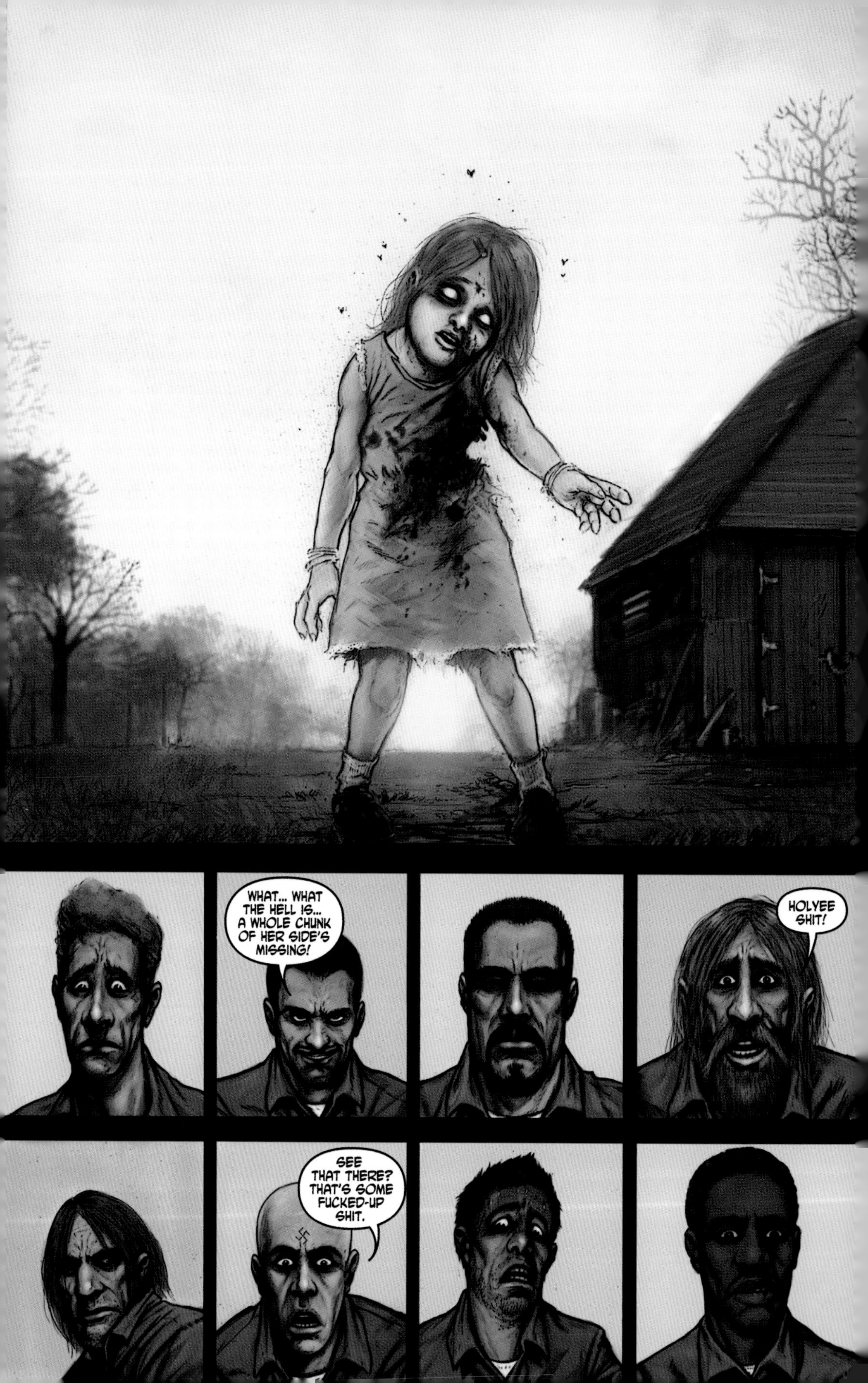
WHAT... WHAT THE HELL IS... A WHOLE CHUNK OF HER SIDE'S MISSING!
HOLYEE SHIT!
SEE THAT THERE? THAT'S SOME FUCKED-UP SHIT.

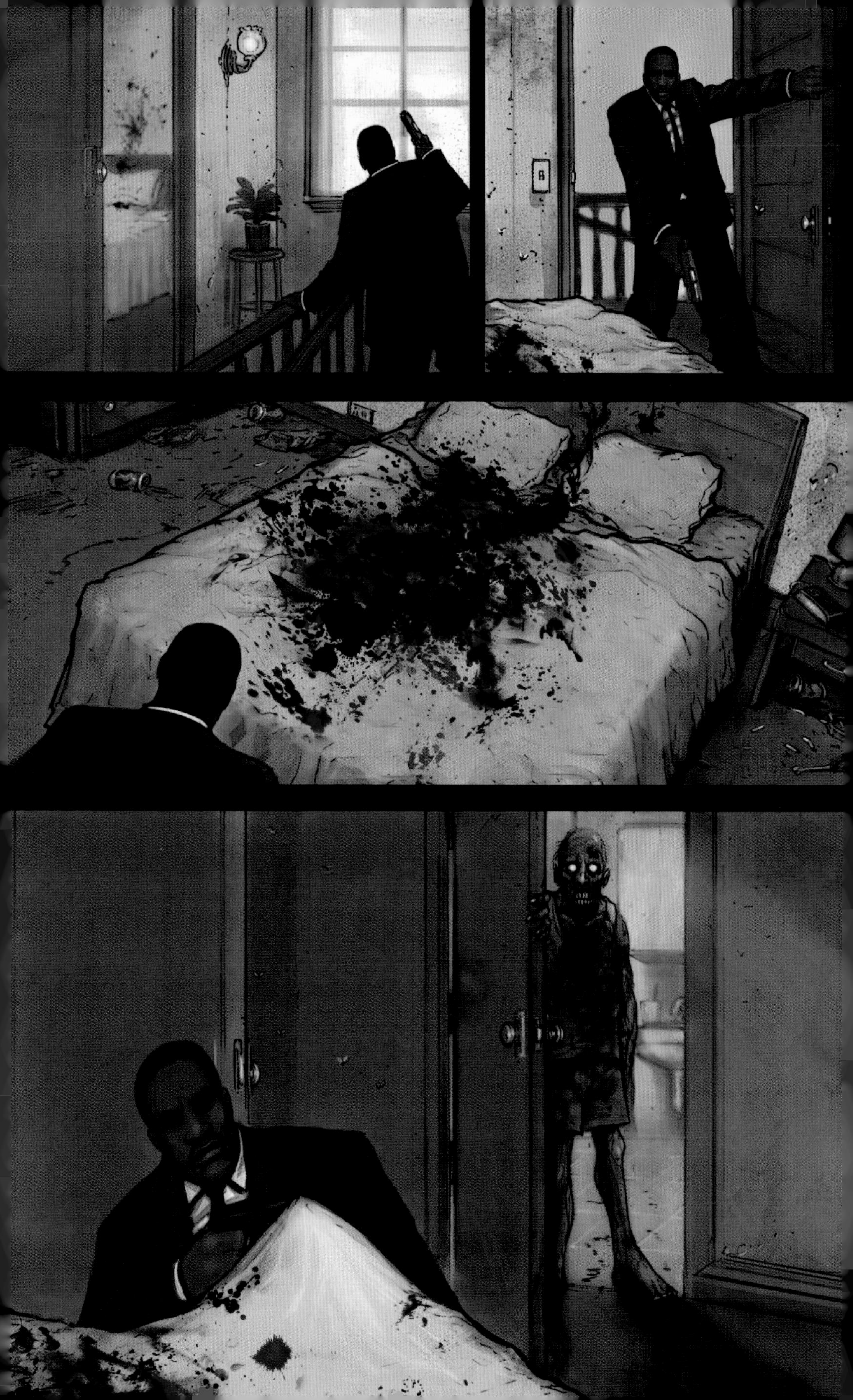

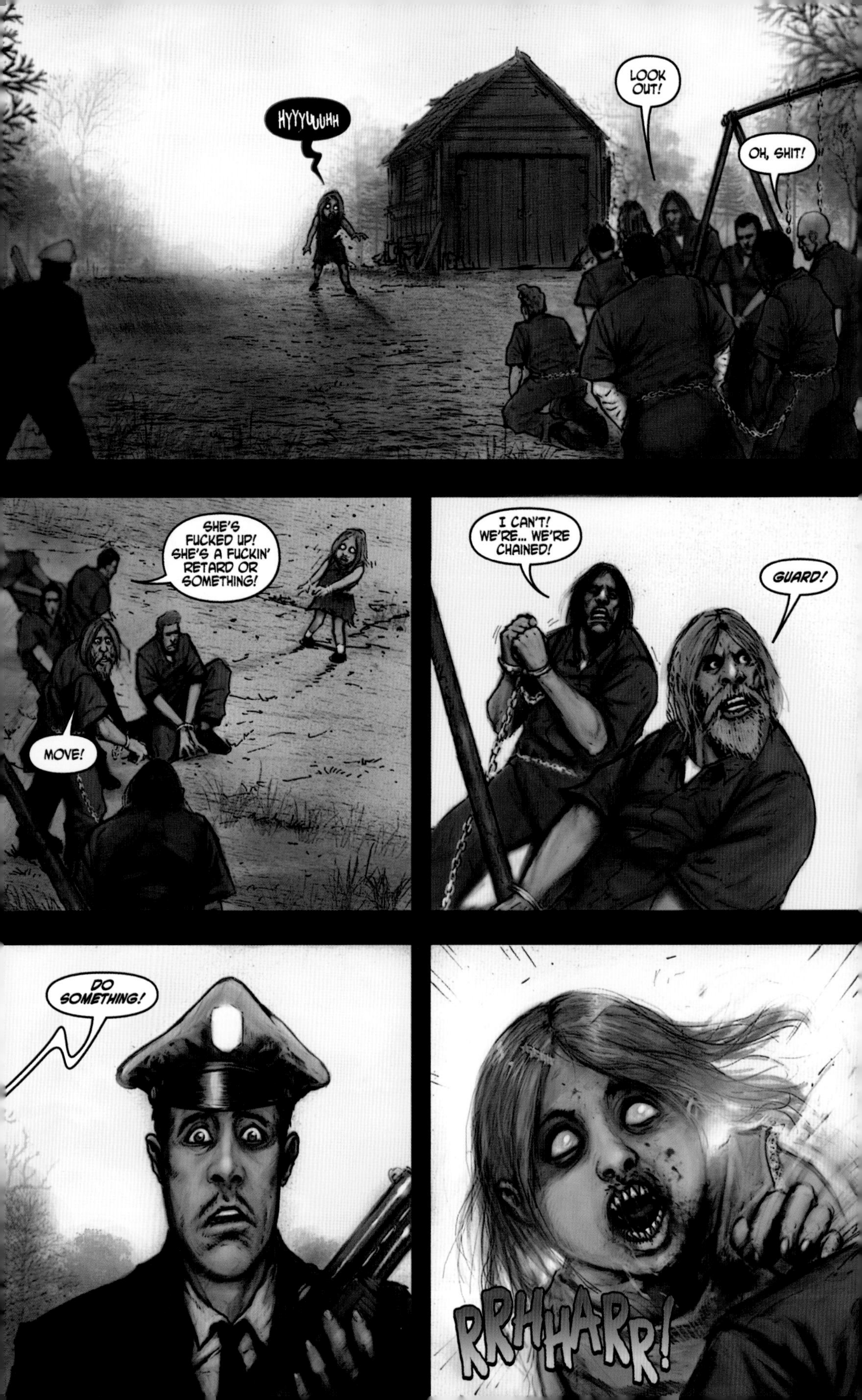
HYYYUUUHH
LOOK OUT!
OH, SHIT!
SHE'S FUCKED UP! SHE'S A FUCKIN' RETARD OR SOMETHING!
MOVE!
I CAN'T! WE'RE... WE'RE CHAINED!
GUARD!
DO SOMETHING!
RRHHARR!

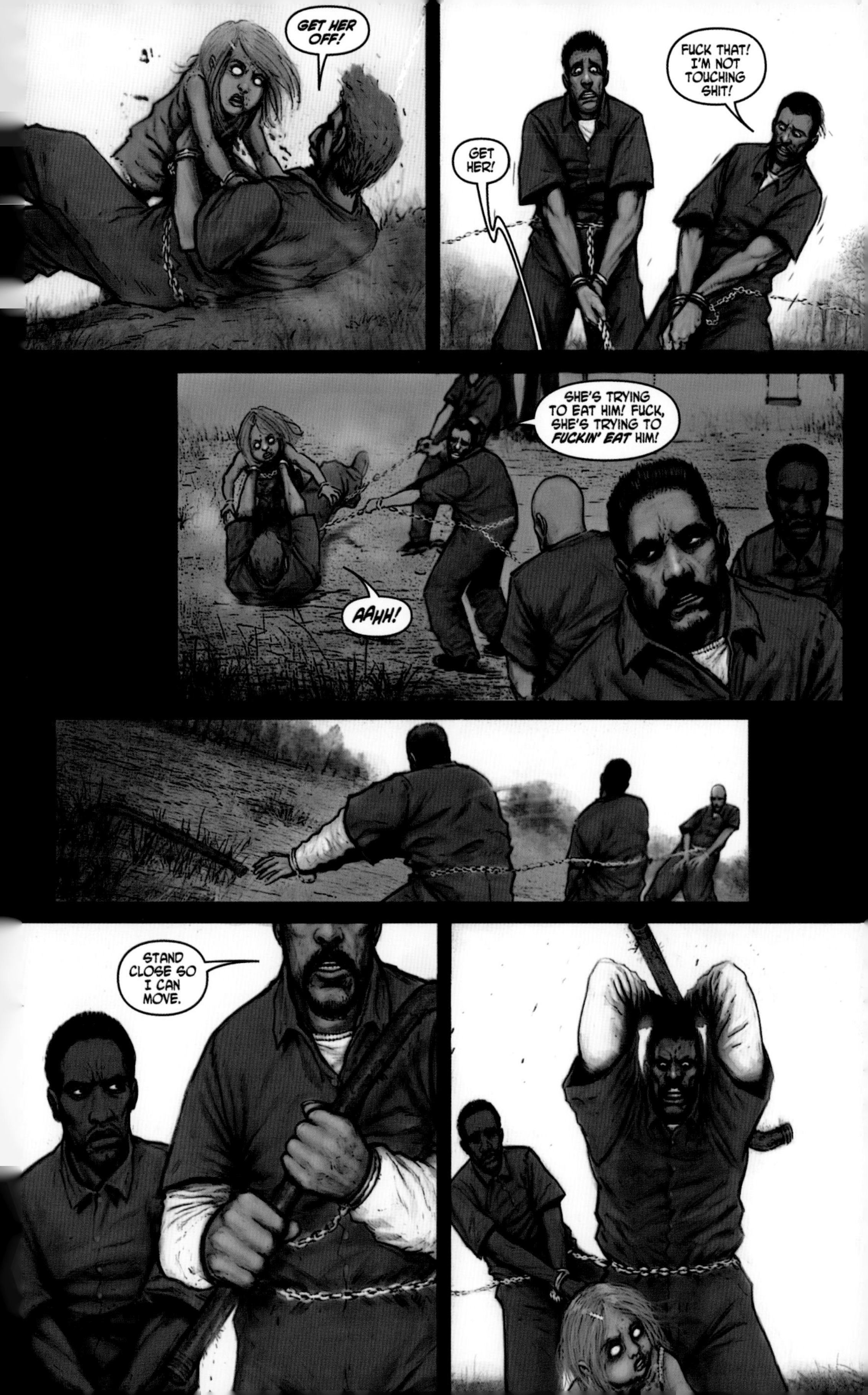
GET HER OFF!
FUCK THAT! I'M NOT TOUCHING SHIT!
GET HER!
SHE'S TRYING TO EAT HIM! FUCK, SHE'S TRYING TO FUCKIN' EAT HIM!
AAHH!
STAND CLOSE SO I CAN MOVE.

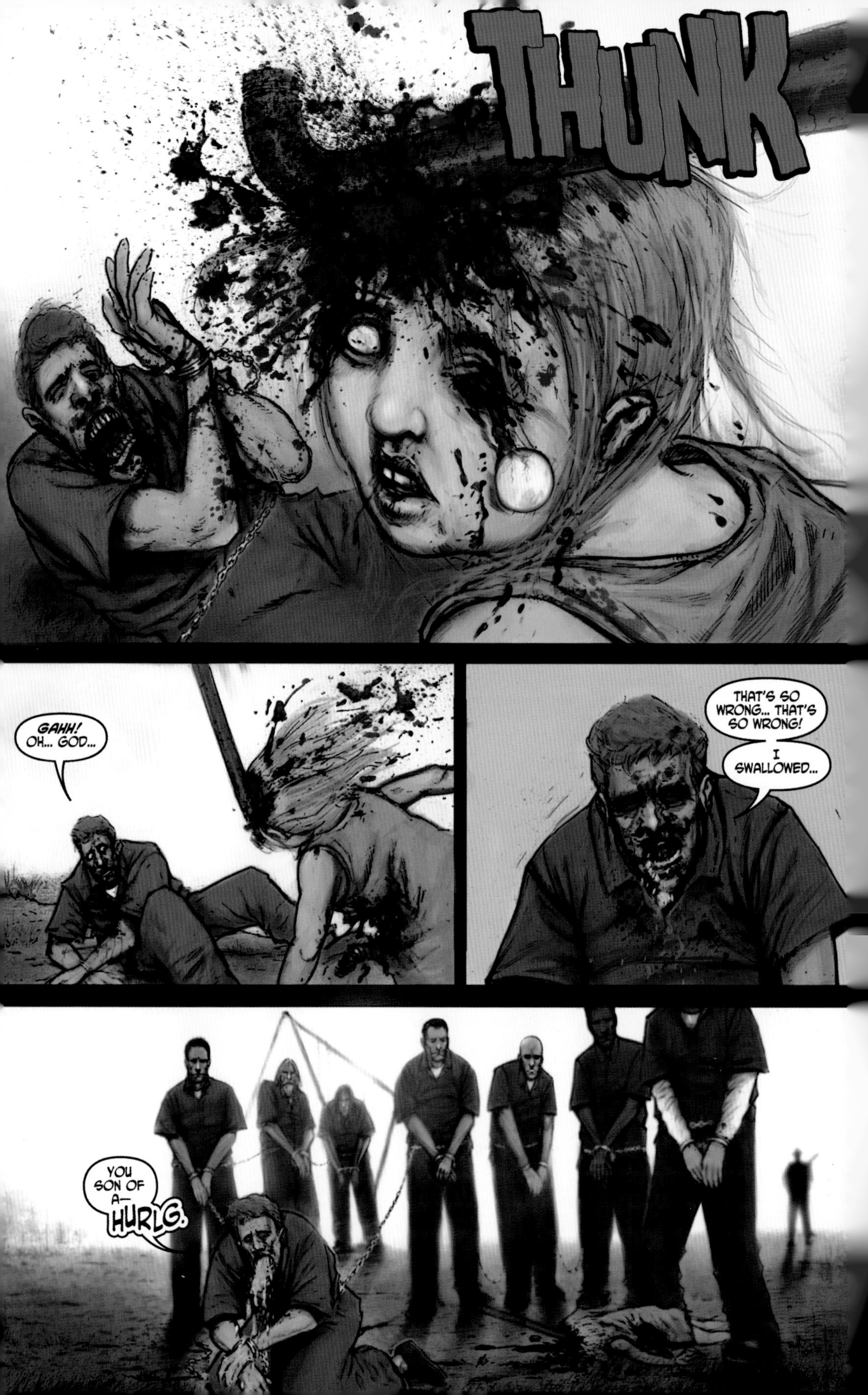
THUNK
GAHH! OH... GOD...
THAT'S SO WRONG... THAT'S SO WRONG!
I SWALLOWED...
YOU SON OF A—
HURLG.

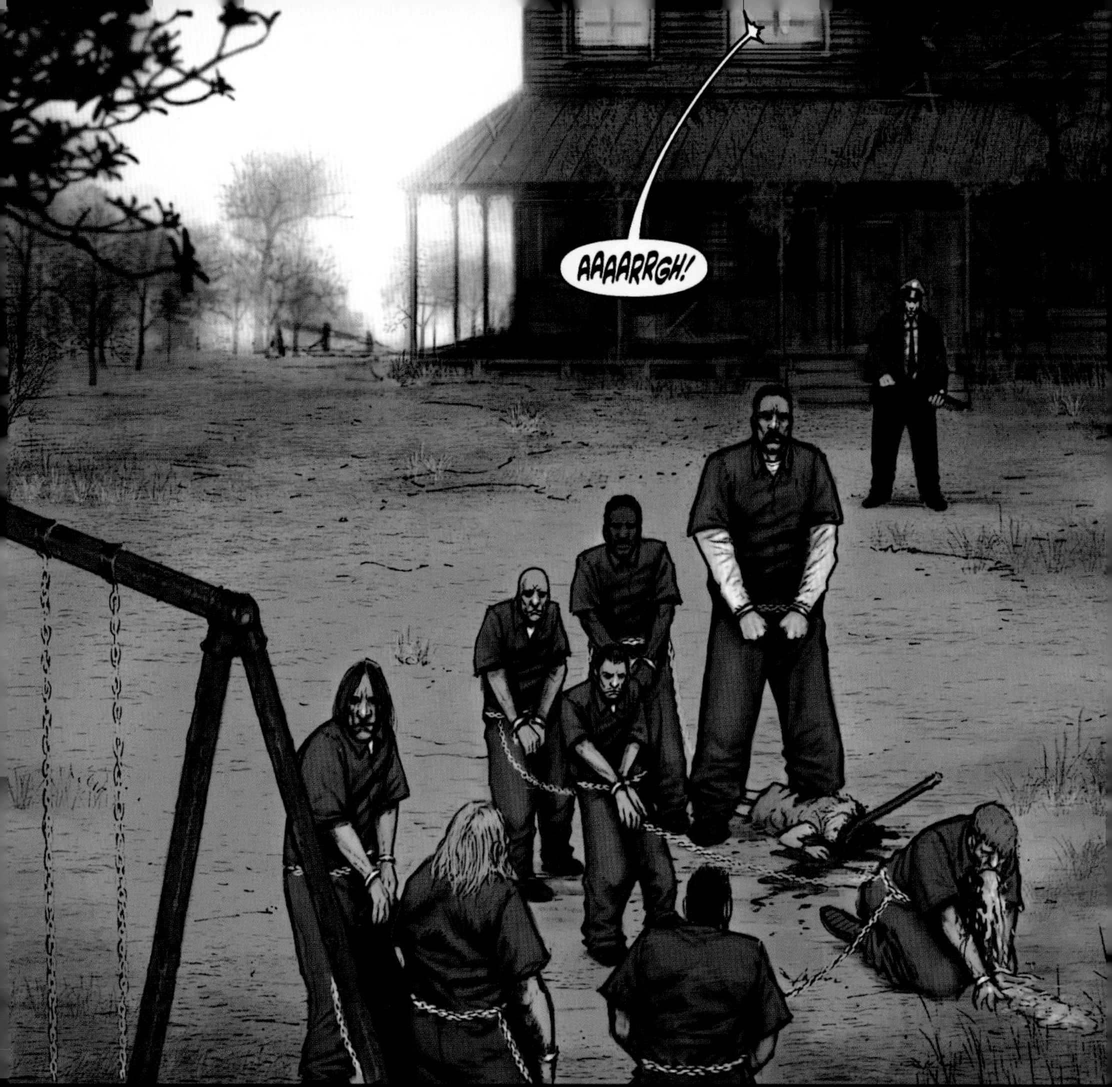
AAAARRGH!

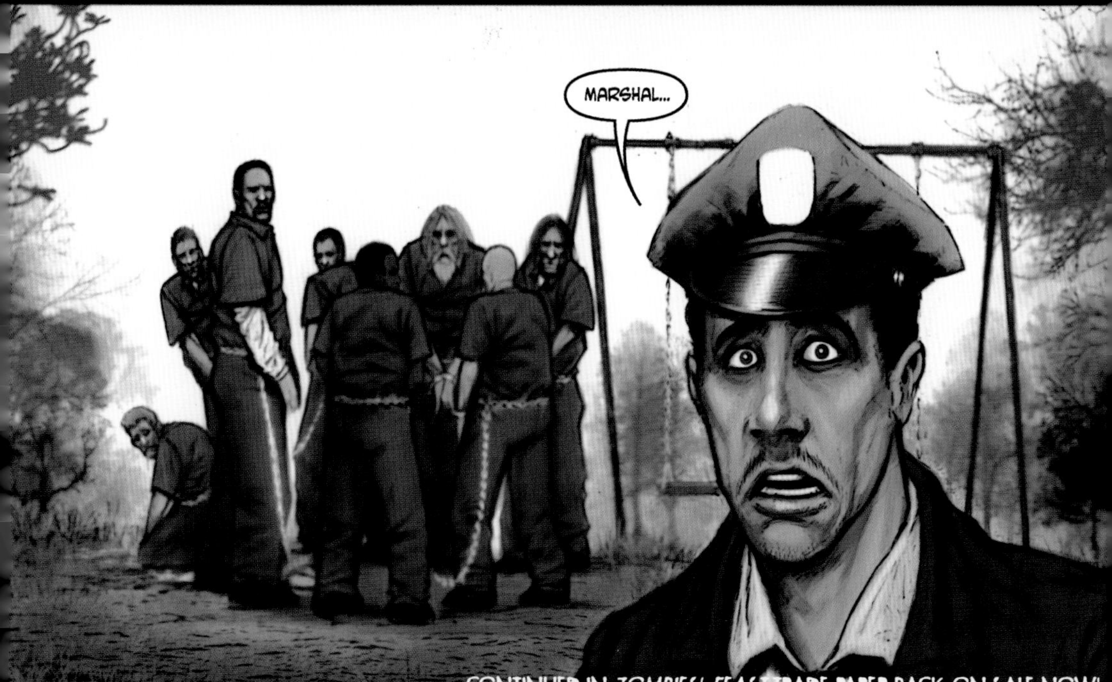
MARSHAL...

CONTINUED IN ZOMBIES! FEAST TRADE PAPER BACK ON SALE NOW!

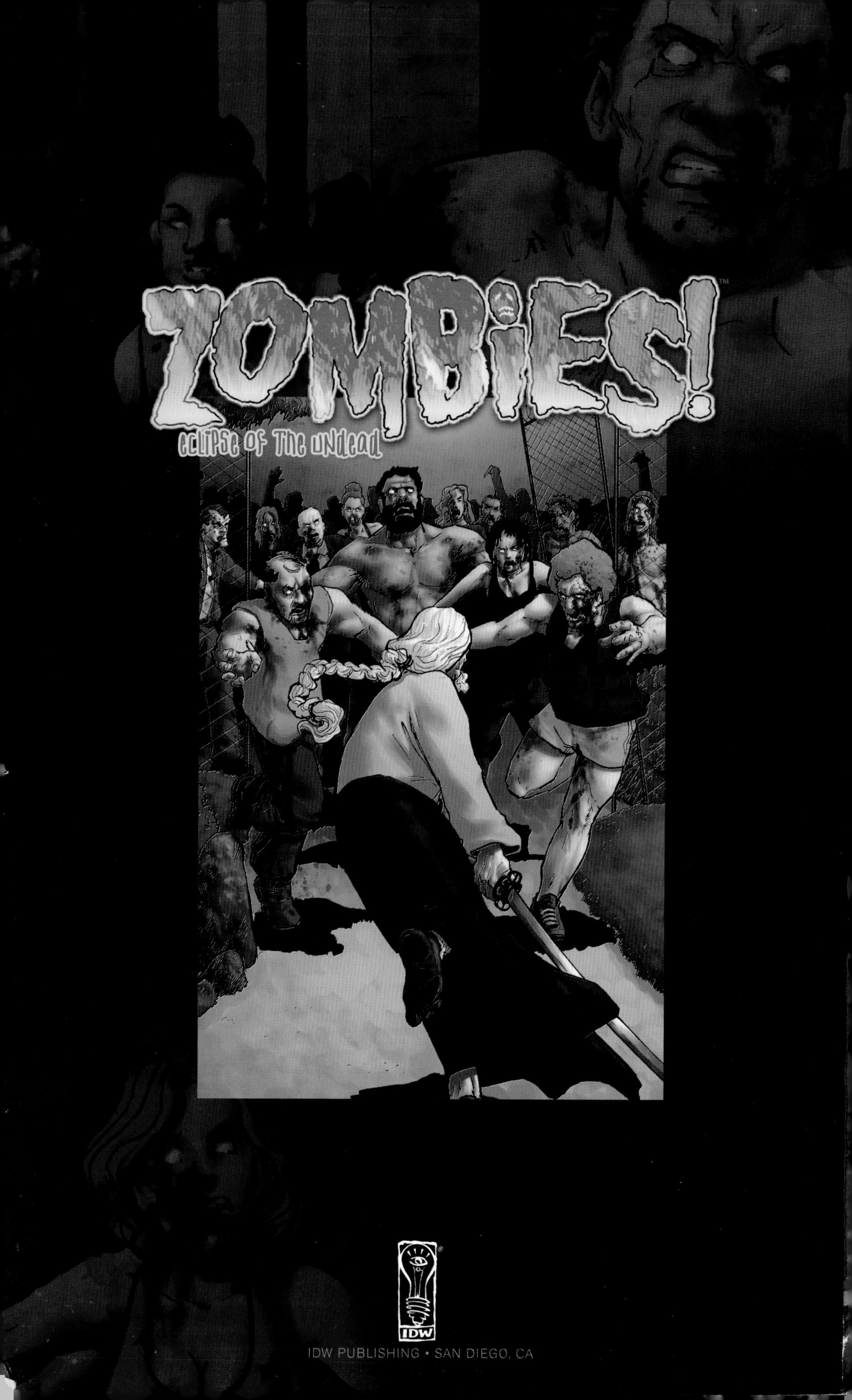
ZOMBIES!™
eclipse of the undead
IDW
IDW PUBLISHING • SAN DIEGO, CA